Strength in What Remains

TRACY KIDDER

Strength in What Remains

P
PROFILE BOOKS

First published in the United States of America in 2009 by
Random House, a division of Random House, Inc., New York

Copyright © John Tracy Kidder, 2010

1 3 5 7 9 10 8 6 4 2

Book design by Casey Hampton

Printed and bound in Great Britain by
Clays, Bungay, Suffolk

The moral right of the author has been asserted.

A CIP catalogue record for this book is available from the British Library.

ISBN 978 1 86197 857 8
eISBN 978 1 84765 313 0

The paper this book is printed on is certified by the © 1996 Forest Stewardship
Council A.C. (FSC). It is ancient-forest friendly. The printer holds FSC chain of
custody SGS-COC-2061

FSC
Mixed Sources
Product group from well-managed
forests and other controlled sources
Cert no. SGS-COC-2061
www.fsc.org
© 1996 Forest Stewardship Council

To Christopher Henry Kidder

Though nothing can bring back the hour
Of splendor in the grass, of glory in the flower;
We will grieve not, rather find
Strength in what remains behind;
In the primal sympathy
Which having been must ever be;
In the soothing thoughts that spring
Out of human suffering;
In the faith that looks through death,
In years that bring the philosophic mind.

—WILLIAM WORDSWORTH, "Ode: Intimations of
   Immortality from Recollections of Early Childhood"

CONTENTS

Out of what I hope is an excess of caution, I have changed the names of many people and places in Burundi. "Goss" and "Fair Oaks Nursing Home" are also pseudonyms.

BURUNDI, JUNE 2006

As we drove through southwestern Burundi, I felt as if we were being followed by the mountain called Ganza, the way a child feels followed by the moon. The road climbed through deeply folded countryside. We would round a corner, and another broad face of Ganza would appear.

Then my companion, Deogratias, would order the driver to stop. Deo would get out of the suv and stand on the shoulder of the pavement, aiming his digital camera at the mountain. Deo wore a black bush hat with a dangling chin strap. I supposed that to people passing by, in the crowded minibuses and on the bicycles laden with plastic jugs of palm oil, he must look like a tourist, a trim young black-skinned rich man from somewhere far away.

Standing beside him at the roadside, I could look down on narrow valleys of cultivated fields and up at steep hillsides, some covered with grass, others quilted with groves of eucalyptus and banana trees and dotted with tiny houses roofed in metal or thatch. Above them rose the flanks and the domed top of Ganza, all but treeless, barren of houses. In Kirundi, *ganza* means "to reign," and the name evoked the kings that once ruled Burundi. The little nation, centuries old, straddles the crest of the watershed of the Congo and Nile rivers, just south of the equator in East Central Africa. It is bordered by Tanzania to the south and east, by the Democratic Republic of the Congo across Lake Tanganikya to the west, and by Rwanda to the north. It's a landlocked and impoverished country with an agrarian economy that exports excellent coffee and tea and not much else—a land of dwindling forests that still has lovely rustic landscapes.

Deo could hardly take his eyes off Ganza. He was thronged by memories. All the summers of his boyhood, once a week and sometimes twice, he and his older brother had toiled over the mountain, climbing impossibly steep paths, their knees shaking under the loads balanced on their heads. Back then, the land out there had all been thickly forested, and in the trees and under them he used to see chimps, monkeys, even gorillas. They were all gone now, he said. But there had been so many monkeys then! One time he and his brother sat down to rest partway up another mountain, and a host of monkeys surrounded them, like a gang of little thugs, harassing them, trying to take their sacks of cassava, even slapping them right in their faces! In the end there was nothing for him and his brother to do but run away, leaving the cassava behind.

When he told me this story, Deo laughed. It was what I'd come to recognize as his normal laugh. It had the same bright, surprised, near soprano sound as his voice when he greeted a friend and cried out, "Hi!," the "Hi!" drawn out as if he didn't want it to end. His English was accented with French and Kirundi and sprinkled with misplaced emphases—as in, "I am laughing when I think *about* it." And many of his phrases had a certain hybrid vigor, a fresh extravagance: "I want to get it out of my chest." "Run like a thunderstorm." "I had to bite my heart."

Deo grew up in the mountains east of Ganza, in a tiny settlement of farms and pastures called Butanza. He had returned to Burundi several times over the past six years. But he had avoided Butanza. He had not visited it for nearly fourteen years. Now he was going back at last. He seemed happy to see Ganza again, but when we drove farther east toward Butanza, he grew, not silent, but increasingly quiet. One noticed this, because he was usually so talkative and animated.

After a while we turned off the paved road onto dirt roads. The dirt roads grew narrower. Finally, as we bumped along up a steep, rutted track, Deo said we were getting close. He said that when we arrived, we would climb on foot to the pasture where, many years ago, his best friend, Clovis, took sick. We would visit the very spot, he said. Then he added, "And when we get to Butanza we don't talk about Clovis."

"Why?"

"Because people don't talk about people who died. By their names, anyways. They call it *gusimbura*. If for example you say, 'Oh, your granddad,' and you say his name to people, they say you *gusimbura* them. It's a bad word. You are reminding people . . ." Deo's voice trailed off.

"You're reminding people of something bad?"

"Yes. It's so hard to understand, because in the Western world . . ." Again, Deo left the thought half finished.

"People try to remember?"

"Yah."

"Here in Burundi, they try to forget?"

"Exactly," he said.

PART ONE

FLIGHTS

ONE

Bujumbura–New York,
May 1994

On the outskirts of the capital, Bujumbura, there is a small international airport. It has a modern terminal with intricate roofs and domed metal structures that resemble astronomical observatories. It is the kind of terminal that seems designed to say that here you leave the past behind, the future has arrived, behold the wonders of aviation. But in Burundi in 1994, for the lucky few with tickets, an airplane was just the fastest, safest way out. It was *flight*.

In the spring of that year, violence and chaos governed Burundi. To the west, the hills above Bujumbura were burning. Smoke seemed to be pouring off the hills, as the winds of mid-May carried the plumes of smoke downward in undulating sheets, in the general direction of the airport. A large passenger jet was parked on the tarmac, and a disordered crowd was heading toward it in sweaty haste. Deo felt as if he were being carried by the crowd, immersed in an unfamiliar river. The faces around him were mostly white, and though many were black or brown, there was no one whom he recognized, and so far as he could tell there were no country people. As a little boy, he had crouched behind rocks or under trees the first times he'd seen airplanes passing overhead. He had never been so close to a plane before. Except for buildings in the capital, this was the largest man-made thing he'd ever seen. He mounted the staircase quickly. Only when he had entered the plane did he let himself look back, staring from inside the doorway as if from a hiding place again.

In Deo's mind, there was danger everywhere. If his heightened sense of drama was an inborn trait, it had certainly been nourished. For months every situation had in fact been dangerous. Climbing the stairs a moment before, he had imagined a voice in his head telling him not to leave. But now he stared at the hills and he imagined that everything in Burundi was burning. Burundi had become hell. He finally turned away, and stepped inside. In front of him were cushioned chairs with clean white cloths draped over their backs, chairs in perfect rows with little windows on the ends. This was the most nicely appointed room he'd ever seen. It looked like paradise compared to everything outside. If it was real, it couldn't last.

The plane was packed, but he felt entirely alone. He had a seat by a window. Something told him not to look out, and something told him to look. He did both. His hands were shaking. He felt he was about to vomit. Everyone had heard stories of planes being shot down, not only the Rwandan president's plane back in April but others as well. He was waiting for this to happen after the plane took off. For several long minutes, whenever he glanced out the window all he saw was smoke. When the air cleared and he could see the landscape below, he realized that they must already have crossed the Akanyaru River, which meant they had left Burundi and were now above Rwanda. He had crossed a lot of the land down there on foot. It wasn't all that small. To see it transformed into a tiny piece of time and space—this could only happen in a dream.

He gazed down, face pressed against the windowpane. Plumes of smoke were also rising from the ground of what he took to be Rwanda—if anything, more smoke than around Bujumbura. A lot of it was coming from the banks of muddy-looking rivers. He thought, "People are being slaughtered down there." But those sights didn't last long. When he realized he wasn't seeing smoke anymore, he took his face away from the window and felt himself begin to relax, a long-forgotten feeling.

He liked the cushioned chair. He liked the sensation of flight. How wonderful to travel in an easy chair instead of on foot. He began to realize how constricted his intestines and stomach had felt, as if wound into knots for months on end, as the tightness seeped away. Maybe the worst was over now, or maybe he was just in shock. "I don't really know where I'm going," he thought. But if there was to be no end to this trip, that would be all right. A memory from world history class surfaced. Maybe he was like that man who got lost and discovered America. He craned his neck and looked upward through the window. There was nothing but darkening blue. He looked down and realized just how high above the ground he was seated. "Imagine if this plane crashes," he thought. "That would be awful." Then he said to himself, "I don't care. It would be a good death."

For the moment, he was content with that thought, and with everything around him. The only slightly troubling thing was the absence of French in the cabin. He knew for a fact—he'd been taught it was so since elementary school—that French was the universal language, and universal because it was the best of all languages. He knew Russians owned this plane. Only Aeroflot, he'd been told, was still offering commercial flights from Bujumbura. So it wasn't strange that all the signs in the cabin were in a foreign script. But he couldn't find a single word written in French, even on the various cards in the seat pocket.

The plane landed in Entebbe, in Uganda. As he waited in the terminal for his next flight, Deo watched what looked like a big family make a fuss over a young man about his age, a fellow passenger as it turned out. When the flight started to board, the whole bunch around this boy began weeping and wailing. The young man was wiping tears from his eyes as he walked toward the plane. Probably he was just going away on a trip. Probably he would be coming back soon. In his mind, Deo spoke to the young man: "You are in tears. For what? Here you have this huge crowd of family." He felt surprised, as if by a distant memory, that there were, after all, many small reasons for people to cry. His own mind kept moving from one extreme to another. Everything was a crisis, and nothing that wasn't a crisis mattered. He thought that if he were as lucky as that boy and still had that much family left, he wouldn't be crying. For that matter, he wouldn't be boarding airplanes, leaving his country behind.

Deo had grown up barefoot in Burundi, but for a peasant boy he had done well. He was twenty-four. Until recently he had been a medical student, for three years at or near the top of his class. In his old faux-leather suitcase, which he had reluctantly turned over to the baggage handler in the airport in Bujumbura, he had packed some of the evidence of his success: the French dictionary that elementary school teachers gave only to prized students, and the general clinical text and one of the stethoscopes that he had saved up to buy. But he had spent the past six months on the run, first from the eruption of violence in Burundi, then from the slaughter in Rwanda.

In geography class in school, Deo had learned that the most important parts of the world were France and Burundi's colonial master, Belgium. When someone he knew, usually a priest, was going abroad, that person was said to be going to "Iburaya." And while this usually meant Belgium or France, it could also mean any place that was far away and hard to imagine. Deo was heading for Iburaya. In this case, that meant New York City.

He had one wealthy friend who had seen more of the world than East Central Africa, a fellow medical student named Jean. And it was Jean who had decided that New York was where he should go. Deo was traveling on a commercial visa. Jean's French father had written a letter identifying Deo as an employee on a mission to America. He was supposed to be going to New York to sell coffee. Deo had read up on coffee beans in case he was questioned, but he wasn't selling anything. Jean's father had also paid for the plane tickets. A fat booklet of tickets.

From Entebbe, Deo flew to Cairo, then to Moscow. He slept a lot. He would wake with a start and look around the cabin. When he realized that no one resembled anyone he knew, he would relax again. During his medical training and in his country's history, pigmentation had certainly mattered, but he wasn't troubled by the near total whiteness of the faces around him on the plane that he boarded in Moscow. White skin hadn't been a marker of danger these past months. He had heard of French soldiers behaving badly in Rwanda, and had even caught glimpses of them training militiamen in the camps, but waking up and seeing a white person in the next seat wasn't alarming. No one called him a cockroach. No one held a machete. You learned what to look out for, and after a while you learned to ignore the irrelevant. He did wonder again from time to time why he wasn't hearing people speak French.

When his flight from Moscow landed, he was half asleep. He followed the other passengers out of the plane. He thought this must be New York. The first thing to do was find his bag. But the airport terminal distracted him. It was like nothing he'd ever seen before, an indoor place of shops where everyone looked happy. And everyone was large. Compared to him anyway. He'd never been heavy, but his pants, which had fit all right six months before, were bunched up at the waist. When he looked down at himself, the end of his belt seemed as long to him as a monkey's tail. His belly was concave under his shirt. Here in Iburaya everyone's clothes looked better than his.

He started walking. Looking around for a sign with a luggage symbol on it, he came to a corridor with a glassed-in wall. He glanced out, then stopped and stared. There were green fields out there in the distance, and on those fields cows were grazing. From this far away, they might have been his family's herd. His last images of cows were of murdered and suffering animals—decapitated cows and cows with their front legs chopped off, still alive and bellowing by the sides of the road to Bujumbura and even in Bujumbura. These cows looked so happy, just like the people around him. How was this possible?

A voice was speaking to him. He turned and saw a man in uniform, a policeman. The man looked even bigger than everyone else. He seemed friendly, though. Deo spoke to him in French, but the man shook his head and smiled. Then another gigantic-looking policeman joined them. He asked a question in what Deo guessed was English. Then a woman who had been sitting nearby got up and walked over—French, at long last French, coming out of her mouth along with cigarette smoke.

Perhaps she could help, the woman said in French.

Deo thought: "God, I'm still in your hands."

She did the interpreting. The airport policemen wanted to see Deo's passport and visa and ticket. Deo wanted to know where he should go to pick up his bag.

The policemen looked surprised. One of them asked another question. The woman said to Deo, "The man asks, 'Do you know where you are?'"

"Yes," said Deo. "New York City."

She broke into a smile, and translated this for the uniformed men. They looked at each other and laughed, and the woman explained to Deo that he was in a country called Ireland, in a place called Shannon Airport.

He chatted with the woman afterward. She told him she was Russian. What mattered to Deo was that she spoke French. After such long solitude, it felt wonderful to talk, so wonderful that for a while he forgot all he knew about the importance of silence, the silence he'd been taught as a child, the silence he had needed over the past six months. She asked him where he came from, and before he knew it he had said too much. She started asking questions. He was from Burundi? And had escaped from Rwanda? She had been to Rwanda. She was a journalist. She planned to write about the terrible events there. It was a genocide, wasn't it? Was he a Tutsi?

She arranged to sit next to him on the flight to New York. He felt glad for the company, and besieged by her questions. She wanted to know all about his experiences. To answer felt dangerous. She wasn't just a stranger, she was a *journalist*. What would she write? What if she found out his name and used it? Would bad people read it and come to find him in New York? He tried to tell her as little as possible. "It was terrible. It was disgusting," he'd say, and turning toward the airplane's window, he'd see images he didn't want in his mind—a gray dawn and a hut with a burned thatch roof smoldering in the rain, a pack of dogs snarling over something he wasn't going to look at, swarms of flies like a warning in the air above a banana grove ahead. He'd turn back to her to chase away the visions. She seemed like a friend, his only friend on this journey. She was older than he was, she'd even been to New York. He wanted to pay her back for helping him in Ireland, and pay her in advance for helping him enter New York. So he tried to answer her questions without revealing anything important.

They talked most of the way to New York. But when they got up from their seats, she turned to him and said, *"Au revoir."* When he reached Immigration and took a place at the end of one of the lines, he spotted her again. She was standing in another line, pretending not to see him. He looked away, down at his sneakers, blurred by tears. The spasm passed. He was used to being alone, wasn't he? He didn't care what happened to him anymore, did he? And what was there to fear? What could the man in the booth up ahead do to him? Whatever it might be, he'd already seen worse.

The agent stared at Deo's documents, then started asking questions in what had to be English. There was nothing to do except

smile. Then the first agent got up from his seat and called another agent over. Eventually, the second agent went off and came
back with a third man—a short, burly, black-skinned man with a
bunch of keys as big as a fist on his belt. He introduced himself to
Deo in French. His name was Muhammad. He said he came from
Senegal.

Muhammad asked Deo the agents' questions and also some
questions of his own. For the agents, he asked Deo, "Where are you
coming from?" When Deo said he had come from Burundi,
Muhammad made a pained face and said to him in French, "How
did you get out?"

There was no time even to attempt an answer. The agents were
asking another question: Deo's visa said he was here on business.
What business?

Selling coffee beans, Deo told them through Muhammad. Just
keep smiling, Deo told himself. He could tell them anything they
wanted to know about Burundian coffee. But they didn't ask about
coffee.

How much money did he have?

Two hundred dollars, Deo said with pride. The cash had been a gift
from Jean. Exchanged for Burundian francs, it could have bought a lot
of cows. But neither Muhammad nor the agents looked impressed.

Where was he staying?

Jean had told him he'd be asked this. A hotel, he said.

The agents laughed. A week in a hotel on two hundred dollars?

In 1994, airport security wasn't what it soon would be. Muhammad said something in English to the agents. His words must have
been the right ones, because after a few more questions, the agents
shrugged at each other and let him through, into America.

He had no idea what he'd do next. After six months on the run,
he was in the habit of not looking ahead. God had taken care of him
so far. And still was taking care of him, it seemed. As this stocky and
serious-looking stranger, Muhammad, walked him out of Customs,

he said that Deo could stay with him in New York City. But Deo would have to wait here for three hours. Muhammad worked at the airport as a baggage handler. He had to finish his shift. Could Deo wait three hours?

Only three hours? said Deo. Of course!

He sat on a plastic chair at baggage claim, his suitcase at his feet, and watched the new world pass by. Wheeled carts in which infants rode like little princes, their parents pushing them. And people in suits, so many people in the uniform of preachers and government ministers. Almost everyone looked happy. Or at least no one looked alarmed. And no one looked terrified. These were people just going about their business, greeting their friends and their families, as if they didn't know there were places where dogs were trotting around with human heads in their mouths. But how could they not know?

"God, why is this?" Deo asked silently.

Muhammad had a big car. He had to be a person of means to have a car, even if it was old and swayed from side to side on the road. So much went by so fast, it was hard to focus on anything, though once, amid all the wide crisscrossing pavements and the great herds of automobiles, Deo saw a car that was nearly as long as a bus. "*Mon Dieu!* What is *that*?" Deo asked.

"Sometimes they're used as taxis," said Muhammad.

Deo sat staring straight ahead, so as to think about this. Then they were crossing a bridge so high he felt as if he were in the airplanes again, and Muhammad said, "Manhattan," and pointed at a horizon of buildings impossibly tall, like giant trees, like a sky of pillared clouds at sunrise in the mountains. After a time Deo began to notice vacant lots, and buildings with wood covering their windows. When Muhammad finally turned off a main avenue onto a side street, Deo wanted to ask, urgently, why they were stopping here. A few yards away, a man stood urinating against the wall of a building. The sidewalk was covered with empty cans and bottles and all sorts of paper trash. Muhammad led the way toward a brick building with broken windows and letters scribbled here and there on the walls. High up on one wall there were three letters painted, as if each letter were swollen: P E N. He followed Muhammad inside, the air reeking of urine and excrement, up a staircase with a busted railing, and finally into a room with a dirty wooden floor, a room with no door and no furniture. At the end of a dark hallway, there was a toilet, completely stopped up.

Muhammad said he stayed here to save money. He didn't have to pay rent for this room. His whole reason for being in New York was to earn and save as much as he could. He would be leaving for Senegal in a few weeks. Deo should do as he had—work here for a while and save, then start a new life. But he should do this somewhere back in Africa, not in New York. "Because it's so hard here," Muhammad said.

In retrospect, the tenement PEN was like a warning of this truth. The next day, Muhammad led him outside and down a staircase in the sidewalk, and introduced him to the subway. They would go in the direction called "Uptown," Muhammad said, speaking the word in English, then translating it: *"Haut de la ville."*

Deo nodded, wondering, "Are we actually going to go *up*? Like flying?"

Muhammad took him to a grocery store. The manager said Deo should come back tomorrow if he wanted a job. The next morning Muhammad told him, "You know how to get there." Feeling that he ought to know—he knew how to find his way around, he was not a child—Deo set off for the grocery store alone.

When he slid one of Jean's twenty-dollar bills into the hole at the teller's window, the woman inside asked him something, he smiled, and the next thing he knew she had shoved a whole pile of tokens back through the hole. Here he was going off to earn money and he'd already spent a fortune just to get there. But he couldn't think how to explain. So he swept up the tokens and turned away, before the teller or anyone else might see his confusion, and raging at himself—"You are mentally retarded!"—too flustered to look for the sign that said "Uptown," whatever "Uptown" meant, he went to the nearest platform and boarded the first train that stopped.

For most of the rest of the day, Deo rode the subways, from one end of the line to the other, again and again. He studied the maps on the walls of the cars. They were hard to read, because they were covered with writing that looked a little like the writing that said PEN. Peering, he realized a map was no good to him anyway, because he had no idea where he might be situated among the multicolored lines and foreign words and symbols. He abandoned his pride and tried to ask other passengers for help, to no avail—and how harsh their voices sounded, even the voices of people who seemed to want to help. A couple of times he disembarked and found himself surrounded by cars and people rushing by in all directions and by buildings so tall he had to search for the sky, and, feeling even more lost up there than on the trains, he went back underground and used up yet another of the expensive tokens. He peered out the train windows, at station signs that came and went too quickly for him to study, at blue and yellow lights flashing by in the tunnels, at the reflection of his own frightened-looking face in the glass. He told himself he didn't care if this pointless journey never ended. What seemed like another voice was saying this was a catastrophe, he might be lost forever. Then he began to feel too weary to argue with himself. This weariness was strong. It was like something outside of him, like the clangings and screechings of the train, of the rocking rolling train. "No one is in control of his own life," he told himself. The thought seemed to comfort him. He dozed off for a while.

It was evening when he finally made a lucky guess and came above ground and saw PEN. Gazing at the façade of the abandoned tenement, he said to himself that he never wanted to leave here again. Just in case, though, he went back down to the station and studied the signs on the walls, memorizing the number and name: "125th Street."

When Muhammad returned from work that night, Deo told him—it felt like confession—"I got lost."

Muhammad was reassuring. He said he'd show him how to find his way around and also help him get a job. He'd do this on his next day off, a week or so away.

In the meantime, Deo stayed close to the building PEN.

TWO

New York City,
1994

Deo felt he wasn't really here, as he left the abandoned tenement in the morning and saw the empty bottles and remnants
of dinner and soiled babies' diapers that other squatters left behind,
and the roaches and rats that skittered away as he passed by. When
he walked out onto the sidewalk of Malcolm X Boulevard, he was
met by a noise as loud and constant as the waterfall on the Siguvyaye River, but much less peaceful: a mingled noise of car horns
and sirens and shouts and babbling voices and a blaring, tuneless
music made up of words he didn't understand, words spoken emphatically over thumping sounds so deep he felt as though he heard
them in his chest. The music came from cars and young men who
walked by carrying boomboxes on their shoulders and basketballs
under their arms and caps turned backward or sideways and pants
riding so low they seemed about to fall down, all walking as if they
had broken their hips. "My God," he thought, "what happened to

these people?" He asked a French-speaking friend of Muhammad's why people were drinking alcohol out of bottles concealed in paper bags, and the man said it was illegal to drink in public. But in public was where most Burundians drank. Everything was so upside down. So many heavy people sat on the stoops of buildings. Some looked almost too heavy to walk. Back home, only the rich were fat, and yet this was obviously a poor part of New York City.

Of course there were a lot of people working, too, in hair-braiding salons, pawnshops, small grocery stores and liquor stores, and there seemed to be at least as many people working at tables on the sidewalks, hawking music tapes, pocketbooks, wristwatches, clothes. There was a group of Jamaicans selling a kind of bread he liked. The biggest table selling clothes belonged to a group of people from Senegal. They were friends of Muhammad's, they spoke French, and they had an apartment in a building a block away from PEN. It was a real apartment, which they had turned into a little factory, half a dozen women and men sitting shoulder to shoulder at sewing machines, making clothes from African cloth to sell at their sidewalk table. There was no question of their inviting Deo to sleep there, the place was already so crowded. But they told him he could do as Muhammad did—leave his suitcase with them, use their phone for local calls, and wash up in their bathroom. One of the men said to Deo, "Maybe you could learn to sew."

Deo understood this as a kindly gesture, not a serious offer. For several days after his long subway ride, he didn't feel up to much of anything except sitting. He chose to do this on the stoop of the respectable building where the Senegalese lived. With Muhammad away at work, these people from Senegal were the nearest thing he had to friends. Their table stood nearby. Deo gazed at the street. Everyone in sight had dark skin. At moments he thought he'd been transported to an African city. Memories felt more present than this place. All by itself and randomly, it seemed, his mind shuffled through pictures of home and his family, and horrible images that he stared at stupefied, as if he were right now standing in gray dawn at the open window of the hut with the smoldering roof, staring in at the bodies on the floor. When two police cars, blue lights whirling, pulled up to the curb in front of the stoop, and several uniformed men came out of the cars yelling, he thought he must be dreaming. He awoke to see a pistol practically touching his nose. A white man in a uniform held the gun, the first white man he'd seen in Harlem. The man was shouting at him.

Over the past six months, in almost every dream he remembered, he was trying with all his will to run and his legs just wouldn't move. This was the most vivid part of his dreams, usually the part that woke him up, legs kicking. He meant to run now. He was going to jump up and run. But then he heard another voice. It wasn't louder than the others, but it was yelling in French: "Deo! *Tu es fou? Haut les mains!*" "Are you crazy? Hands up!" It was one of the Senegalese men at the clothing table. Deo's hands shot up, as if all by themselves.

He was handcuffed and frisked. His mouth was forced open, a flashlight shined into it, his passport and visa examined—thank God, he had kept them in his pocket. Finally, a policeman's face came up close and spat fierce-sounding words. Then the patrol cars drove off.

The cops were looking for narcotics, the Senegalese man explained. They were angry because Deo hadn't obeyed their orders quickly enough.

It was a while before Deo's hands stopped shaking. But the policemen didn't put a stop to the train of his memories. The policemen seemed to have come right out of his memories. He sat again on the stoop. There was nowhere else to go. A weariness surrounded him. It felt stronger than any he had known, even on the run. It dulled his senses. It cut him off from the present. He wondered what was happening to him. No one was chasing him with a machete now, he thought. Now his body was at rest. Now it was his mind's turn to run.

If only he could surrender himself to sleep. He had slept on dirt

floors most of his life, and in forests and fields, but it was hard to
surrender to sleep on the piece of floor that Muhammad had staked
out inside the tenement. At night the adjacent rooms filled up with
other squatters. Lying awake in the dark, on his blanket, his mind
cycling through images he couldn't find a way to stop, he heard babies crying, drunken voices arguing, muffled moans and grunts that
he recognized as sounds of sex, disgusting because public. Usually
he dozed off only a little before dawn. Awakening at first light, he
was apt to think, "Oh, it's *samoya.*" The word meant "one o'clock"
literally, but on the hill where Deo grew up there were no clocks,
and *samoya* was the name for the first hour of daylight. For a moment he was himself again, a medical student with a family that
loved him and owned a fine herd of cows. Then he'd realize that the
light was coming through the broken windows of the tenement, and
he wondered who was Deo now.

Muhammad reminded Deo a little of his favorite uncle, a man of
few words and completely reliable. On a Saturday morning,
Muhammad handed him a subway map, and Deo spent the day
learning how to read it, as they rode the trains beneath Manhattan.
Along the way he followed Muhammad to a store named Gristedes,
on the Upper East Side. The job was delivering groceries, and the
terms were twelve hours a day, six days a week, fifteen dollars a day,
no lunch break.

At a bookstore near the grocery, Deo bought a pocket-size
French-English dictionary and a little notebook. "Slow" was one of
the first words he looked up. It also had a practical meaning at the
grocery. When one of the cashiers made a sour face and declared,
"Slow," she was saying that there weren't many customers around,
and this meant that Deo would be ordered to stock shelves or be
sent to the basement to clean up or, once in a while, be dispatched
to another store, called A&P or Sloan's or Food Emporium, which

all seemed to be connected somehow. The A&P was across town. He'd be driven there in the back of a van, riding among brooms and other tools. There was no seat. He tried to brace himself against the walls, but the first time the van made a turn, he lost his balance and slammed into one of the walls, clattering among the tools. One of the men riding up front—he was African and spoke French—called back over his shoulder, "Hey! Careful with the tools back there!" Sounding worried, the man asked, "Did one of my brooms fall out?" In his mind, Deo answered, "No, it's just me." He laughed to himself—this was the way you managed discomfort back home— and thought: "Somehow I wish I could be treated like a broom."

Mostly he delivered groceries, from seven in the morning until seven at night. He had looked up the essential words. These were "service" and "entrance" and "delivery." "Where is the service entrance?" was the first English phrase he mastered. Having no one else to tell them to, he told himself his jokes. "Delivery," he decided, was his American name. Out on foot with his grocery cart, he would ring the bell at the door or metal gate that read "Service Entrance." A voice would growl through the intercom, "Who is it?"

"Delivery."

Some addresses were better than others. Some were only a short walk away, some had service entrances at street level which weren't hard to negotiate, some were easier than others to find—along Park Avenue, for instance, the street signs showed the numbers on a block. By the end of his day, though, it seemed as if every delivery was fifteen blocks from the store and every entrance was like the one off Park Avenue that had a wrought-iron gate fringed with barbed wire and a sign by the bell that read "Please wait five minutes for superintendent." The first time Deo came there, he took out his pocket dictionary and spent the five minutes looking up those words. Now he simply stood and waited at the iron door, weary in his legs, weary all over, feeling a wave of nausea waft upward toward his chest, threatening to turn into tears. When the superintendents arrived, often after more than five minutes, Deo would say, "Hi"—according to his pocket dictionary, this was a friendly greeting—but as often as not the superintendents wouldn't bother to answer. They unlocked the gates, but only a few held the doors open for him. Deo would lift the bags of groceries out of his shopping cart, hold the gate open with his foot, and inch down narrow, clanging metal stairs. He'd shoulder open the next door, make his way past the trash cans of an untidy, gray basement, ride up on the service elevator, then lug the bags down carpeted hallways to apartment doors. Behind some of them he had glimpses of rooms that looked like pictures he'd seen at school of Belgian palaces. Most of the people who opened the doors were polite but brusque and almost never friendly. Many just looked at him oddly when he offered his "Hi." Sometimes as he walked back toward the store near the end of another long day, he'd stop and stare at the canopied, carpeted front entrances of Park Avenue apartment buildings, and bitter thoughts rose up: "I just do *not* deserve to use an entrance like that. And yet I am bringing them their *food*. Don't respect me, but at least respect your food."

To return to the Gristedes was no relief. The manager was a white, middle-aged man whom everyone called Goss, and right from the start Deo knew that Goss hated him. The man kept a long wooden pole near his desk. Deo would see the tip of the pole coming at him and force out a smile, wanting to break the pole in half. Goss would poke him with it to get his attention, to send him in one direction or another, or sometimes, it seemed, just for fun.

Deo searched his dictionary for English equivalents to *adieu*. He wanted something with more feeling than "goodbye." He settled on "I'm finished" and "See you tomorrow." Maybe if he said those words to Goss at the end of the day, the man would realize Deo was a good person and would keep him. Deo couldn't afford to lose his pay, and he couldn't bear to think he might be judged unfit even for a job as a grocery boy. But the farewells did no good. If anything,

Goss seemed to hate him more. Goss would say something loudly, and the cashiers and the other delivery boys would turn and look at Deo and everyone would laugh—even the fellow delivery boy who also came from French-speaking Africa and who Deo thought was his friend.

When no one else was nearby, when he and the other young African were stocking shelves together, Deo asked in French what it was Goss said about him that made everyone laugh.

His friend looked away as he spoke. "For example, he says that the people where you come from are starving, and that's why they're killing each other. So they can eat each other."

Most of the other workers, Deo thought, couldn't really be amused by a joke like that. They were only trying to please Goss. They were probably afraid for their jobs, too. And, Deo realized after a while, every delivery boy wanted Goss to favor him with the good deliveries, the deliveries to customers known for giving tips.

Deo had a lot of experience with bargaining, but the whole idea of soliciting tips was new, and, once he understood it, repugnant. His French-speaking African friend at the store explained. No one could survive in New York on fifteen dollars a day. You had to get tips. You lingered in doorways, you cleared your throat, sometimes you asked for a tip outright. But this was the same as begging, Deo thought. Back home a self-respecting person didn't even yawn in public, because to yawn meant you were hungry, and to admit that you were hungry was to admit that you were incompetent or, worse, that you were lazy. The beggars you saw in cities like Bujumbura were mainly displaced country people who had lost their pride. The first time a customer in a doorway held out a dollar bill toward Deo, he raised his hands as if to push the money back, and said in his thickly accented English, "No. No. Thank you very much. Eeet is okay."

But this didn't happen often. It wasn't hard to tell that whenever possible Goss sent him to tipless destinations—to addresses where a doorman took the groceries and delivered them himself and got the tip, or where customers received the groceries and quickly shut the door or said they were sorry but they didn't have any change. It was also clear by then that the other delivery boys were usually the ones Goss picked to work at one of the other stores on days when the cashiers declared, "Slow." Not that Deo liked riding in the back of the van across town to the A&P, but he felt wounded. By now it seemed obvious that a delivery boy belonged to a layer near the bottom of New York's hierarchy, and also that there was a bottom to that near-bottom, which he occupied. Standing at another service entrance—they all might as well have been fringed with barbed wire—waiting for another brusque superintendent who would hardly even look at him, he wondered whether this could really be the station he had been put on earth to occupy. Not long ago he had been a student so accomplished he'd been offered a scholarship to college in Belgium. Not long ago he had been a medical student at the top of his class. "And here I am," he thought, "being treated as someone who has a primate brain." "God," he said silently. "Take my life."

"A New Yorker." Deo had heard the phrase around the store. Even Muhammad used it, and the Senegalese tailors and sidewalk merchants. This world, he was beginning to understand, was divided, among other ways, between people who were "New Yorkers" and people who weren't. Within a couple of weeks, he felt he had all but mastered the subway. The trains ran like rivers, taking you *anywhere*. To look at his subway map was pleasing, like looking at a set of differential equations he'd solved. Never mind that he had solved only one, his route between Harlem and the Upper East Side, or that he always rode in the first car, so as to gain a little extra time to peer out the windows at the station signs and decide whether he'd reached the right stop. Riding along, subway map sticking out of his hip pocket, Deo told himself he was becoming a New Yorker, too.

He had discovered Central Park. The first time he'd walked into it, curious about the trees on the other side of Fifth Avenue, he had thought, "My God, I just discovered a forest!" It had become one of his favorite places, along with bookstores.

Some of the stores were like forests themselves, forests of books, more books than he'd thought there were in the world, and all in one place. He often went to the stores in the evening after work, just to recover from being poked with Goss's stick, just to walk among the tables and shelves and pick up books and turn the pages and imagine he was reading them. The stores he liked best had chairs where he could sit and look at books he hoped one day to read. Sometimes he fell asleep in the chairs. Bookstores, he found, were one place he could sleep, but never for long, before a clerk or manager woke him up and asked him to leave.

He always spent some time with the dictionaries. Many people had looked at him oddly when he'd said, "Hi." There had to be something wrong with the way he was saying it. At the Barnes & Noble on Eighty-third Street, he found a dictionary with an international phonetic alphabet, something his pocket dictionary didn't have, and after a little study it all came clear. He had been pronouncing the word as if it were French. He'd been saying "Hee" instead of "Hi." He looked around in the store for the cheapest dictionary that contained the phonetic alphabet. But it was an English-only dictionary, and after he spent half a day's pay to own it, he realized he had solved only half his problem. When he heard a new word, he would if possible get someone to spell it for him or guess at the spelling and write the word in his notebook. Then he'd look it up in his new English dictionary and learn how to pronounce it. But most of the time he couldn't decipher the English definition in his little phrasebook. So he'd take his notebook to the bookstore and look up the word in a French-English dictionary. It was a laborious process. Performing it was often the best part of his day.

Many evenings he composed English sentences out of dictionaries and wrote down the words and sounded out the pronunciations in his mind. Some of the sentences he made up produced puzzled looks when he tried them out at the grocery or on a customer, but he managed to explain to a pharmacist—in a low voice so no one else would hear—that his feet were afflicted with a disgusting fungus. The cause was obvious to Deo: six months on the run in wet sneakers.

When he had left Bujumbura, a close friend from medical school named Claude had been living in an apartment with other displaced young men. The apartment had been equipped with a telephone. Deo had made sure to take the number with him. He kept it on a piece of paper in his pocket. He asked the Senegalese clothing merchants whether he could call from the phone in their apartment. Too expensive, they said, but they showed him how to make a streetcorner call from Harlem to Bujumbura. You went out to the sidewalk to one of the open telephone stands and right away someone, almost always a man, would come up to you. He'd get you to write down the number you wanted to call, and he'd take the phone and punch in a bunch of numbers. Usually, the phone man would turn his back as he dialed—so that you couldn't see the numbers he was pressing, Deo figured. He didn't want to know the details of the phone men's business, because if they were doing something illegal and he knew it, he wouldn't want to use their services, and he didn't know any other way he could afford to call Burundi.

The first time Deo made a streetcorner call, the phone man demanded five dollars. Deo parted with the money reluctantly. Miraculously, the phone rang on the other end, and a voice answered in Kirundi and said that, yes, Claude was there.

The news was bad. Civil war continued. Claude came from the same region as Deo. To speak to him was almost like speaking with family. Deo could have talked to him for hours. The phone man was making a fuss, though, telling Deo his time was up—the man's tone of voice was unmistakable. Deo gestured him away. There was a

woman standing near the phone man, drinking from a bottle in a
paper bag. She began yelling at Deo. He was telling Claude that he
would call again soon, when from the corner of his eye, he saw the
woman throw her bottle at him. He was wearing flip-flops. The bottle shattered at his toes. Deo let out a yell, turning angrily to face the
woman. She was laughing at him. Deo even raised a fist. Seeing this,
one of the Senegalese vendors walked over, telling Deo in French
not to mess with that woman. There was a reason why it was the
woman and not the man who had done that to him, the street ven-
dor said. Here in the U.S., you don't touch a woman. It didn't matter whether you were the victim or not. If a woman attacked you
like that, the best thing to do was to leave.

Selling streetcorner calls was a competitive enterprise. Once he
realized this, Deo haggled every time he made a call. He could almost always find a phone man who would connect him for three
dollars, four at most. But that was still almost a third of a day's pay.
The money he'd brought with him was long gone, and his wages
seemed to evaporate no matter how careful he was. Money went for
the antifungal salve, for antacids to lessen the chronic churning in
his intestines, for the food he could stomach, for his dictionaries, for
subway fare. He studied the dictionary one night and the next
morning descended the stairs to the subway outside the tenement
PEN and tried to bargain with the teller over the price of tokens. The
teller was firm but polite; maybe he wasn't the first who had tried to
bargain with her, that part of the city harbored so many Africans.

He stopped turning down tips. They weren't easy to come by,
partly because he would never allow himself to ask for one, partly
because of Goss. But the more deliveries he made the more chances
he had, he reasoned. For a time he worked on Sundays. But only for
tips, and Sundays were so slow that the most he could hope to get
was about four dollars. A dollar was a big tip, fifty cents a decent
one. The transactions were almost always short and impersonal.
Once in a great while, a customer wanted to talk—for instance, a
white Frenchwoman in a very tall building on 110th Street. She

talked on and on to him in French, while a baby cried in another room. She seemed to view him as a compatriot. She said she knew the grocery stores treated people like him badly. He should go to the French consulate and get them to help him find a better job. She meant well, he thought, but clearly she didn't understand. France was the friend of the *génocidaires* in Rwanda, and therefore his enemy. She was Catholic and would pray for him, she said. When he left, she tipped him a dollar.

And then there was the American woman who appeared on a day when he happened to be working at the A&P on the Upper West Side. Deo was assigned to carry her groceries to her apartment. She was, he thought, quite beautiful to look at, a middle-aged woman with wonderful posture. "So elegant," he thought, as he walked along beside her, her bags of groceries in his arms. She asked him a question. He didn't understand it, all he could do was smile. But she smiled back, as if she actually enjoyed his company. He had picked up a baseball cap somewhere, an "I ♥ New York" cap. When they got to her apartment and he had put the groceries in her kitchen, she looked at him quizzically. She must have been looking at his cap, because she asked, "Do you really love New York?"

This he understood. "Oh, yes!" He put on his best smile. At the moment, he felt that his answer was true, or true enough.

She walked him to the door, and he went out to the hallway, thinking he didn't care this time that he wasn't getting a tip. But then he heard her say, "Wait." He turned back. She said something he didn't fully understand. The gist seemed to be that she didn't believe he loved New York, and she wasn't sure if this would really help him. She was holding the door open with one hand, and extending the other toward him. He stared at her hand. He couldn't believe it. She was giving him a twenty-dollar bill!

He took it. He was speechless. He was wishing he knew the words to thank her—stronger, better words than the English equivalent of *Merci beaucoup*.

"*Bonne chance,*" she said.

Did she speak French? If she spoke French, he would love to talk with her. But before he could get the question out, she had closed the door.

He was living mostly on milk and bread and cookies. Once in a while he took a carrot or a few grapes from the produce bin at the grocery store. Everyone did that. It occurred to him there might be ways to steal most of his food from the Gristedes or the other stores where he worked, but that would be risky and worse than begging. Out of mild curiosity, on his way to work, he had looked at a menu posted outside a fancy restaurant on the Upper East Side. In a place like that, his day's pay wouldn't even buy a napkin. A place like that, he thought, might as well be on another planet, along with the juice bars, coffeehouses, hot dog stands, pizza shops he passed every day. He hardly noticed those places anymore. They weren't just too expensive for the likes of him; they didn't offer anything he wanted. He could remember caring about food and wanting certain foods, but over the past months he'd lost his appetite. He hadn't studied the physiology of appetite, but it seemed as if a switch in him had simply been turned off. On the run, he'd learned to stifle hunger, and now he often had to force himself to eat, even on days when he was feeling well. It was a good thing, he thought, that his system still had lactase. Lately, milk was one of the only things he could bear to taste.

He had felt puzzled at first at the skinniness of so many of the well-dressed women he saw on the streets and in the apartments of the Upper East Side, a skinniness that would have marked them as impoverished back home. He himself was downright skeletal, even thinner than when he had arrived in New York. Some days he would rise very early and walk the thirty blocks or so to the grocery. Once in a while, he'd walk back at the end of his twelve hours of

work, to save the subway fare and to prolong the time before he arrived back at the tenement. Sometimes he'd ride the bus instead of
the subway, because the bus took him back there much more slowly.
His knees ached constantly. He still couldn't sleep for long on the
floor of the filthy room he shared with Muhammad, and when he
did nod off he often wished he hadn't, because of the dreams that
came. He would start awake from nightmares, without much memory of the dreams themselves but with a residue of dread that felt
like something interfering with his breathing, that made him afraid
to go back to sleep.

And now Muhammad was heading home to Senegal. The apartment of the Senegalese would still be a refuge, with a shower and a
functioning toilet that Deo could use. But he didn't like the prospect of sleeping in PEN, among the drunks and drug addicts and
prostitutes, without his burly friend and protector. Muhammad
himself didn't think this was a good idea. Before he left, he took
Deo to another abandoned tenement in Harlem, on 126th Street,
and introduced him to the men squatting there. They were all African-
Americans. None spoke French. Muhammad called them "friends,"
but they were not friendly once Muhammad left. Almost at once
they began making jokes about Deo. He couldn't understand the
jokes, but he knew they were directed at him. After he'd spent a
few nights there, one of the squatters told Deo he had to pay him
rent. Deo pretended not to understand. On a morning soon afterward, another of the squatters came up holding a knife and asked
Deo for money. The man was big—bigger than Deo, anyway. His
smile was nasty. Deo said he didn't have any money. The man jig-
gled the knife in one hand and slid the other into Deo's pocket.
"Unh-hunh," he said, as he pulled out the cash Deo had managed
to save that week. "Yeah! You have money!"

After that, Deo kept his cash in his underwear. And he moved, to
another abandoned tenement, another reeking, rat- and roach-
infested place, on 131st and Third Avenue. He had found a piece of

floor inside. On his second or third evening there, sitting by a broken window on the second floor, he heard gunshots. He knew the sound at once, an all too familiar sound. Deo looked out the broken window and saw people running in all directions and, on the sidewalk just below, a body lying in a spreading pool of blood. He thought, "I can't believe it. I can't believe I'm seeing blood again." There were sirens. Police cars arrived, then an ambulance, and when those were gone, a crowd gathered around the pool of blood. For hours Deo lay on the floor listening to the excited voices of the sightseers on the sidewalk below. He had to get away from this place. He had to get away from Harlem.

On mornings when he walked to work, he always went through part of Central Park. He would go down Malcolm X, and when he reached 110th Street, he would climb a stone stairway, overarched with leafy trees. Right there, where Central Park butts into Harlem, he had seen small groups of men, some sitting on benches, some still sleeping on blankets in the grass nearby, each, it seemed, with his own black plastic bag of belongings. It was Muhammad who had explained to him that some people actually lived in the park. The day after Deo saw the body on the sidewalk, he went to the West Africans' apartment, the clothing factory, and retrieved from his suitcase the things he thought he'd need—a change of clothes, his toothbrush, his blanket. He put them in a plastic bag.

He slept in Central Park that night, near the 110th Street entrance. He awakened with a foul odor in his nose, which followed him all day. He realized the grass he'd chosen to sleep on was a place where the other homeless people usually went to urinate. The next evening, literally following his nose, he found a better spot, a lovely spot, a grassy slope beneath tall trees, near a public swimming pool. But in the morning he discovered the reason that place smelled better: the police didn't tolerate camping there. He saw the police before they saw him, and quickly moved away. He understood. It was a nice public swimming pool, and it was beautiful because the police kept the area clean, and the way they kept it clean was to prevent people from shitting in it. He himself used the toilet at the store or at the apartment of the Senegalese, where he still went regularly to bathe.

The first few nights, Deo avoided the shadowy figures of other men who were living in the park. Gradually, he began to observe them from a little distance. He'd hear them talking to each other. Little by little he made out some of the words they used most often. Most weren't in his dictionary, though, words like "mothafucker." He could tell this was a bad word, from the way the homeless men would use it, when they were yelling at each other for instance. But he didn't see real fighting. Actually, most of them seemed to be generous with each other, even with him, proffering their bottles wrapped in paper bags, or whatever it was they were smoking. He would say, "No, thank you." They called him "bro," as in, "Hey, bro, where you from?" They'd say, "Whassup?" And when he walked away from them, "Take it easy."

"Take it easy, bro," he'd reply, wondering, "What are they talking about?"

They weren't much help in learning English. But they didn't frighten him after he got used to them. Some could even be trusted to watch his plastic bag of stuff while he went off to deliver groceries. He supposed that they felt sorry for him, as he did for them. All of them were black. Most of them, he thought, suffered from one form of mental illness or another. If he got too close, he'd find himself breathing through his mouth so as not to smell them, but he felt much safer sharing the park with them than he had in the abandoned buildings, among men like the one with the knife who had robbed him.

He found places that felt private, spots of grassy or leaf-covered ground hidden by bushes. Lying on his back, looking up through leaves and branches at the stars, he felt almost at home, almost as if he'd been restored to his proper element. But always memories troubled him, even more than they had in PEN, and especially on nights when there was a moon. It was automatic: every time he saw the moon, he thought of a moonlit night when he was a little boy, lying on a mat of banana leaves in the grass of a mountain pasture, feeling utterly safe because he was with his grandfather Lonjino. Staring up at the sky, Deo had seen something he'd never noticed before, a profile of a rabbit on the face of the moon. He had told Lonjino, and Lonjino had exclaimed, "Yes, this is a rabbit!" Lonjino was certainly dead. When the militiamen came, he would have refused as usual to run away, right up until the last moment. He'd have stayed near the family compound, guarding the cows with his dogs and his spear, until it was too late.

In the park Deo found what he thought of as his own peaceful corners. Some days after work and on Sundays when it didn't seem worth working, Deo would sit facing the fountain in the Conservatory Garden. It was kept locked at night and was therefore a place where, as he thought of it, his receptors could recover from urine-saturation. He would sit and sometimes manage not to think of home or horrors, but simply gaze at flowers and close his eyes and doze to the sound of the fountain, like the lapping waves on the shore of Lake Tanganyika.

He discovered the big pond in the park, the Jacqueline Kennedy Onassis Reservoir. He would stand at the railing and gaze out at the water and his thoughts. Now and then he would join one of the passing groups of runners, jogging along with them for a while by the pond, for the sake of what he thought of as "psychological friendship." A curious tableau, the joggers in their shorts and spandex, Deo in his long pants and sneakers and "I ♥ New York" cap. It made him feel as if he belonged there, as if he were like everyone else. He couldn't run far anymore. Even the slowest crew of joggers would eventually leave him behind, but that was all right, he'd tell himself. There was always another group coming along that he could join.

He had acquired other spots for long thoughts. Making deliveries on the Upper East Side, he often found himself in the vicinity of a small Catholic church, St. Thomas More. Occasionally, he would park his grocery cart and go inside and say a prayer for himself and his family. In motion again, he would pass by the window of a children's clothing shop. One day he stopped. Looking through the glass past his own reflection—he couldn't have weighed more than sixty kilograms now, far too little for a man of medium height—he peered in at the little dresses and young gentleman's jackets and at the price tags attached to them, and his anger flared. "Look at how little you are making, sweating, smelling like a dead body, and you can't even buy more than a button."

It was clear that to be a New Yorker could mean so many things that it meant practically nothing at all. He had studied the graffiti on the outer walls of subway cars, noting especially the crude, sexually explicit drawings and the vulgar words that his dictionary did contain. He had come to think of these as messages, sent from people uptown in Harlem to people downtown who shopped in places like that children's clothing store. A phrase he'd put together out of his dictionary kept coming to him. "A different planet." New York had many planets. Better, he thought, to be in Burundi, if Burundi were at peace, than to live on the wrong, impoverished planet in New York. This place made you feel like you were simply not a human being. How could you be a human being like everyone else, if your circumstances were this different?

He stood on the corner of Fifth Avenue and Ninety-sixth Street and looked at the traffic. What was going to be his future? His life and the future he had imagined had been, not interrupted, but wiped out. There was no future now that he cared to occupy. When would his life be over? Would God please hurry up and end it? It was getting dark. Rush hour was past, and cabs and cars were racing by. Maybe it would be a good idea to close his eyes and run out into the middle of the street.

He waited for the traffic light. There was an entrance to the park right in front of him, the Ninety-sixth Street entrance, a passage into the darkness beyond the streetlights. As he approached it, he felt embarrassed again, and annoyed at himself for the feeling. Anyone who happened to see him walk into the park at this hour would guess he was a homeless person. So what? He didn't really know anyone in New York City. But as usual, he looked around, to the right and left and behind him, to make sure no one was watching.

THREE

Burundi,
1970s

"Deogratias, thanks be to God" was Latin his mother had learned in church. She had nearly died during his gestation and birth; his name was her thanksgiving. In Deo's Burundi, the Burundi of ordinary farmers and herdsmen, many names told stories. Deo grew up with a boy whose mother called him Good Road because he had been born by the side of a trail. Some names were like social commentary, such as Nzokirantevye, which means I Won't Be Rich Soon. And some names were harsh. He knew a boy named A Hungry Street Dog, and another called Shit. At an early age he understood the reason. These were *amazina y'ikuzo,* "names for growth." Parents were saying, "This child tastes bitter, Death. You don't want to take him."

Villages were called *collines,* hills. Deo's home was a compound on ground carved out of the *colline* Butanza. A large part of his extended family lived together there—his paternal grandparents, his parents, a growing number of children, including several sons of deceased relatives, and also his grandfather's dogs and the family's cows, many long-horned *inyambo* and *ankole* cows. A wall of hardened clay reinforced with saplings surrounded the compound. The human beings lived in wooden buildings with thatched roofs. The smoke from cooking fires rose through holes in the centers of the roofs. The largest building was the barn; the ferns that covered its floor made soft beds for the cows, and were replaced daily by Deo and his siblings. Each cow had its own name. Among others, there was Jambo, whom his grandfather doted on, and Yanzobe, whose name means "Light-Skinned," and Yaruyange, "Beautiful Grasses."

In Burundi, land was the only natural resource and, along with cows, the only wealth. Cows had long been the traditional form of large currency, the essential gift by which chiefs—and many others as well—had secured loyalty and service. Deo's family's herd was numerous but didn't yield a great deal of milk, just enough to feed them all and to make butter, with some left over to give away to impoverished neighbors. Certain traditions applied to cows, at least in Deo's family. One couldn't take money for the milk, and no cow could be slaughtered for food, though rarely one might be sold to buy a piece of arable land or for some other truly important purpose. The family was paramount—one member's disgrace or success belonged to all—and the herd of cows was his family's pride, like a bank account made public, one from which you rarely made withdrawals: a source of prestige, and insurance in times of scarcity.

None of the children wore shoes, and all knew hunger, at least from time to time. August and September were arid months, when hardly anything grew and one ate mostly beans or peas that had been dried and stored. By December, in large families especially, the supplies would be depleted. Seeing neighbors whose teeth were stained green in December, you would know they had been eating leaves. It was the season for *umukubi,* the leaves of bean plants. You grazed like a cow, people would say.

The settlements lacked electricity, of course, and safe water supplies. The water Deo and his brothers and mother lugged home came from a stream that ran a steep two kilometers away from their hut. Infectious and parasitic illnesses were ubiquitous, and there was no public health system to measure their extent or even to identify them, let alone a clinic in the area to cure them. Every child knew the pain of illness, and, as some names implied, almost all parents knew the pain of losing a child—and many children the pain of losing a parent. Deo fetched water in the evenings after school, always racing to get to the stream before sunset, because there were frogs in the water, and if he couldn't see them, he might scoop up tadpoles and messes of eggs along with the water. His father had received some training in veterinary medicine. He knew the germ theory of illness, so they always tried to boil their drinking water, but this was hard to do in the rainy season when firewood was usually wet.

The elders would say, "When too much is too much or too bad is too bad, we laugh as if it was too good." As long as you could say this, you didn't feel you were really poor. If you didn't know what electricity was, you didn't feel its absence. Deo and his siblings slept on woven straw mats on the dirt floor by the embers of the cooking fire, fighting for a corner of the blanket they shared. On nights of heavy downpours, he'd be awakened sooner or later by a raindrop hitting his ear and would know that more were coming. At least one nearby family was better off than his. Deo first realized this when he visited the house of a schoolmate and heard a strange pinging sound, which close examination showed was the sound of rain falling on that family's metal roof. Many families were obviously poorer than his, families without cows or enough food even in the bountiful seasons. But for the most part, the differences seemed small, at least during his years of elementary school.

He first heard the term "Hutu" on a day in the summer before he began middle school. He was carrying a sack of grain from Butanza to another town, a hike of several hours. Passing through a grove of towering trees, he came upon an elderly woman, bent over, a load of firewood on her back. As he passed her on the trail, she yelled at him. "What are you saying? What are you saying?"

Deo looked back at her. He'd never seen her before, and he hadn't said a word. He was frightened. Was she a ghost?

"Did you say that I'm a Hutu?" she yelled angrily. "Did you say that I'm a Hutu?"

Deo dropped his bag of grain and ran all the way back to Butanza. He found his father working on the barn and told him what had happened. "Hutu," Deo said. "What is that?"

His father glared at him. "Shut up!" he said, and went back to work.

A year or so later—maybe it was at school or in the schoolyard—he heard the term again, along with the term "Tutsi." Evidently, these were the names of different kinds of people in Burundi. He took his question to his father again. "Which are we?"

"Tutsi," his father said, and added, "Don't you have anything better to think about?"

The names seemed to have something to do with cows. If a man gave a cow to his brother, the giver might call the other his Hutu. If a family had no cows, others who owned cows might call them Hutus. It followed that people with many cows were Tutsis. Deo tried out this theory on his grandfather once, saying of a certain neighbor, "He is a great Tutsi because he has so many cows."

His grandfather, who was usually fairly gentle with him, actually spat in his face, and said, "This is prejudice! Shut up! Who is teaching you this?"

Deo asked his older brother in private about the man with many cows. Wasn't he a Tutsi? Deo asked. His brother said no, actually that man was a Hutu. And according to his brother, so was the family with the metal roof. It was all very confusing. Everyone he knew lived much the same life—though his older brother, Antoine, insisted that he and Deo had to work a lot harder than other boys. Deo was inclined to agree.

Farming was difficult in that region, the terrain very steep, the soil poor. Deo's father had raised some cash—probably by selling a precious cow; Deo was too young to know—and had bought a hectare of fertile land near the shore of Lake Tanganyika, where the family grew cassava and rice and beans and bananas, also some oranges and mangoes. There was no house or even a hut there. When it came to a home, his father preferred the mountains. One did not ask many questions of one's father, but gradually the reasons became obvious: the mountains' relative lack of mosquitoes, and their distance from the big towns and cities, full of malign influences for growing boys and girls and potentially more dangerous for everyone, given the country's recent history of violence—a history largely unknown to Deo, and indecipherable, like the whispers of an overheard conversation among elders.

Most of the food raised by the lake was for the family and had to be carried to Butanza, a trip that for a bird would have measured about twenty-five kilometers. But on foot the trip was nearly twice that long and full of steep climbs and descents. It took about fourteen hours. Deo made it for the first time when he was about ten and many years of going barefoot lay before him. They would set out before *samoya,* and he soon learned to feel relieved when they left in moonlight and he could make out stones and roots on the paths. Inevitably, when there was no moon, he stubbed his toes. He knew by then that crying aloud was not acceptable. He'd fall to the ground curling up over his wounded toes, struggling not to cry, and then would get up and go on, hurrying after the others, sniffling until the pain subsided.

Soon he and Antoine were making the journey once a week and alone. Both of them were still small, too small to lift a sack of cassava onto their heads without help. On hot days they took off their shirts and used them to cushion the loads. Sometimes they made head cushions of banana leaves, called *ingata.* On the first stretch, climbing up from the lake, they had to cross footbridges of logs over the streams that fed the Rwaba River, and sometimes, especially if it was raining and the logs were slippery, one of them would lose his balance and his load. Then they would have to go back to get more cassava. To arrive in Butanza without food meant trouble, and shame.

After the Rwaba River came the mountains. Three stood out. Honga was first, a long and arduous climb and the most frightening, because from a certain cliff near the summit on stormy days Deo really feared he would be blown off and come to rest like the blackened and now rusting skeleton of the automobile that lay on a grassy slope down below.

An uncle, a brother of Deo's father, had owned that car, and had died in it—in 1972, it was said. Deo had been just a baby, and didn't remember his uncle, only the good stories about him and, cars having been a very unusual sight, an image of his uncle's car, a Volkswagen Bug, which was white before it got burned. People said that his uncle had been sent by priests to Europe for some medical training and that afterward his uncle had come back and worked as a doctor. People feeling ill in Butanza would say, "Oh, we miss your uncle. Oh, if only your uncle were alive." How could Deo not ask for the story? For a long time he was told his uncle had died in an accident. Then when Deo was about twelve, one of his younger uncles said, out of everyone else's hearing, "No, he was killed." Crossing the summit of Honga, Deo would tell himself not to look, but he always would. He'd see the car's skeleton in the mountain grass, then avert his eyes and look at Antoine and see that his brother was doing the same. He and Antoine would pass by without speaking, as solemn as if they were in church.

He couldn't recall hearing any other stories about killings, even such cryptic stories, during those years of hiking the mountains. They always encountered many others who were hiking in the same direction, up and down the paths and dirt roads. Most became friends for the duration of the trip. When they were still small, there were grown-ups and older kids willing to help them put their sacks of cassava back on their heads after a rest. In later years, there were fellow teenagers to trade jokes and stories with. All were comrades in toil, Deo felt. He respected especially the men who carried palm oil up from the lakefront on bicycles, great loads of yellow jerry cans tied onto their bikes, the barefoot men pushing their loads up the dirt roads toward Kirimiro in Gitega province for days on end. He remembered this as a time of *amahoro,* of peace, when, as he later put it to himself, people were still people.

After Honga, there was Ganza. More than once on the upward climb Antoine suddenly cursed, threw down his load, and stalked off up the trail toward the summit. Deo would sit down and wait. After a while Antoine would return. Deo would say, "Were you looking for some fresher air?" And they would load up again, and go on.

The last of the truly difficult climbs was the mountain named Kabasumyi—"The Challenge of the Shepherds." It would be dark or nearly dark by the time they trudged up the last paths to home. Antoine would often say to Deo, speaking of their parents, "I'm afraid we are not really their children." What parents would work their own flesh and blood so hard? Antoine would say. Often as they scrabbled up the last incline, they'd see their mother standing at the top of the trail, awaiting them.

———

Deo was still in elementary school when his father built another traditional, thatched-roof hut and moved them a kilometer or so away from the family compound in Butanza—a steep climb away, to the top of Runda mountain. The cows had more room to graze there, and maybe his father felt safer: there were fewer neighbors, and there was a forest nearby. Partly, Deo guessed, they moved for his mother's sake, to give her some distance from her mother-in-law.

Summer mornings on Runda were often windy and chilly. Deo and his brothers and younger uncles would lie around in the sun in the lee of the house before getting to work. Finding them there one morning, on her way to get water from the stream half a kilometer away, his mother put down her clay pot and gave the boys a long stare and compared them to lizards lying in the sun. He could not remember a harsher scolding from her.

There were eight children eventually, three of them cousins his parents adopted, all but Antoine younger than Deo. It seemed to Deo that he spent more time with their mother than the others did, helping her plant beans and talking with her. People said he resembled her, both in looks and—this was a mixed compliment—in temperament. She was emotional. She cried easily, as he did, and he imagined people saying, "What's her problem? She has children; she has a strong husband." She could be counted on to feel sorry for neighbors' misfortunes, and, though his voice was never as soft as hers, maybe the habit of sympathy was a weakness he caught from her, along with her tendency to get upset when even little things went wrong. Looking back, Deo felt she was both beloved and ridiculed by neighbors, because she was always giving things away, such as milk and especially salt, the sine qua non of the local cuisine, sold by the pinch in the markets. To have to beg or borrow salt was utterly demeaning. To curse someone doubly, one would say, "May you spill borrowed salt"—may you lose what you humiliated yourself to obtain. But his mother was artful. She would take pinches of salt from the supply that his father bought for the cows and wrap the salt in a banana leaf, then slip the package into the needy housewife's hand when no one else was looking. Word had long since got around. Some people, Deo suspected, wouldn't spend their own money on salt because they knew they could get it from her. And her generosity could leave his father fuming in the cow barn, yelling at her, "I bought salt! Where did you put it?"

Once, only once, he overheard her arguing back at his father. She told him he was working her sons too hard. "You're killing my children," she said.

His father was utterly different. If you were playing in the hut or the barn and knocked something over, he'd grab you and shake you. "I could kill you!" he'd say. Then he would visibly catch himself, and say, "Don't do that again." An hour or so later he would find you and apologize, and then you would probably cry. One time a man on their hill, drunk on banana beer, was beating up another neighbor, and Deo's father grabbed the drunk, a much bigger man, and threw him to the ground. Deo watched, sick with fear—fear for his father, fear of his father. Another time, his father roughed up the local Belgian priest. Deo's baby brother had started squalling while being christened, and in irritation the priest had slapped the baby. After the ceremony Deo's father belted down some banana beer, then strode right into the priest's house. The priest banished him from church, where he rarely went anyway.

His father was well-off by local standards, but he had a lot of children to feed, and he was rather profligate with money, giving it away or buying rounds of drinks. Deo would sometimes hear his grandfather scolding his father, saying, "You shouldn't hang out with people, drinking like this." But Deo's father wasn't a drunk, and if he worked his children hard, he worked himself harder. He had saved enough to acquire the land by the lake and later, to buy another smallholding, on a hilltop not far from the lake in a town called Kayanza, where little by little he was building another house. He was often away, farming the land by the lake or tending his cows. More than by anyone else, Deo was raised by his *sogo-kuru*, his grandfather Lonjino.

Not all the treks Deo and his older brother made were between Butanza and the lake. In late May, when the grass had been over-grazed and had turned into yellow stubble, various members of their extended family would set out with their cows, sometimes for their land by the lake, but often for nearer mountainsides, only four or five hours away instead of fourteen. Often Lonjino would have charge of the family's herd.

They would stay out for months, trading milk and manure with farmers in return for the use of their grazing land, and live on milk themselves, also on beans and cassava that Deo and his brother would carry from home. Sometimes he and Antoine would carry cooked mashes of cassava, beans, and potatoes—food so hot when they started out they'd think the tops of their heads were being burned, but often cold and smelly by the time they arrived at the camp of the herders. When Deo wasn't carrying food, he was herding cows with his grandfather, sleeping on beds of banana leaves under the stars, wary of the dangerous snakes—cobras and mambas, adders, vipers, and asps—and frightened routinely by the harmless chameleons camouflaged in the leaves, which at first touch felt like snakes.

In the suitcase he carried to New York, Deo had packed a photograph that someone had taken of his grandfather. Lonjino was sitting on a rough wooden bench, dressed in a homemade chamois coat, a straw hat, and a scarf: mornings and evenings, a chill descends on the mountains of Burundi. In the picture, Lonjino looked elderly and thin. His chin was lifted, and he wore a look that Deo knew well, a mixture of dignity and tight-lipped amusement at his own pretensions to dignity. It was the same face Lonjino wore when he had been listening for too long to someone he disliked and would say, "May you have an interesting life." The same face he'd put on when his wife, Deo's grandmother, was railing about something or other, and he'd whisper to Deo, "Stay quiet. Let her talk to herself."

Lonjino was friendly to most people. He was adept at listening. If he was talking and someone broke in and then apologized for interrupting him, Lonjino would say, "No, no, go ahead, go ahead." When he spoke, his voice was so quiet and sure and his words so succinct that Deo felt that he wanted to lean toward him to listen, even when Lonjino was scolding him: for bringing back water full of tadpoles, or for stealing a bunch of bananas from a farmer whose land they camped on. Deo's punishment for the bananas was a huge pot of milk, fresh from the cows, sickeningly warm, which Lonjino make him drink, and go on drinking even after he threw up. There was no punishment, though, for slipping on a pile of manure in the family compound and breaking Lonjino's special banana-beer pot. Deo cried out when he fell, less from pain than fear of Lonjino's disappointment in him. His grandfather came right out and picked him up, and said nothing about the pot.

By the time Deo was traveling with Lonjino, the cow Yaruyange was old and useless, so decrepit you had to lift her with a stick to get her on her feet. Lonjino sold her to some strangers. The money changed hands, and then, while the other buyers sharpened their machetes on a stone, one of the men grabbed Yaruyange's long horns and twisted her head halfway around. The cow was bellowing, the men were laughing, and Deo ran, covering his ears with his hands so as not to hear any more. Then he heard the muffled sound of Lonjino's voice, calling, "Deo!"

"Yes, Sogo-kuru," Deo called back.

"Run and tell those men to wait for me before they slaughter Yaruyange."

The tall grass whipped Deo's cheeks as he ran. The men were still sharpening their machetes when he got to the clearing. "Just wait. Just wait. My granddad has something to tell you."

Deo watched as Lonjino gave the men back their small wad of Burundian francs. Then Lonjino led Yaruyange back to the barn in the compound. The old cow died peacefully, and unprofitably, a few days later.

Deo became, thanks to Lonjino, a connoisseur of banana beer. Deo didn't like the drink himself, but he knew Lonjino's taste so well that the old man would send him off to fetch beer without even telling him where to buy it, knowing that Deo would find the brew with just the right bitter taste. Sometimes, out in the mountains, Lonjino would go himself to a village and fetch his own calabash of beer to savor at the end of a day. Once, up near the waterfall on the Siguvyaye River, Deo sat with Lonjino in the shade, and figuring his grandfather might be softened up from the beer he was drinking, Deo asked—it was a momentous question—"Sogo-kuru, can you give me just one cow?"

"I didn't know you were that drunk," said Lonjino.

"I'm not drunk!" said Deo. He hadn't even had a sip of the beer.

Lonjino gave him the look. For a time they sat there in silence. Then Lonjino said, "I'll give you a cow when you finish school."

There were many times with his grandfather in the mountain pastures when Deo felt in no hurry to become someone else. Times when the cows would take a break from grazing and lie down, and Lonjino would sit and play his flute. Back in the village, Lonjino played accompaniments on his flute while his best friend played the stringed *inanga* and sang the traditional songs in the traditional whispery voice. This best friend of Lonjino's was especially equipped for traditional singing. Years before, so the story went, someone had tried to strangle him and had injured his vocal cords. Lonjino made his own flutes and many of his own melodies. It was said that one should not play flutes in the wild because snakes would come to listen. Lonjino would play anyway, and Deo would feel afraid at moments. But then he'd forget about snakes and listen to the rush of the waterfall and the flute music. Often a gaggle of colorful, long-legged birds would gather nearby—*musambis,* with their spiky-looking hairdos, Deo's favorite animal after the cow. He would try to persuade the birds to dance. The trick was to wave your arms up and down, while you sang a traditional song. "*Dambira musambi dambira. Dambira musambi nzoguhera. Nzo-gohoya akogorika yinankonge.*" ("Dance for me, please. I will give you maize with the beautiful colors, if you dance for me.") And more often than not the musambis would oblige, prancing around and flapping their wings.

Deo looked forward to those times after sunset, when, all the chores done, his grandfather would tell stories, out in the mountains and especially back in Butanza. Children were warned not to traffic in made-up stories during daylight hours. If you did, you'd never grow up, the adults said. But fictions were permitted at nighttime, especially stories told by elders. Inside Lonjino's house, seated with his siblings on the dirt floor around the cooking fire, Deo would wait for his grandfather to begin, thinking, "This is going to be so much fun." Deo would feel like laughing in anticipation, trying to keep silent—or if he couldn't, he'd go outside for a moment to get rid of his laughter, because Lonjino would be offended, even angry, if you laughed during his stories, and especially if you laughed beforehand.

Sometimes Lonjino would weave a story together about events of the day. Sometimes he'd tell stories from the past. There was fiction in all of them. Some were fables, even if Lonjino pretended they weren't:

Once, Lonjino said, he had a neighbor here in Butanza. Deo and his siblings never knew him; he'd died long ago. The poor man had two lazy sons, but as he lay dying he came up with a plan to reform them. He told them he had buried money in cow horns all over his land and they could have all the money they found. So the sons dug and dug, turning over the earth everywhere, each staking his claim to a part of the land by planting trees and crops on it. The old man died, and they kept on digging and planting until they had created a sizable forest and a much improved farm. Only then did their mother tell them, "There is no money. Your father just wanted you to do something worthwhile."

Lonjino told that story more than once, and always ended it the same way, saying to Deo and his siblings, "Love work, and keep doing more. Don't wait for your parents to lie to you and tell you they have money buried."

Sometimes Lonjino would begin his stories by saying, "It used to be . . ." Deo sensed pain in these words. And sometimes he heard indignation—when for instance Lonjino told stories about colonial days and the Belgians. Back then, Burundi and Rwanda were essentially tiny adjuncts of the vast Belgian Congo. Like many other Burundian men, Lonjino had worked in the Congo tapping rubber trees. Unlike some others, he had survived the experience intact, returning home unharmed after a year. Lonjino told of a fellow worker, a huge, powerful man, whom the Belgians beat to death with the *kamoke,* the whip. If you were late to work, Lonjino said, they would make you

lie down, and beat you from the legs up to the neck, eight times. Top
to bottom and bottom to top. And each full circuit was counted as
one, so it was really sixteen beatings, Lonjino would say. The victims
would lie bleeding from their heels, naked on the ground. Other men
would go back home after months of this abuse, and they would beat
their wives and their children, destroying their families.

From Lonjino, Deo first heard about the onerous taxes the Belgians imposed, how small owners of cows or crops had to turn over
the best part of their milk, produce, and meat to the local Burundian chiefs, who administered the hills for the colonists. Lonjino
talked about how, during the struggle for independence, in the late
1950s and early 1960s, Belgian helicopters sometimes appeared
overhead—"like bees," he said. And he seemed to be in mourning
himself when he told of how the nation grieved after Prince Rwagasore, the man leading Burundi to independence, was shot to death,
with an elephant gun, at a restaurant by Lake Tanganyika. Shot by
a man from a place called Greece, but Lonjino believed that the Belgians arranged the killing. Finally, there was the happy ending—
independence, the time, Lonjino would say, when he and his family
could at long last drink as much of their own cows' milk as they
liked.

Lonjino had a whispery laugh, nearly soundless. In the glow of
the cooking fire, Deo would see his grandfather's shoulders shake
and his fine white teeth light up. Knowing that Lonjino was laughing, Deo knew that all was right with the world.

On an evening when Deo was five or maybe six years old, his
mother hovering over the fire, cooking supper, he heard a man's
voice call his father's name from outside. "Prosper! Prosper!" It was
his mother's cousin, from many kilometers away. He was breathing
hard. He stood at the fence outside the compound, panting and
shouting angrily at Deo's father, saying words like these: "What are

you doing? You are going to be burned down in your house with your children and your wife! How stupid are you? What are you doing? Can't you go out and know what's going on?"

Deo's father was easily provoked, as a rule, but he didn't answer. Deo's mother listened quietly and then she said to her cousin, "Thank you."

The memory of that evening had lost some detail by the time Deo was a teenager. But he remembered the men of the family removing the pile of wood that blocked the lone entrance to the compound, and being hustled out into the dark toward a place with tall trees while his grandfather's dogs barked. He also remembered hearing his older brother ask the adults what was going on—and the adults didn't answer.

For what seemed like a very long time, his family and several others camped out among nearby wooded hilltops, moving again and again. Most of the men of his family had taken the cows somewhere to safety. He and the rest of his siblings stayed with the women. There were downpours and lightning at night. In the daytime, one or another of the adult women would leave them and return with food from their gardens—squashes, bananas, potatoes. The women kept watch from the hilltops. He'd hear them asking each other whether they saw houses burning. When they finally went home to the compound, their cow barn had in fact been burned. Only Lonjino had stayed there, with his dogs and his spear. He must have left at the last moment and hidden out in the banana groves.

The barn was rebuilt, and normal life resumed. No one told Deo exactly what had happened, and, being a very obedient child, he didn't dare to ask. In second grade you were obliged to read a book of fables. All of them frightened Deo, especially the one entitled "What Killed You, Head?" The fable went like this:

There once was a man who went out walking. On the trail, he met a head rolling across his path.

He started bothering the rolling head with questions: "What killed you, head?"

The head replied: "Would you keep going and stop reminding me of unpleasant things? I died a hero, but you will be killed by your own tongue."

The man continued his walk. When he arrived at his destination, he told the people there: "Do you know what I saw? I met a rolling head on my way here, and I asked it: 'What killed you, head?' And it replied: 'I died a hero, but you will be killed by your own tongue.'"

The people told him: "If you don't show us this talking head, *we* will kill you." And the man said: "Let's go. If you don't find the head talking, do whatever you want to me." And the people said: "Let's go!"

When they came upon the head, the man started talking to it, but the head said nothing. The man insisted, but the head did not say a word. Upset because the man had lied to them and wasted their time, the people beat him. They beat him until he was unable to walk. After they had left, and the man was writhing on his back on the ground, the talking head laughed at him and said: 'Didn't I tell you that you would be killed by your own tongue?'"

You were warned not to talk to others about problems in the family. "Keep it in the kitchen," you were told. You might not be praised for being a quiet child, but if you talked a lot you were scolded. *"Hora!"*—Shut up!—"You talk like birds in the morning," his father or grandfather would say. Or: "You talk as if you were raised by a widow." Or, more gently: "Better not to ask a question, because you might not like the answer."

FOUR

New York City,
1994

Deo pushed the grocery cart down the sidewalks of Eighty-
ninth Street. There were times when he felt crushed by the
height and humiliated by the splendor of the buildings in this part
of New York. They reminded him he was alone and completely out
of place. There were also times when he didn't see the buildings or
other people passing by, but rather a parade of his family: his
mother smiling shyly, showing her glossy teeth, which people in Butanza praised; his elder brother, Antoine, short, stocky, emphatic
about everything, joking that all the loads they carried on their
heads as little kids had stunted his growth. He could hear Antoine's
big laugh so clearly! But then his mind would take a wrong turn.
Once again he would be looking in the window of that hut with the
roof that had been burned, the memory that kept surfacing. The
family mutilated on the floor. What had become of his own family?
Then he would imagine them, Antoine and his mother and sister

and little brothers and his father and grandmother and Lonjino, lying violated and dead in the dirt. And then he'd realize that his cheeks were wet, that he'd been crying in public, while pushing his cart down the sidewalk, making a spectacle of himself.

But today, a day in late June 1994, he felt too sick to think about anything but the causes of gastrointestinal pain. He gritted his teeth, his stomach muscles flexing around his rising nausea, trying to strangle it. He hadn't been able to eat all day. He imagined worms gnawing on his intestines. He probably had intestinal worms or amoebas, he thought, from all the dirty water he'd had to drink on the run. A doctor could find out for sure with stool studies—tests he could do himself, if he had the equipment. He had seen the names of doctors around Park Avenue, on little brass plaques. Whatever they might charge would be more than he could pay. He knew the broad-spectrum antibiotic to rid the gut of parasites. But did you need a prescription to buy Flagyl in America? What would the drug cost here?

At least this wasn't a difficult delivery, only three crosstown blocks, and he already knew the address, right next door to that peaceful little church, St. Thomas More. And there was no service entrance, just a front door, a few steps up from the sidewalk.

A woman opened the door almost at once, and she held it open for him as he shouldered his way in with the bags. She was smiling.

"How arhh you?" said Deo. He had added this to his repertoire. He still struggled with the "are," however. He'd worked so hard from childhood to pronounce the French "r" just so.

The woman smiled and said she was fine, thank you. She said something about showing him the way to the kitchen. He asked her if this was a church, and she said, yes, this was the rectory. Wanting to make a good impression, he said he was very interested. She had a friendly-sounding voice—the voice of a good tipper perhaps. He didn't notice much else about her until, after he'd deposited the groceries and was walking back with her toward the door, she asked him, *"Parlez-vous français?"*

"Mais oui!"

Her name was Sharon McKenna. She was dressed in a skirt and blouse. She was slender, and she had very pale skin and very blond hair, so blond he couldn't see if it was turning white or not. She might be as old as his mother, she might be ten years younger. Her French wasn't impeccable, but good enough for a conversation. She asked him get-acquainted questions. Carried away by the chance to speak, really speak, feeling too sick to remember his lessons, he told her more than he ever told a stranger now—not only that he came from Burundi but that he had escaped from the violence there and in Rwanda. Before he left, she gave him a five-dollar bill, after rummaging around in an untidy-looking bag.

Maybe it was just the tip that made him carry away an image of a beautiful person, of a woman who would look elegant even if she were dressed in an old blanket. But it was more than the money. She had seemed interested in him, and worried by his circumstances. Deo thought he would be welcome if he went back to see her again. Which he did, a few days later.

He found himself telling her he had been a medical student. He said he was determined to go back to school and become a doctor, and she seemed so enthusiastic about this that for the moment he felt it might actually be true. But then she asked him about his parents, and he didn't know what to say. She said she'd been hearing a lot about Rwanda on the news. He thought, "God, what should I tell her?" Everyone was dangerous, maybe even this woman. He felt like running away. He answered as vaguely as he could. When he left, she gave him a hug.

It had been so long since anyone had touched him with affection. But, no, he thought, she asked too many questions. If he saw her again, she would *gusimbura* him for sure. But clearly she was someone who would help him if she could. He decided to write her a letter. His African friend at the grocery wrote it for him. Deo looked up some of the medical words, though most were cognates of the

French. He copied the letter out carefully in his own hand. He had beautiful penmanship when he tried; maybe she would notice.

Dear Sharon McKenna

I'm very glad to find this short time in order to tell you that I've some troubles which make me too hurt (bad)

In fact, since before yesterday, I feel pains around intestines and have difficult to go to the toilet (constipation) I'm telling you all these problems about my health.

I spent all this last night without feeling asleep even if I worked hardly. I think that these pains are caused by intestinal parasites like especially AMIBES or ENTAMOEBA HIS-TOLYTICA because of all these symptoms.

In this way, I'd like I have a treatment against these troubles, but unhapply I don't see how I can find a Doctor for consultation on one hand, and how I can pay him on the other hand because it may be very expensive while I'm too poor to pay. So, I don't know if you could find for me medecines called FLAGYL or help me in other way.

I am here to SLOAN'S even if I'm ill. That's a pity!

Thanks a lot for your best comprehension.

God bless you.

He brought the letter to the rectory in the morning and left it with the receptionist. The very next day, Sharon appeared at the store. Her doctor, she said, had agreed to see Deo for free. The man was pleasant, and the examination was thorough. On the walk back, Sharon told Deo that the doctor didn't think there was much wrong with him, except that he was far too thin. The doctor had told her, "Your job is to fatten him up." She also said that she'd told the doctor Deo's story, hoping to get him interested in a potential future colleague, but all the doctor could suggest was that Deo's chances might be better in Canada. Sharon drew a map that showed where Canada was in relation to New York. Just to look at the drawing made him weary. He didn't want even to try to imagine the journey. A few days later, Sharon took him out for a walk. She showed him her doctor's report and translated it. "The tests are normal. Let me know how I can help you."

So his problem was maybe part exhaustion, and maybe lack of protein, and certainly psychosomatic. He wasn't sure this was good news.

Then Sharon asked him whether he liked girls.

For a moment Deo couldn't speak. The doctor must have told her that Deo might have AIDS, and Sharon must be thinking the same—that he had been a philanderer back in Africa, where AIDS was mainly a heterosexual disease, or that he had been selling himself to men here in New York. How could she think that? She wasn't the person he'd imagined she was.

Yes, he liked girls, Deo said aloud. He wouldn't speak to her again. He couldn't bear even to look at her. He would avoid her from now on.

But in fact he couldn't. He wasn't going to forgive Sharon, but when he went to see her the following week and she said she had missed him, he had to admit to himself she was a beautiful person after all, and that he had missed her, too.

He had told her he had to learn English to get back into medical school. She took him to an odd little store, full of old-looking lamps and furniture but with a rack of shelves of old books, where together they found a bilingual copy of *Le Petit Prince*. She bought it for him. It didn't cost much. He devoured it, first reading it in French, then memorizing the English text. Another time he took her to the huge Barnes & Noble and showed her a physiology textbook he'd found some weeks before. He thought he only wanted to share his enthusiasm for this book. He wasn't asking her to buy it for him. It cost eighty-one dollars; it was hard to believe that a single book could cost that much. But Sharon said, "Let's get it!"

This was a sackful of borrowed salt, but Deo couldn't help himself. "Oh, that would be so great!"

The text was written in English, but he could study the drawings and photographs. He took the book back to the apartment of the Senegalese, where he stored it in his suitcase and visited it from time to time.

He brought Sharon words he'd written down and asked her to translate them into French. One time he was talking to her inside the rectory and asked her the meanings of some of the words he'd been hearing in the park. He should have known better; there were other people around, including a priest.

"What does this word, 'motherfucker,' mean?"

Her face turned red. She whispered hastily, emphatically, "I'll tell you later."

Sometimes he wished he hadn't asked for Sharon's help. She decided to teach him to pronounce "are" correctly. She kept making him repeat after her, as persistent and patient as she'd probably be when helping a child. She handed him pages written in English. "Okay, now read this," she'd say, just as if he were in first grade.

Sharon was like the brother you fought with for your share of the blanket at night and thought you never wanted to see again, you hated him so much, and then felt so glad to find in the morning lying on the mat beside you. More to the point, she was like a mother, who couldn't stop worrying about you, who couldn't help reminding you that you still needed her help, which was infuriating because in fact you did.

They often went for walks. One day she told him, in her cheery, raspy voice, that she was going to show him Central Park. He ended up sitting on a bench with her—she'd brought sandwiches for both of them—and listening to her say, "Oh, look at that pretty bird" and "Look at these pretty flowers." She was trying to distract him, he knew, trying to cheer him up. At the same time, he was thinking:

"I hate this woman. This woman is crazy. I'm not five years old. I know what a bird is. Yes, I know that is a flower. And I know Central Park better than you do. I sleep here."

He would never let her in on such thoughts. And she must never know he slept in the park. When she had asked him where he was living, as she was bound to do of course, he had told her he slept on the floor of an apartment in Harlem. He gave her the address and phone number of the Senegalese clothing factory. But he made the mistake of also telling her that he had seen a person killed in Harlem, right outside his window. From then on, she gave him no peace. She was going to find him a safe place to stay, if it killed both of them.

He disliked spending time with her inside the rectory, because invariably a parishioner or priest would happen by and Sharon would say, "Oh, Father So-and-So, this is Deogratias," and then he would have to listen, half comprehending by now, as she told what she knew of his story, and often the third party would say he'd heard about genocides over there in Africa and that terrible thing between Hutus and Tutsis, and which was Deo, Hutu or Tutsi? Just hearing those terms made him start inwardly. He would feel completely alert—that would be adrenaline. Often the aftermath was a throbbing headache.

Sharon decided he should write a brief account of his life, which could be used to help him with potential benefactors. This struck him, forcefully, as a very bad idea.

It scared him to tell anyone he was a Tutsi. How much worse it would be to write down the fact on a piece of paper with his name on it and tell what he had witnessed. Especially since by now she was calling people all over New York, trying to get him help. God only knew how many people she was calling. Just the calls she told him about included priests and official-sounding organizations, and even—this was chilling—the Burundian consulate and the Burundian Mission to the United Nations. She could end up talking to someone who could get more information about him and come and find him and kill him. Or hurt relatives or friends in Burundi. If he wrote down his story, there was no telling who would see the document.

He wanted to tell her: "Look, just do what you can to help me, don't even talk to other people about me." But he couldn't. She was so warm and generous, never neglecting to give him a hug before they parted, and so sure that this document would help, that he decided to comply. But not entirely. He didn't use the real name of anyone in his family, he omitted many details and changed others, and he completely altered the geography of his life. Mostly he wrote about what a good student he had been. Sharon enlisted the services of an elderly priest, to refine her translation of Deo's French and type up the thing.

She was inflicting the Talking Head on him. And she was trying to borrow salt all over town. She described some of her schemes. In English, they would have gone like this: There was a woman, a friend, she was a little unstable, she drank a little too much, but Deo shouldn't worry about that, but anyway this woman had said Deo could do some work, like painting, around her apartment, which was a very nice apartment, and of course the woman would like him and find a little spot in her apartment for him to stay.

The result that time was both good and bad. Good because the woman paid him six dollars an hour, bad because he went to her place and painted woodwork after twelve hours of delivering groceries. And the woman didn't seem to like him. He'd be painting away and without any warning she'd say in a rather harsh tone of voice, "It's time to stop. Now go."

He was working there one evening when Sharon appeared, saying he had to stop work and come with her right away. There was this nice old dentist she knew whom they were going to call on. Maybe he would have a place for Deo to sleep.

He didn't want to go. What had she said about him to this stranger? Deo told Sharon he was tired. She said the dentist's place wasn't far away. This at least was true. The three of them sat in a tiny kitchen, Sharon and the elderly man talking and talking in En-glish, Deo trying to pay attention but losing more and more ground. So he had no idea what was coming when the retired dentist leaned across the table, reached out a quavery hand, and hooked Deo's lower front teeth with an index finger.

Sharon translated. The old dentist said that Deo needed braces.

Deo felt a flash of anger. What else would he have to endure? What further insults? For the rest of the time there, Deo kept his mouth shut tight. For the next several days, he was aware of trying not to smile in public.

Of course, the dentist wasn't about to take him in. But some-thing promising came out of the encounter. Sharon said she knew how he could get his teeth straightened for free, if he wanted them straightened—at the New York University dental school. He wouldn't mind, but dentistry was for later. The search for a place continued.

She took him to see a nun who ran a boardinghouse of sorts. Sister Leontine. "She's great," Sharon said.

Sister Leontine had a place in Harlem, which she had turned into a refuge for homeless people just out of prison. A basement place and packed with people. The sister probably was a great person, Deo thought. And it was wonderful of Sharon to take him there. Sharon could live in this chaos happily enough. She was a person who would just come shining and smiling into hell, he thought. But he didn't want to be in this place. He'd rather be alone. He'd rather sleep outside.

Fortunately, Sister Leontine said that Deo could stay but would have to sleep on the floor because all the beds were taken. So he was able to decline the offer politely and still let Sharon know he was grateful.

Declining wasn't always so easy. A wealthy friend of Sharon's was having a birthday party in Central Park, a real fête. Sharon's friend had said she could bring Deo. It would be a wonderful party, Sharon said, it would be good for him, he'd really enjoy himself.

Deo thought fast. He said he couldn't go, he didn't have a dress shirt or a tie or a jacket.

But Sharon said that was no problem. St. Thomas More collected old clothes for the poor. And a lot of the clothes were very fine, she said, because this was a wealthy part of town. Sharon said something about having gotten her own "start in clothes" this way. She took him down to the church basement and rummaged cheerfully through a pile of big plastic bags and outfitted him.

How much energy the woman had! Deo wanted to ask her to stop trying so hard. But he hated the idea of hurting her feelings, and the weariness surrounding him made it too hard for him to resist her. The only way to keep her from doing too much was to avoid her, and he tried that, but then he would go back to see her when he needed something. But this made him feel he was behaving like a spoiled child. The only solution was to let her do as she pleased. As she sat with him and told him about yet another possibility for housing, he would let his thoughts drift away. Eventually, she'd ask him in French, "Do you understand?" Sometimes she'd have to repeat the question. "*Quoi?*" he would say, as if startled out of sleep.

She seemed fretful, even at times a little discouraged by the search for a bed for him, but by now he knew she wouldn't quit. He thought, "She wants this more than I do." How was this possible?

Summer had arrived. One day when they were out for a walk, Sharon said, as if she had suddenly remembered, that she had a friend she called a brother. Chukwu. He came from Nigeria. He was a math professor now, at North Carolina State University, but he had spent some tough times in New York.

Deo said that perhaps she should call this Chukwu, knowing she would anyway.

As usual, the result was another hot trip through the city, this time to the office of a lawyer, named James O'Malley. Evidently, Chukwu had told Sharon that Deo should see this man.

Deo wasn't sure exactly why he needed a lawyer. He wasn't a criminal. Something to do with immigration, he gathered.

It was a fine-looking office. The lawyer called James, small and stylishly dressed, sat behind an enormous desk. Deo could tell that Sharon was telling James his story. He caught words like "Burundi" and "Rwanda" and "medical student." Then Sharon told Deo that James would like to see his passport, which Deo still always carried.

How did he come by a business visa? James asked through Sharon.

Deo told the whole story.

For a minute or two, James sat frowning down at the visa. Then he lifted his eyes and smiled and said something that made Sharon smile. She translated: "James says he will take your case if you promise to be his doctor."

Deo felt elated. Was James saying that Deo was going back to medical school? Maybe he did need a lawyer!

Chukwu had given Sharon another suggestion, which sounded altogether familiar, even depressing. She only told him about it when it was a fait accompli. Deo had been invited to have dinner with people named Nancy and Charlie Wolf. Old friends of Chukwu's, and, as it happened, acquaintances of Sharon's. Nancy was an artist, Sharon said, Charlie a sociologist. They were very nice. And they had invited Deo to dinner at their apartment. It was a subway ride away, downtown, in a place called SoHo. Sharon had written down the address.

Deo looked at it. How to get out of this?

He had never been to that part of town, he said. "And how am I going to talk to them? What am I supposed to say?" All this was true. She couldn't deny it.

"I'll go with you," said Sharon.

FIVE

New York City,
1994

You rode up to the Wolfs' place in a noisy old elevator, which opened into a room with large windows on one end and hundreds of books on the walls. Deo thought, "Maybe I can ask for a book." He didn't notice much else. He might have just awakened and found himself standing in front of these strangers, shaking hands. Mrs. Wolf, Nancy, was blond and thin and rather tall. Her hands looked busy even when they weren't doing anything. She seemed to have a hard time standing still. She smiled and laughed a lot, sometimes in a nervous-sounding way. But she spoke too fast for him to understand the words, and it wasn't long before he quit trying to catch up. But Mr. Wolf, Charlie, spoke to him very slowly. One word at a time. And Charlie would gesture at things to make sure Deo understood. Something about him seemed familiar and comforting. When Nancy interrupted him, Deo noticed, Charlie would stop speaking at once, and if she excused herself, he would tell her to go on. The second or third time this happened, Deo thought, "He's like Lonjino." There was gray in Charlie's hair. He seemed completely calm.

At the dinner table, which was just big enough for four, Deo tried to tell them some of his story. He was sick of feeling silenced in these situations. He thought, "I'm just going to make noise." These people might think, "What the heck is he talking about?" But he didn't care. As always, it felt dangerous to try to describe the violence he had seen. Mainly he tried to tell them about cows and medical school. His English kept failing him. Nancy looked more and more agitated as he talked. Suddenly, she said to him, "Never mind talking. Just eat!"

For a while after that, he gave up on talking and tried to listen to the others. He was pretty sure that Charlie spoke about working in Africa and even living and working along with Nancy in Nigeria. But most of the conversation went on without him. Then he realized that Charlie was asking him a question, enunciating the words carefully.

"What can we"—Charlie pointed at himself and at Nancy—"do to help?" He pointed at Deo. "You."

Deo understood, and then again he didn't. Did this man really want to give him help? What made him think he could? Deo said he didn't know.

Charlie asked the question again.

In broken English, feeling rather irritated, Deo asked if Charlie really wished to know.

Yes, said Charlie. Of course!

Well, Deo told him, there was only one thing. It was impossible. To go to school.

Charlie shook his head. Deo was wrong. "This is a country of second chances," Charlie said very slowly.

Second chances? Deo said.

Many opportunities, said Charlie. Of course Deo could go back to school.

Afterward, Deo wasn't sure what he had said aloud to Charlie then and what he had wanted to say to him but had spoken only in his mind. The gist of it went like this: "That's the only thing that would really help me, just to heal my brain, my mind, would be to sit down in a classroom." He remembered how it felt to be in a classroom. Perhaps it felt better in memory than it ever had in fact, but now it seemed like the greatest pleasure he had known.

On a hot afternoon not long after Deo first met Sharon, Goss ordered him to go outside and load a truck. As he worked, Deo noticed that he wasn't sweating, a bad sign. Buried in heat, hefting boxes, he found he was crying, and through the film of tears he saw the faces of Goss and a couple of the cashiers in the front windows of the store. They were watching him work. They were smiling and laughing as they watched him. Then he heard Goss calling out to him from the doorway, "Hey, looks like it's hot for you. Isn't it hotter than this in Africa?"

Deo thought he would celebrate the news that Goss had died, preferably killed by heat. His mind remonstrated with him over this thought, that part of his mind trained by his mother and his church. But the other part stood firm: No, I will not regret thinking this.

Soon afterward, Goss sent him out on a delivery. Deo managed to get the groceries to the address. Afterward, he walked with his cart to the post office near the store, another of his peaceful corners. The place was air-conditioned. He sat inside for hours, unmolested—though after an hour or so one of the clerks did ask him what he was doing there. When the office was about to close, Deo walked away, leaving the grocery cart behind. He wasn't going back to the Gristedes.

He stayed away for five days. When he walked through the door again, the assistant manager said, "We don't know you. You don't work here." The job was harder now than before, not just because he had to beg to get it back, or because Goss gave him more to do around the store, still poking him with his long stick, unnecessarily because Deo's English vocabulary by now encompassed the functions of a grocery. He had known more difficult toil in the mountains of Burundi and worse humiliations in grade school, but always then he could believe that enduring those would lead to something better. You mastered one set of skills, in order to master bigger ones. Now he knew how to be a grocery delivery boy, and he could see nothing more ahead.

Life seemed like an endless chain of moments, as it had when he was on the run, except that most of the moments now weren't threatening, just dreary. In the midst of them sometimes—loading up the grocery cart, standing at a service entrance—he'd be arrested by memories of himself before the wars began, a person with dreams and plans. He'd awake from memories of hope and find himself right there, waiting for another superintendent to open up the gate, and he'd sneer at himself. Those dreams were gone. Ashes. This was it, this grocery cart, this service entrance. His life from now on was going to depend on how strong he was physically, working in a grocery store, being paid fifteen dollars a day. More and more, living felt to Deo like a job he couldn't wait to finish. "Be brave," he thought. "It's time for you to die."

He thought he should be more grateful for Sharon. In her company, sometimes, he could talk as if he still imagined himself becoming a doctor, even though, as it had been from the start, this was usually just a way of telling her who he used to be. She seemed so sure they'd find a place for him, and she led him around the city so cheerfully and energetically that he couldn't help but borrow a little of her optimism. But the rejections mounted up. What did it say about him that no one was willing to lend him a bed? The feelings that came from this weren't entirely different from the feelings that came from having people try to kill you. You wondered who they thought you were and who you were in fact. You felt utterly alone. And you felt indignant. He didn't need borrowed salt. He could get along by himself. He knew how to survive, if he wanted to go on surviving.

He was tired of following Sharon around, like a calf behind its mother. But she just wouldn't quit. She kept making calls. She took him to the office of a place called Catholic Charities. A harried woman there said she'd never heard of Burundi. Why did Deo come to the United States? the woman asked, irritably.

Sharon said she still had hopes for the Wolfs. She said Deo must have made a good impression on them, because they called her quite often in the weeks after the dinner party, to ask if she had found a proper place for him. Deo knew this must be right, because the Wolfs called him, too, leaving messages at the apartment of the West Africans in Harlem. As with Sharon, he had let the Wolfs think he was borrowing a piece of floor there. To tell them that he was really sleeping in the park would be inconsiderate, and as shameful an act as crying aloud when he'd stubbed his toes at night as a child. There were things about you that other people wouldn't want to hear and things you wouldn't want them to know. Often they were the same things. He thought of them as "things I keep for myself."

Returning the Wolfs' calls was hard sometimes. He knew he wouldn't be able to understand Nancy. He'd think, "God, I'm a grown man. Why am I unable to communicate?" Several times when he called and it was only Nancy who answered, he simply hung up without speaking. But usually both Charlie and Nancy would pick up the phone, and usually Deo got the gist of what Charlie said. Sometimes the Wolfs just wanted to know how he was doing. They had suggestions, too. They told him about a library up in Harlem, the Schomburg Center for Research in Black Culture—Nancy's idea. And one day Charlie asked Deo to meet him at the New York Public Library, the landmark branch, the one with the carved stone lions out front. Charlie showed him the reading room.

"*Ooh la la!*"

Deo remembered the two libraries in Bujumbura. The country's largest was at the university. Most of its collection had been donated, as he recalled, by Muammar Khaddafi, the dictator of Libya, back in the early 1980s, and he thought it probably hadn't received any books since. The other was a one-room library in the center of Bujumbura, which was open to the public. He had preferred the smaller one, but both were like shabby used-book stores compared to the place that Charlie showed him. Deo felt a pang—"Oh, my poor country"—when he gazed at the New York library's reading room and thought of the Bujumbura libraries. And a pang sometimes when he gazed at those stone lions outside the entrance. All his youth he'd heard Lonjino's stories about lions and wished he'd had a chance to see one—but by the time Deo was born, lions had long since become part of Lonjino's "used to be."

The library vastly improved New York for him. He could go inside without paying. He didn't take out any books, and he still couldn't read much English, but Charlie had shown him how to use the card catalogue and order a book, so he could sit in the reading room with a book that he thought he would like to read and turn the pages, imagining that he was reading them. And when he fell asleep, it usually took the staff longer to ask him to leave than at the Barnes & Noble. He had never much liked Bujumbura, a city where nothing worked right, a city that had seemed like an incipient hell when he had left it. When he thought of home, he thought, yearningly, of the palm groves by the light blue waters of Lake Tanganyika and the grazing land in the mountains. At night in New York's great park, he could almost imagine himself back there, and when he came out onto Fifth Avenue early in the morning, he felt at moments not only weary but also nearly happy to be in this city that wasn't Bujumbura. He was still amazed at the constant motion of the place. Always going going going going. Running like a river. He thought of all the people hiding out in abandoned buildings, all the people burrowing into little corners of the park. There was always a space for someone. It was an amazing example of human organization, deeply flawed but still amazing, and amazing to think that he had become a small part of it. Having a few friends helped.

One time Charlie met up with him and bought him an ice cream cone. Deo had yet to see a dentist, and he knew he had cavities.

When the first bite hit his molars, he almost cried out. He clenched his jaw and managed a smile, and waited until Charlie looked away. Then he tossed the cone into a trash barrel. Moments later Charlie turned and looked at him and did a double take, then declared that Deo was clearly a man who loved ice cream. On another occasion, Charlie arranged to meet him at the library, and arrived with a small mattress, a camping mattress that could be folded up into a little bundle. It was for Deo to use in the apartment in Harlem, Charlie said.

Deo slept on the mattress that night, in the park. He had tried out five or six sleeping places in the park. Each, it seemed to him, represented an improvement. When he found a better one, he'd think, "I'm making progress." He had found a good place over on the West Side among some boulders, shaded by a tree. Napping there one Sunday before work—stuck to the ground like a frog—he had seen a woman in a burqa disrobing in front of her lover. "Now you're thinking right," he thought, stifling his laughter. He didn't watch the rest of the proceedings. He'd found a better spot since then, the best so far. It was just off Fifth Avenue, near some benches and a towering bronze statue. He didn't always have the place to himself. Other homeless men sometimes sat on the benches, but this spot was adjacent to very fancy neighborhoods, a spot that the police would pay attention to, so the men wouldn't sleep there, and they'd speak only in whispers, and the area was clean. He could lie down on his mattress behind some bushes near the statue and sleep peacefully. In the morning he put the mattress in a plastic bag and left it hidden in that spot. For three nights running he found it there when he returned. On the fourth it was gone. But he didn't much care about not having a mattress, so long as Charlie didn't find out.

It was near the end of summer when Sharon told him their search was over. The Wolfs had invited him to live with them. He was glad. Only good people would do this, and they must think he was a good person, too. But the news was tempered by that dulling, heavy weariness—as if every present thing were connected to his aching legs—and by the feeling that he'd bridled at since arriving in New York, that he was being forced into the position of a child. He didn't get to decide whether the Wolfs would take him in. And he didn't get to choose whether to accept their invitation. He didn't want to be a person who needed rescuing, but he knew he did need it—and later he'd realize he hadn't known the half of it; when he had heard people talk about "winter" in New York, he'd wondered if this meant there was a rainy season. To him just then only one thing seemed to matter: the Wolfs might help him go back to school.

He was about to call Nancy and Charlie, as Sharon told him to do. Then he remembered the stolen mattress. In Burundi, household items were precious. If a family took in an orphan and the child broke a plate, the hosts might throw the kid out. Deo had known of such cases. No telling how Nancy and Charlie would react if they found out what had happened to their mattress. If he told them the whole story, they'd realize that he had lied to them, or at best misled them. They would know he had been sleeping in the park, and no one was going to know that about him.

He consulted his dictionaries and prepared a question. Over the phone, he asked Charlie what he should do with the mattress.

Charlie paused, and then, to Deo's great relief, Charlie said, "Leave it."

SIX

New York City–Chapel Hill,
1994–95

The apartment was very long and rather narrow. At one end were the living room and kitchen and a sleeping loft, at the other Nancy's studio, full of her paintings and drawings, which were all about buildings, detailed and fascinating. Deo slept in the room in the middle. To satisfy the building code, a small opening had been cut high up on one wall, but otherwise the room was windowless. It had been Charlie's office. Charlie and Nancy called it the Black Hole. A bed and a small desk were wedged between the books that covered the walls.

It was the most comfortable room he'd ever slept in, a room fit for the end of a journey of the body, but also for the continuation of a journey of the mind. Again and again, on the perimeter of sleep, he was visited by sudden vivid images, of machete and flesh, and by those dreams in which, sooner or later, he had to run but couldn't move. He would get out of bed and tiptoe to the bathroom and take a cold shower, as cold as he could stand, then try to stay awake. He had a radio on his desk in the Black Hole. Playing it very softly, turning the dial, his ear bent to the speaker, he discovered a station called Radio France International and on it a show called *Afrique.* It came on after midnight. Sometimes it carried news of the civil war back home. Terrible news as a rule, but he became, as he thought of it, addicted to the show. Charlie read *The New York Times* daily, and sometimes Deo would look through the paper for the name Burundi. He wouldn't find it. Rwanda, yes, but almost never Burundi. He listened to the radio partly to hear the name Burundi, partly to stay awake and safe from dreams.

Sometimes when Deo sat up with the light on, Nancy would knock at the door and come in and sit beside him on the bed. His English wasn't good enough for extended conversations, and he didn't usually feel like talking much at those times. But Nancy didn't seem to mind. She'd simply sit with him. Some nights he fell asleep in spite of himself, at the desk, with his head on his arms. Other nights, after the radio show ended, around three A.M., he sat waiting for dawn, watching the clock, now and then looking out from the door of the Black Hole to the windows, thinking, "Why isn't it coming faster?"

He wasn't near the equator anymore. The nights grew longer and longer. One day Nancy called to him from her studio, "Deo, come look."

He peered out the studio windows at snow. "Where is this coming from? It's something that comes like rain?"

Nancy and Charlie had wanted him to quit his job. He had simply stopped going to the grocery store. But this meant he had to accept gifts of spending money. "I am like a parasite," he thought when he pocketed it. "Probably it would be better for me to go back to Central Park." Nancy and Charlie told him to use their phone to call Claude in Bujumbura, but he did so only once and never again, because he found out that it cost something like five dollars a minute. So from time to time he took subways up to Harlem and made streetcorner calls.

At the bottom of the last page of the account of his life that he'd written for Sharon, the account full of deliberate inaccuracies, he had written with complete truthfulness: "I pray God to learn me some good news about my family, or I will surely die. Too tired!" The news from Claude was almost always bad, though, and sometimes dreadful. One day he learned over the phone that a cousin had been killed and beheaded. He'd been telling Nancy about that same cousin over coffee just the day before, and he simply was unable to stop weeping before he got back to the apartment, or to keep the news for himself when Nancy came out of her studio to see what was wrong. She hugged him for a long time.

The world was full of dangers. Nancy's asthma began to worry him. Winter seemed to worsen it. Then she came down with a cold. Listening to her wheeze, Deo felt increasingly alarmed. He told her she had to go to a doctor. She demurred, and he thought, "All right." He went into the Black Hole, pulled his suitcase from under the bed, took out his stethoscope, and returned with it around his neck. "Maybe I can listen to your lungs." He didn't think he heard sounds of pneumonia. He still thought she should go to a real doctor. She wouldn't.

Deo had shown Charlie the books he'd carried from Burundi in his suitcase, and Charlie had said to Nancy, in front of Deo, "This man loves books. He needs to go to school." Since then, a friend of the Wolfs had helped Deo enroll at Hunter College in an English as a Second Language class, and Deo knew he must be doing well, because within a week he had been promoted, and his teacher had taken him to a lunch with other teachers—to show him off, it seemed.

On Saturdays, he walked with Charlie to the greenmarket on Union Square. Charlie had been a university professor of sociology. He knew a great deal about the city. Deo didn't understand everything Charlie said, but he liked to listen to Charlie discourse on the history of the streets they crossed. They'd stop at a café and chat over coffee, then stroll over to the Strand and spend an hour or two looking at books, and sometimes on the way home they'd stop at the Warehouse to buy some beer or a bottle of wine, which they'd finish slowly, after dinner at the table. There, almost every night, Charlie would use an expression new to Deo, such as "Indian summer" or "break a leg." Nancy would turn to Deo and begin to offer a definition, and Charlie would beg to differ with Nancy. Or Deo would interrupt Charlie and ask a question: What did "beating a dead horse" mean? Well, it was a colloquial expression, Charlie would say. What did "colloquial" mean? Deo would ask. It was a cliché, Nancy would answer. No, Charlie would say, a colloquial expression was different from a cliché. Often the argument went on and on. At first, Deo sat there feeling frustrated, wondering when they'd ever get around to answering his question. But then this situation began to seem interesting: two people unable to resolve a question about their native language. He'd listen to them wrangle, his spirits lifting. Even native speakers had something to learn. His question had been a challenging one after all. He wasn't stupid for not knowing the answer. His situation wasn't hopeless.

Deo lived with Nancy and Charlie for about five months before he decided he should leave, to continue his quest for school. Charlie said he'd been speaking to an old friend back in his hometown, in Chapel Hill in North Carolina. His friend thought Deo ought to come down there. It would be good for him to get out of the big city, said Charlie's friend, and it would be easy for Deo to enroll at the university there. Deo sensed that Charlie and Nancy didn't want him to leave. On the other hand, Charlie seemed to think highly of North Carolina and of his own education at its great university. In the end, what Deo heard most clearly was the word "university."

Charlie and Nancy had spoken about his "going to college" in New York. It seemed to him that he was now being offered a choice between college and university. He didn't ask for a definition of the word "college," because the word was the same in French, and since the French *collège* meant "secondary school," his choice was clear. A university was what he wanted. Nancy and Charlie took him to the train station. On the platform, Nancy burst into tears and Charlie pulled out his handkerchief and staggered backward slightly, and Deo, putting on his toothiest smile, climbed aboard, hoping they would decide for him that he shouldn't go, right up until the train departed.

Charlie's friend had found free lodgings for him, in the house of a ninety-year-old man, rather crotchety as it turned out. At night Deo would tiptoe around, moving so quietly he thought he could have heard a bird fly past, but in the morning the old man would say, "You woke me up." Once, he accused Deo of eating his watermelon. When, some months later, Deo tried a slice of watermelon for the first time in his life, he took one bite and threw the rest away. Deo would have put up with far worse—he would gladly have lived outdoors again—if only he could have gone to a university. Soon after he arrived, though, Charlie's friend said that getting him enrolled was going to be harder than she'd thought. Actually, it turned out to be impossible. He didn't fit into any category, and the rules were rigid. The closest Deo got to his dream was the main library at the University of North Carolina, where he would go before or after working his shifts as an aide at the Fair Oaks Nursing Home.

He knew right away he was the lowliest employee, the one the nurses and other aides, almost all of whom were African-American, would summon to clean up the ugliest messes, the urine on the floor, the shit in the bed, the food the old people spilled, the food that dribbled down the old people's chins. He imagined the other staff thought he was dim-witted. That was what so many assumed when you didn't speak their language well. So many people, he thought, don't listen to the content of what you say but only to the noises you make. The very idea of the place puzzled him. He remembered how hard it had been for his parents to move out of his grandparents' compound to the mountain Runda, how they'd been obliged to leave several children behind for his grandparents to care for. He looked at the so-called "residents" slumped in their wheelchairs around the nursing station, and he wondered, "Are all these old people actually going to be here until they die? They are not going to go home?"

The job wasn't all bad. The nursing home was an hour's walk from the old man's house, but Deo liked a long walk again, now that he had gained some weight and his nausea had mostly lifted. He usually worked twelve hours a day, for five dollars an hour, a fortune compared to his pay at Gristedes. He didn't mind dealing with the messes human bodies make. It was, in a general sense at least, what doctors did. On breaks, he liked to read the residents' medical records and pretend he was their doctor. He liked taking temperatures and blood pressures and writing down the numbers on the appropriate form. He liked evaluating TB tests. "I'm becoming an intellectual again," he'd say to himself. Sometimes he'd pore over chest X-rays just for fun, and even on occasion, in spite of his English, he would try to talk about one resident or another to the doctor who visited periodically—just as if he were an intern on rounds. It had been a long time since he'd been the one dispensing help, not the one asking for help.

He received a lot of blessings from the residents. And he made a friend, a dignified octogenarian named Martha. Soon after she arrived, she said something he didn't understand, and she smiled at him and said, "You have no clue."

"No *clou*?" he thought. "No nail?"

"Do you know what a 'clue' is?" Martha asked.

"Yes!" He made as if to drive a nail with a hammer.

She laughed, but in such a happy way he couldn't feel offended. "No," she explained. "It means, you have no *idea*."

He spent his breaks with her. She improved his English and his mood. Then one day another aide, a hefty African-American woman, got impatient with Martha and gripped the old woman's arm and twisted it, right in front of Deo. Martha bled.

The aide tried to get Deo to lie about what had happened:

"You're talking about a white person," she whispered fiercely. He had only vague notions about the history of race relations in America, but he understood the words. The aide seemed to be saying that since Martha was white and Deo was black, he should automatically take the side of a fellow black person. And this was because white people had long oppressed black people. This was madness, he thought. How many wholly innocent Burundians and Rwandans had been slaughtered because of offenses their fellows had committed? The aide told him if he didn't take her side, he'd better quit this job and leave. She was going to get him in big trouble if he didn't quit. He shouldn't just quit, he should go back to Africa!

Deo followed her advice, in part. He told the authorities the truth, and not long afterward he called up Nancy and Charlie—they had been calling him regularly the whole four months. Would it be all right if he came back to live with them?

They met him at Penn Station and took him back to SoHo. When the elevator door opened into the apartment, there were a lot of people there, friends such as Sharon and the lawyer James O'Malley and O'Malley's wife, Lelia. On the table there was a big cake spiked with candles, surrounding the figure of a little cow resting on the frosting. Someone said, "Blow out the candles, Deo."

"What?" he asked.

Lelia made as if to blow, and he understood.

Later, as they were cleaning up, Lelia asked Deo to pass her a paper towel. He couldn't think what a paper towel was. He made as if to search, to look as though he knew what it was she wanted. Then he said, "There's nothing." Lelia smiled at him and walked over and got the paper towel herself.

He thought he must go back to school or die.

Soon after Deo returned from North Carolina, Nancy and Charlie asked a friend to take him on a tour of the city's colleges. The second stop was Columbia. When Deo passed through its stone gates, he cried out, "*This* is a university!" There was no need to go further.

Deo enrolled in Columbia's American Language Program, an ESL program essentially, but more rigorous than most. Nancy and Charlie paid the tuition, about six thousand dollars. There were still nights he couldn't sleep or didn't dare try, but he could use those hours now to read and write his papers. He studied English through the spring and summer of 1995. Meanwhile, he had applied to become an undergraduate in Columbia's School of General Studies, a program fully integrated with the college proper, created for students whose college careers had been interrupted. The standards for admission were rigorous, but the deadline for applying was June instead of January.

Nancy and Charlie and another friend of theirs, a neurologist at Columbia's medical school, helped him fill out the forms, but he had to prove he'd been to school before, and he didn't have any of his transcripts from Burundi. He made several streetcorner calls. A friend of Claude's went to the medical school in Bujumbura—the school was functioning again, marginally, Deo was told. At first, the administrators there refused to give up any of his records, because according to their files Deo was dead. When the records finally came, he found among all the other papers a photograph of himself, a picture of his own face with a cross drawn over it in black ink. Deo usually saved everything—receipts, letters, snapshots. You never knew when a thing of the past might be useful to the future. But after staring at the picture of himself dead, he tore it into several pieces and threw it in the trash.

He had to take the SAT and a bunch of special Columbia admissions and placement exams. He finished the calculus test with time to spare. He was checking his answers when he saw a tall, well-dressed man come into the room, a black man in a three-piece suit, clearly a personage around Columbia. The man stood near the front of the room, beside the desk of the man who was monitoring the exam. The big man seemed to be eyeing the would-be Columbia students, all bent over their desks, hurrying to finish on time. But Deo was done. He slid out of his chair and carried his answer sheet to the monitor. As he turned to go back to his desk, he heard the big man say to the monitor in a low voice, "Is he done, or did he just give up?"

"No. It looks as if he's done."

"Let's see."

Deo watched from his desk as the two men graded his answer sheet. Then the big man looked up, smiling across the room at him. "De-*oh*-Gratias! Well done!"

SEVEN

Burundi,
1976–93

By rights Deo should have hated education, and he might have, if all he'd ever known had been the brick single-story grade school in Sangaza. It had six classrooms all in a row. Each room had two windows, covered with metal grating but otherwise open to the air. Looking into any of the rooms would have been for an American like looking into a one-room New England schoolhouse preserved as a museum: a slate blackboard, rows of battered wooden desks with inkwells.

The school had been owned and run by the Catholic church. Yearly tuition was roughly the equivalent of a U.S. dollar, a large sum. Deo's parents said they couldn't afford to buy him a pen, only one pencil, but they were determined to send their children to school. And so were many other families in the region, too many by the time Deo was six years old and eligible for first grade. Since there wasn't room for all the applicants, the authorities seem to have reasoned that some children either weren't old enough or

weren't ready for school. They had a peculiar way of weeding those
kids out.

On the morning of enrollment day, Deo stood on the dirt field in
front of the school in a line of about seventy-five boys and girls, all
jostling each other. "I was ahead of you!" "No, you weren't!" Parents hovered at the fringes, whispering commands to their children:
"Be quiet!" "Stay in line!" Preoccupied with keeping his place in the
line, Deo didn't notice the procedure being enacted up at the head of
the line. Before he knew it, he was standing there alone. From his
vantage point, only a few feet above ground level, everything looked
enormous—not only the building but also the steps in front of him,
and especially the bearded white man, the *muzungu,* who was seated
in a metal chair at the top of the steps just outside the metal door to
the first-grade classroom. This was the local Belgian priest, nick-
named We Can't Escape You, conducting interrogations in Kirundi.

"Touch your ear like this," said the man to Deo. The white man
quickly bent his right arm over his own head and briefly touched his
own left ear.

Deo stared at him, astonished.

"Out!" said the man.

Deo just stood there, staring.

The man was sitting with his legs crossed. He lifted a foot off his
knee and brushed Deo aside with it. *"Out!"*

Deo was led away by his mother. She was in tears. His father
bent over him. "Are you stupid? Why didn't you stretch your skinny
arm?"

Deo never did learn the provenance of the touch-your-ear-with-
the-opposite-hand theory of human development. His parents had
him practice the procedure at home. He started school the next year,
at seven.

One pair of shorts and a T-shirt lasted a year. He or his mother
would wash them at night. In the morning when he took them

down from the rope that hung over the cooking fire, his clothes were never quite dry and he'd smell the smoke in them all day, but you went to school in washed clothes or else. He got his copybook, gathered his lunch of beans wrapped in banana leaf, and headed out. On the way, he broke off a twig of an especially fragrant variety of eucalyptus, mashing one end with his teeth, then brushing his teeth with it as he walked along.

School lay three long descents and three steep climbs away. Down from the compound in Butanza—the family hadn't yet moved onto the mountain Runda—up along paths that cut through pastures and banana groves and gardens of beans, and quickly through a dense wood where, he'd heard people say, bad spirits lurked, then down again to a stream bottom, a small piece of open flat land, where sometimes he and his classmates would meet up with kids from the Protestant school in Nanga and play soccer, or fight, or both. (The Protestants usually won. Deo and his classmates would go away saying to each other, "Oh well, what do they do, these stupid kids from Nanga? They spend all their time just fighting and playing.") He climbed through more woods, through a field of ferns with huge fronds, then crossed a barren, stony hilltop whose trees, people said, had been cut down before he was born and turned into charcoal. This spot marked the beginning of the last leg. If he had been punctual, he could relax when he got here.

But things went wrong sometimes. When it was raining, it was easy to slip and fall in the mud, and then he'd have to stop to wash off his legs in a stream and to reassemble his lunch. Sometimes he'd stub a toe, and then have to walk slowly for a while—walking, as he pictured himself, like a chicken that had lost its other leg. And there were so many distractions—the crowing of cocks, the crying of babies in houses below in the valleys, a wildflower, birdsong, chimps—so much coming in at his eyes and ears and nose and asking for examination, that he could forget momentarily the object lessons against tardiness he'd witnessed at school the day before. So he didn't always get to the top of the bald hilltop as early as he meant to.

From that summit, he could see across the next valley to the schoolyard, and in the distance he could make out the miniature figures of schoolmates on the bare ground in front of the building, the field that served as their playground. From across the valley, he heard the ringing of the metal head of the hoe that served as the school bell. He saw his classmates already forming into lines at the classroom doors. Then he ran. Headlong down the hillside, legs brushing through knee-deep grass, across the muddy bottomland, and gingerly across the slippery logs spanning the stream, trying to make his feet prehensile, praying, "Please, God, don't let me fall. Please, God, don't let me be late."

But once across, he knew there was no hope. Small eucalyptus trees bordered the path up the last hill. He stopped and broke off a long thin branch and stripped away the leaves. He also broke off a twig and put it in his pocket, and walked slowly on. A couple of other boys were crouching among the brush and saplings beside the path. He wasn't really tempted to join them. They'd have to hide there all day, because going home before the end of school would bring approximately the same penalty from their fathers as arriving at school late would bring from their teachers. Sometimes a student hoping to escape a punishment would duck into the latrine off to one side of the campus, but the teachers knew that trick. If they caught you hiding there, they'd sometimes make you stay in the reeking hut for the rest of the day.

Entering his classroom, Deo offered the eucalyptus branch wordlessly to his teacher, who wordlessly accepted it for use later that day.

In his memory, a couple of the teachers were French, one was Belgian, and the rest were Burundians. He and most of his classmates tried to make good impressions on their teachers. He sensed before he understood that the Burundian teachers tended to be cruelest because they were trying to impress the white ones. Maybe beatings were less common than he remembered. And yet in retrospect, it seemed as if a day never passed without someone being punished. No matter how hard he tried to be perfect, the rule seemed to be that everyone must be beaten.

There were so many rules that you couldn't help breaking one now and then. There was arriving late or arriving without your homework done—and arriving in either condition without a eucalyptus switch, the tool for your own punishment, got you a double whipping. The teachers would sneak around, trying to catch kids speaking Kirundi instead of French, a punishable offense. Forgetting to bring your lunch was bad, though not as grave as what one schoolmate did, in a hungry season when his family had run low on food. A teacher discovered that the boy had filled his package of banana leaves with cow dung instead of beans. "Eat it!" the teacher commanded. The child refused, he was suspended, and to get him reinstated his mother had to come and watch him be beaten with the eucalyptus in front of the whole school. From then on everyone called that boy Fumier, "Manure." The name would have been the hardest thing to take, Deo thought, though he laughed at his schoolmate, too.

Punishments were at least as varied as infractions. Whippings with the eucalyptus switch across your bare legs and sometimes your back. Hard pinches on the arms and cheeks. Teachers would lift you by the skin at your jawbones and give you a good shake or force you to kneel on the ground in front of the school and hold a rock above your head for an hour. If a rooster shat on your copybook while you were trying to do your homework by the light of your family's cooking fire, you might end up the next day with your hands on your desk, your teacher beating your knuckles with his ruler. Biting down on a twig of eucalyptus helped you not to cry, but Deo hadn't brought one the time this happened to him, and the more he cried, the harder the ruler struck. By the end of that day, his fingers were so swollen he couldn't hold a pencil, let alone do his chores at home. He made the long walk toward Butanza, crying out silently, "What am I going to say to my dad?" But he was saved. He kept his hands behind his back and told his father he was sick, and was excused.

He knew he had it easier than some other kids. Some kids had cruel fathers, whereas his was merely stern. And Deo's father believed in education. His own schooling had ended after sixth grade, when he was obliged to go to work tending Lonjino's cows. But Deo's father had insisted that his own younger brother get educated. He'd fought with Lonjino and won; that younger brother, Deo's favorite uncle, had made it through the national university and become an economist. As for Deo's mother, her education had begun and ended with a year of catechism class. Sometimes Deo would come home from school, thinking, "I'm learning things my parents don't know." Sometimes he'd hand a textbook to his mother and ask her to read it, and she would hold it upside down. But she forgave him. She told him once, "If I can send my children to school, then no one is ever going to tell me that I didn't go to school. If my child went, I am educated, because I have an educated child."

On most days Deo's father let him stay at school for an extra half hour, so he could do his homework while there was still light. And Deo's daily walk was manageable, whereas other kids had to come from mountains twice as far away. Those were the ones most in danger of the eucalyptus switch, the kids he was apt to see hiding on the way to school, caught between the fear of teachers and the fear of fathers.

Many students dropped out. In Deo's memory, many also died. One day he would come to the room and a classmate would be missing. For the next several days Deo would keep glancing at the empty seat. The school was attached to a church. There was a graveyard filled with wooden crosses just a short distance away.

Through the grated windows of his classrooms he would hear the ululations from funeral processions, high-pitched, two-note sounds of grief played on fluttering tongues. The sound went right to his stomach, especially on windy days. People said the wind could carry the thing that had killed a person. He pictured this thing floating like a leaf on the wind, up from the graveyard and through the classroom's open windows.

Some other students were differently affected, like the brother of the most popular girl in the school. That boy sat in the classroom, studying, on the day of his sister's funeral, as if he didn't hear the cries of mourning that Deo was hearing all too well. How could you lose your sister and go to school during her funeral? That boy never cried when he got beaten, and there were some others like him. Their numbness had seemed strange to Deo, because numbness hadn't overtaken him. Looking back, he thought he understood the condition and its consequences: "Some people wonder why so much anger in my country, and really there is something that is rooted, from the way you grow up in the beaten conditions."

His best friend, Clovis, died on the evening of a completely normal Sunday. They had spent it minding their families' calves on a slope of the mountain Runda, their usual Sunday job, a good job for a pair of fourth graders. They took turns retrieving the calves that strayed near the edges of ravines. They spent the rest of the time playing cards and wrestling around on the ground. Near sunset, with no warning at all, Clovis began shivering and sweating and weeping, moaning, "I don't feel good."

Deo wanted to run away. Maybe the thing on the wind had caught Clovis. Maybe it was going to catch him, too. Oh, God, would he be next? He began weeping with Clovis and calling frantically for help. For a long time, all he heard were his own echoing cries, and then at last his father's voice called from an adjacent slope. Several men came and carried Clovis away. After Deo and his father had put the cows safely in their pens, they went to Clovis's house. Deo stood in the doorway of the hut. Inside, torches made of tightly wrapped dry grasses were set into the dirt floor. In the wavering light, Deo saw a neighbor he recognized attending to his friend; people called this man a doctor, but Deo's father had said he was really just an herbalist. The man was forcing a green liquid into Clovis's mouth. Clovis wasn't moving. Perhaps he was already dead.

Standing there in the doorway, watching the herbalist administer his potion, already suspecting that this medicine was worthless, Deo thought, "God, what is killing him? What can I do, what can I do?" Deo was an altar boy, in spite of his father's banishment from the church. He asked God for a favor. "I wish I could have some magic to get my friend back to life."

For years afterward he would visit the graveyard by the school and remember the funeral—the women wailing, everyone weeping—and he would think of Clovis and of the prayer he had said in the doorway.

The first time Deo came down with malaria—perhaps the cause of Clovis's death, he'd later learn—he felt as if a layer of his skin had been stripped off, as if the breeze blowing on him were a thornbush. He was on his way to school when he collapsed. His fierce little grandmother found him and carried him home piggyback. His father was away, but the people carrying loads through the mountains formed a virtual telegraph service, which brought his father home in time to have Deo treated at the hospital in the provincial capital. His father knew malaria, its treatment and its cause. His grandmother, however, believed differently. She blamed a neighboring family. "That family, they hate my grandchildren," Deo would hear her say in a low voice for years afterward. "They gave him poison."

Looking back, he saw this as a typical event in the annals of such allegations. His grandmother didn't approve of the way his mother was raising her children. Deo's mother must have exposed him to members of that neighboring family, who must be jealous of Deo's family's cows and must therefore have poisoned Deo. What was frightening and confusing to him then became dreadful in his memory. How, out of love for her grandchildren, his grandmother was bound to start a small feud on their hill. And surely the same sort of thing had been happening in other huts and houses in those mountains all during his childhood.

Most of Deo's classmates who didn't die or drop out of the elementary school progressed from room to room down the length of the building and after six years headed off into the mountains to eke out a living raising crops or herding cows—if their families had some land or cows. Whether they finished school or dropped out, many left Butanza for the towns or the capital, where the usual choice was a menial job or, for Tutsis at least, service in the army.

During the years when Deo was growing up, a succession of military dictators ruled Burundi. All belonged to a group called the Tutsi-Hima. Records from the era show that in all of Burundi there were only a few dozen secondary schools and one university, and that Tutsis occupied the majority of places in them. No doubt this favoritism gave Deo advantages that most schoolchildren didn't share. It seems strange to think of Deo enjoying anything that could be called privilege, but in a small, crucial way that was the case.

His family didn't belong to the ruling group of Tutsis; they had no political connections. For a boy like him, the only ticket onward was good grades and a high mark on the nationwide exam administered to sixth graders. Only Deo and one classmate scored well enough to make the cut.

He excelled in middle school, too, and was admitted to one of Burundi's best high schools, situated two days' walk from home. Deo boarded there. School became genteel. One wasn't beaten, and one wore shoes. He ran barefoot, though, in races. He ran for fun as well, sometimes with friends and often alone in the surrounding hills. He was no sprinter, but he could run for hours. He liked to boast that his feet were so tough you couldn't drive a nail into them. In a sense, he had been in endurance training ever since his first hikes with cows in the mountains. That kind of training continued when the school year ended and he and Antoine went back to carrying food and cowherding for the summer.

At high school his world expanded, partly under the influence of a bishop named Bernard Bududira, a big figure in the region, the man in charge of all its Catholic schools. Deo felt he'd known Bududira for most of his life, ever since third grade, when the bishop had visited the school in Sangaza and Deo had been chosen to present him with a gift. At the high school, priests got to select their spiritual advisees. Naturally, Bududira got the first picks. He chose Deo and one other boy. He spoke to them about God, of course, but with an emphasis on what God asked human beings to do for themselves and what God would have bright young students do about poverty and injustice in Burundi.

"There are many ways in which poverty finds its way into the bodies of the destitute." This was a favorite saying of Bududira's. He traveled widely through his territory, visiting many hills, and he would talk to Deo and the other boy about what he saw, especially about the almost universal need for clean water and medicine. He told them he was distressed at the great numbers of impoverished children who joined the army at twelve or thirteen, and told them about his campaign to build alternatives in the form of technical schools.

At the end of eleventh grade—high school ended with thirteenth—Deo started his own project, an attempt to build a clinic in Sangaza that would serve the surrounding hills. He dreamed of inspiring other communities to do the same throughout Burundi—starting small but thinking big. He talked half a dozen classmates into joining him, and even got his father to let him spend the first weeks of summer vacation on the construction. He worked at trying to build the clinic for parts of three summers, right up until graduation. He didn't manage to get a building erected, but it wasn't for lack of trying. He told himself he would get back to a project like this one day.

Deo received a very high grade on the national post–secondary school test and was offered a scholarship to a university in Belgium, to be trained there for the priesthood. No doubt Bududira had a hand in this, but Deo wanted to go to Burundi's medical school instead. Bududira heartily approved.

In 1988, during Deo's senior year in high school, Bishop Bududira had written a bold public letter, urging the government to abandon its "deliberate refusal to talk about ethnic antagonism." The subject, he wrote, had become "a taboo," and meanwhile, Hutus were being systematically harassed. They were suffering "deliberate injustices in the distribution of positions of responsibility in favor of Tutsi elements." (There was also blatant discrimination against Hutus in all aspects of education, even in the grading of the national tests.) Ethnic antagonism, the bishop warned, had become "extremely acute." His pastoral letter was prophetic. That summer, a large Hutu rebellion erupted in the north. Tutsis were slaughtered indiscriminately, and the army retaliated with even greater brutality, killing perhaps as many as fifteen thousand Hutus.

Deo happened to be at home on Runda when the massacres in the north began. Neighbors who he had long since learned were Hutus—whatever that actually meant—warned Deo's family that the trouble might spread. He and his family spent a few days and nights in the woods, all except for Lonjino, who as usual kept a vigil over the compound. Nothing happened around Butanza, but in the aftermath Deo began asking questions and for once received some answers. He also did some reading. Later, he called this time "an awakening."

In school, he had learned a basic version of Burundian history. Even at the time some of the lessons had seemed weird, particularly when it came to colonization. The basic facts were clear: Germans had claimed the kingdoms of Burundi and Rwanda at the very end of the nineteenth century, and were replaced after World War I by the Belgians, who ran the countries from 1918 until the early 1960s. His teachers said that the Belgians had "tortured" Burundi. Nonetheless, students were taught songs extolling the greatness of Belgium, and the teachers would speak longingly of going to Iburaya. And now those high school history lessons also seemed strikingly incomplete, all but devoid of explanations for the terms "Hutu" and "Tutsi," and of facts that Deo gradually ferreted out. He learned that Hutus made up about 85 percent of the country and Tutsis about 13 or 14 percent; that for decades Tutsi big shots had controlled both the army and the government; that there had been many bloody Hutu uprisings, followed by even bloodier army repressions. This pattern had turned into a bloodbath back in 1972, when Deo had been a baby. That was the year, Deo already knew, when his uncle the doctor had been killed. Now he learned that Hutu militiamen had dismembered his uncle and left him to die in his little car on the mountain Honga. His uncle had been just one victim of a gruesome Hutu rebellion, which the army had put down with gruesome efficiency. They had killed all the Hutu politicians and intellectuals they could, even schoolteachers and nurses, and many schoolchildren—at least 100,000 Hutus in all, and some said 200,000 or even 300,000; many other Hutus had fled to neighboring countries such as Rwanda and Tanzania.

Why had he known almost nothing of this? Had he heard more than he'd allowed himself to remember? It was a frightening subject for everyone: for Tutsis who were outnumbered by Hutu neighbors, for Hutus who knew the army was never far away. And by the time Deo was born, the Tutsi-dominated government had decided its own purposes were best served by silence on the issue of ethnicity. Among other things, they had done away with the Belgian practice of putting "Hutu" or "Tutsi" on citizens' identity cards.

It was a shock for Deo to realize the depth of the divisions in his country, a shock to think how virulently people must have spat out the term "Tutsi" around cooking fires in some neighbors' huts in Butanza during the years of his childhood. And yet, for all the suffering the division had apparently caused, he still felt puzzled as to what "Hutu" and "Tutsi" actually meant. Had the Hutus been the original, the true Burundians, and the Tutsis more recent conquerors from the region of the Nile? It was said that Tutsis kept cattle and Hutus farmed the land, but many people around Butanza, Hutu and Tutsi, did both. It was said that Tutsis were tall and slender with thin noses, whereas Hutus were short and chunky and broad-nosed, with hairlines that ran straight across their foreheads. But in Deo's experience the stereotypes didn't hold. He thought he knew of more exceptions than examples. He himself was close to being a hybrid, at least according to the standards laid down by some Belgian colonials, who had weighed and measured Burundians and Rwandans and come up with averages for features such as height—1.7586 meters for a Tutsi, 1.6780 for a Hutu. By those definitions, most of Deo's brothers were too short to be Tutsis, and he was just barely tall enough. He was thin, but not as thin as many people around Butanza who were said to be Hutus, and his nose was neither narrow nor very broad.

Deo suffered another bout of malaria and put off medical school for almost a year, during which he taught elementary school in a remote village. He had no idea which of his pupils were Hutu, which Tutsi. And he didn't care, nor did anyone else in the village, so far as he could tell. He didn't think about *ubwoko,* about "ethnicity." To him, the pupils were simply poor, and already demoralized by poverty, especially the girls and the ones with physical handicaps, whom he tried to help. He spent a fair amount of his meager pay buying banana beer for their fathers so they would listen as he praised their children.

When Deo finally arrived at medical school in Bujumbura, he began to learn what a rube he was, a country boy with mud between his toes. Some of his classmates also seemed to struggle financially, but everyone had better clothes. He owned only one shirt with a collar. He would wash it at night in his room and let it dry in his open window. He made one pair of pants last his entire first year, by sewing patches on them. "So many patches," he later said, "it was impossible to tell which was the original."

He underwent the standard hazing from the older students. They ordered him to sit beneath a dining table, to put his plate full of rice on top of his head, then to feed himself by hand, grasping handfuls of rice from overhead. "So you think this is bad?" said one of the upperclassmen. "How often do you have rice at home?"

This was a standard question. Deo got the answer wrong the first time it was asked. He said what was true, that his family grew some rice and did sometimes eat it at home. For this, he was kicked. The next time, he managed the exchange correctly.

"How often do you eat rice at home?"

"Only on Christmas Day."

Rice was often served in the dining hall. He understood the implication. He was being inducted into a superior group, which deserved special privileges.

He had always made friends easily and was making many now, among them Jean, who had a Burundian mother but was a *muzungu* because his father was French. (*Muzungu,* which comes from Swahili, originally meant a person who moves from place to place, but it had come to signify a white European. And because, where Deo grew up at least, one assumed that anyone with white skin was rich, *muzungu* was often used to signify any wealthy Burundian—it was like calling that person white.) Jean had his own car and his own apartment near the campus. He was a good-looking, light-skinned young *muzungu* with money and a car, in a city of beautiful young women. He was often out on the town. This was the era of AIDS, and Deo felt more worried than disapproving, though he did disapprove. He didn't remonstrate with his friend, though. He was a country boy who knew how to grow beans. Who was he to lecture a civilized boy?

The medical school itself was a paradise to Deo. The principal building was practically brand-new. It had a well-stocked library, and a room full of microscopes and other gear for studying bacteriology. The buildings of the university hospital that surrounded the school weren't as elegant, but a large staff kept them clean, and there were only two patients per room on the wards. Each class had about a hundred students, about as many of them young women as men. About a hundred and fifty professors worked full-time or part-time teaching them. Many of the professors were French, and they were like gods, not to be crossed. Just as in high school, if you asked a question, you got an answer. One never heard a professor say, "I don't know." Often the answer would be, in effect, "Shut up." Early on, one of Deo's classmates asked a question, and the professor wrinkled his nose and said, "First of all, learn to speak French properly." Deo spoke impeccable French, but after that he didn't often feel like raising his hand.

He lived in a dorm and spent most of his time in class and in the library and on hospital rounds with professors. Grades were posted periodically for all to see, on a bulletin board. His name consistently appeared in the top five. He had a plan by this time: on the day of graduation he would marry—he didn't yet know whom—then he would go to work helping the poor. He had dreamed of building clinics for the country ever since that abortive attempt to build one in Sangaza. In the present, medical school comprised a world all its own, both to him and, he thought, to most of his classmates. It claimed most of his time and energy. But by now even he couldn't help paying some attention to politics, first of all to nearby international politics.

There was war up north in Rwanda. Its roots lay in the late 1950s and early 1960s, when colonial rule had ended. In Burundi, Tutsi elites had claimed power. But in Rwanda the opposite had happened: Hutu elites had supplanted the former Tutsi aristocracy.

In Rwanda, during the struggle for power, thousands of Tutsis had been killed, and hundreds of thousands had fled. Some had settled in Uganda. For decades, Rwanda's governments had refused to repatriate those refugees, and like most countries where exiles tried to make new homes, Uganda didn't want them either. Now a force made up mainly of descendants of the Tutsi exiles in Uganda was attempting what one scholar describes as "an armed repatriation." The group called itself the Rwandan Patriotic Front, the RPF. Its largely Tutsi army, the Rwandan Patriotic Army, had invaded Rwanda in 1990. The RPF was supported quietly but effectively by Uganda's government. Its army was much smaller initially than Rwanda's, which was supported fecklessly by Zaire, to a greater degree by Belgium, and robustly by France. (The colonial language of Rwanda was French, that of Uganda English. A main tenet of French policy in Africa seems to have been the preservation of French-speaking governments at all costs. In French political circles, the RPF invasion was called "an Anglo-Saxon invasion.") Even so, the RPF had grown and become formidable. It had taken territory and seemed certain to take more. Many Tutsis had been arrested in Rwanda in retaliation for the RPF's successes. Hundreds, at least, had been killed. The so-called international community had sponsored on-again, off-again peace talks.

Deo followed the events, desultorily. Once in a while he listened to accounts on Rwandan radio stations. Several times he heard Rwandan officials or commentators say, "Slowly we will finish them." But he assumed the Rwandan speakers were talking about defeating the RPF, not about Tutsis in general.

These were unsettling times, but they only rarely frightened him. His first shock came on a day in the spring of 1991. He was waiting for a bus in front of the Coca-Cola stand across the street from the medical school. A fellow classmate, a casual friend, came up to him and said in a whisper, "Here, look at this." He handed Deo a folded newspaper and quickly walked away.

It was a tabloid-style paper, folded open to a page with this headline: "The Hutu Ten Commandments." Deo had heard of this newspaper, the international edition of a Rwandan paper, sanctioned by the Rwandan government and called *Kangura*—the name meant "wake up." The newspaper was distributed, Deo had heard, by a Burundian Hutu-power group, outlawed by Burundi's Tutsi government and headquartered in refugee camps in Tanzania. The group called itself PALIPEHUTU, an acronym for, roughly, "Liberation of the Hutu People." The Hutu Ten Commandments had circulated widely throughout Rwanda, but this was the first Deo knew of them. He read them surreptitiously on the bus and reread them several times back in his dorm.

The first commandment stated: "Every Hutu should know that a Tutsi woman, whoever she is, works for the interest of her Tutsi ethnic group. As a result we shall consider a traitor any Hutu who: marries a Tutsi woman, befriends a Tutsi woman, employs a Tutsi woman as a secretary or a concubine." Other commandments laid out additional reasons that Tutsis should be feared, despised, and shunned. They didn't actually suggest killing all Tutsis, but the eighth commandment declared, "The Hutu should stop having mercy on the Tutsi," and the ninth read, in part, "The Hutu must be firm and vigilant against their common Tutsi enemy." Other writings in the paper referred to Tutsis as "cockroaches," an old epithet in Rwanda.

Where was this coming from? Deo wondered. Was this sort of hatred going to burst out in the open here, in Burundi? Did some of his family's neighbors believe this stuff? If he traveled back home, would he be in danger on the way? Who were his fellow students and where did they stand on all of this? He kept the paper hidden in his room for several days, then handed it quietly to another classmate, one he happened to know was a Tutsi.

Some of his classmates openly discussed the ethnic issue. Several made no secret of the fact that they came from Tutsi families who had fled from Rwanda to Burundi during one or another pogrom.

They worried openly, saying, "Is it going to happen here?" But Deo didn't know the classification of most of the others at the school. If you were out on the street and you guessed that everyone you saw was Hutu, you would, after all, be right about 85 percent of the time. And he thought he could identify some classmates by stereotype. But most people's looks fell, like his own, in a middle ground. He wasn't even sure about every neighbor's ethnicity back in Butanza. Here in Bujumbura, the only way to know for certain was to be told by the person in question, and he wasn't about to go among his classmates asking, "Are you a Hutu or a Tutsi?" The worry he'd felt when he read the Hutu Ten Commandments didn't pass entirely, but it abated.

Deo began to notice what seemed like a new fad around the university and in the city. He would be out walking with student friends, often a mixture of Hutus and Tutsis, at least as far as he could tell, and they would encounter other friends or strangers who would raise one hand to the top of an ear, then make a fist and raise the hand higher, saying as they did this, *"Inivo nu gutwi,"* which to Deo meant "At the level of the ear." And then they might say, "Oh, hi!" Deo and his friends would laugh and repeat the gesture. Once in a while he would be sitting with friends on the wall outside the medical school or on the grass outside his dorm, or he'd be standing with friends on the street, and strangers passing by would smile and say, *"Susuruka,"* "Warm them up."

Deo assumed this was just a new greeting to go with the fist-raising gesture. *"Susuruka,"* he'd reply, and then do the fist-raise.

It was only much later that Deo was able to make some sense of what had been going on around him outside the medical school classrooms. He would come to feel that history, even more than memory, distorts the present of the past by focusing on big events and making one forget that most people living in the present are otherwise preoccupied, that for them omens often don't exist. "Everyone has a different story," he'd come to think. "It's not like for one team if you are playing football, one team here and one team there. No. It's a chaos. And everyone says something depending on what they saw or lived or felt." Most people probably understood *"Inivo nu gutwi"* and *"Susuruka"* as political slogans, or even as Deo did, as new and friendly greetings. It was only later that Deo came to think that "At the level of the ear" was code for a machete's proper target, and "Warm them up" meant "Pour gasoline on Tutsis and light a match."

In Deo's third year of medical school, a big moment in Burundi's political history arrived. In the aftermath of 1988—the massacres of Burundian Tutsis and counter-massacres of Hutus—there had been international condemnation of Burundi's military government. In Burundi, as in much of Africa, foreign aid had long been a principal source of wealth for the wealthy. Burundi's unelected Tutsi leaders had responded to the pressure by creating a new interim government, led by a Hutu and composed of equal numbers of Hutus and Tutsis. A constitution providing for multiparty democracy had followed, and then a general amnesty, and finally, in early 1993, national elections.

There was some trouble, of course. Hutu refugees were returning, some with their Ten Commandments memorized, many with bitter, horrifying memories of 1972 preserved. Ideologues of Tutsi rule attempted a coup to prevent the election. But the voting went on, and a Hutu named Melchior Ndadaye defeated his Tutsi opponent. Inevitably, ethnicity figured in the election campaign, but after Ndadaye had won 65 percent of the vote, he immediately began preaching peace. Thousands of Tutsi students and members of the losing party held a march in Bujumbura to protest Ndadaye's election. A month later, a small group of Tutsi soldiers attempted another coup, which also failed. Ndadaye appointed a cabinet of seven Tutsis and fifteen Hutus, with a Tutsi as prime minister. On

July 10, 1993, at his formal swearing-in, Ndadaye and the losing Tutsi candidate, a former unelected president, hugged in front of the cameras.

Deo hadn't joined the Tutsi protest. He didn't have any special feeling for either candidate. But not everyone at the school was as indifferent.

He had a classmate who liked to declare that he was a Hutu and would say, "We need to share the small cake." *Le petit gâteau.* Deo had never eaten cake, but he understood: Burundi was poor, only a handful could be wealthy in Burundi. Right now Tutsi elites were enjoying almost all the scarce wealth and privileges. They needed to share the small cake, not with the Hutu people in general, but with Hutu elites.

Many students in Deo's class thought this fellow difficult—cold and haughty, always spouting off about the virtues of the rebel group PALIPEHUTU and taking it upon himself to discover his classmates' ethnicities. Deo had the impression that most self-identified Hutus in the class disapproved of the young man. Deo had avoided him, but evidently he had his eye on Deo and knew Deo was a Tutsi. On a day soon after Ndadaye's election, he came up to Deo in a hallway and, letting loose a burst of toneless laughter, said, "This is your end."

Deo knew he was talking about the election. He figured the guy just wanted to crow a little. "The end of what?" asked Deo. "In power, or what?"

The young man laughed again. "You don't get it," he said. "You are like the tail of a beheaded snake."

Deo knew his snakes, the mambas and cobras and other venomous species, and he knew the proper response to an encounter with a snake, which was either to run or to chop off its head. Evidently, this Hutu classmate was a country boy, too. No doubt he was imagining the same thing as Deo at that moment—a decapitated snake with the tail still wriggling around, as if the tail didn't know it was part of an animal already dead, as if it didn't know there was no hope for it. "My God," Deo thought, "are we Tutsis going to be wiped out? Struggling on the ground?" He had always tended to feel fear in his belly. He felt as if his stomach had filled all at once with acid. He felt like running away from this guy. He couldn't think of a word to say. After that, whenever he saw his radical classmate he saw a beheaded snake in his mind.

EIGHT

New York City,
1995–2000

Improbable as it would have seemed to almost anyone else, the fall of 1995 found Deo entering his freshman year at Columbia University. It seemed improbable to at least one of his classmates, who asked Deo if he was the son of an African king. Deo said he wasn't. Well, the classmate asked, how did he come to be at Columbia? Deo didn't tell him that only a year ago he'd been delivering groceries and sleeping in Central Park, or that a combination of student loans, scholarships, and Nancy and Charlie's money was paying his way. To explain would only have left his classmate more confused and more inquisitive. Deo simply smiled and said brightly, "I don't know why I'm here, but I'm here!"

Deo hadn't known he'd accomplished anything special when Columbia had accepted him, not until he met a few people from other New York colleges and realized they were impressed— "Really? You're going to *Columbia*?" Even then, the fact of being at college didn't seem extraordinary to him. He had already gone through three years of what in the European system constituted both college and medical school. Starting college over again, as a freshman with at least four years between him and a return to medical training, didn't seem like a big deal. It felt like a demotion. And because he was in a hurry to catch up, he got a little ahead of his abilities with English.

A few days after his first chemistry test, the professor took him aside and told him he had answered almost every question wrong. When Deo said this was impossible, in an accent that was unmistakably French, the professor looked at him quizzically, then smiled and said, *"Je parle français aussi."* In his answers, Deo had written down the names of chemicals as he had learned to do in Burundi—he'd written "chloride hydrogen," for instance, instead of "hydrogen chloride." The professor regraded his test and his score went from a zero to an A minus, but the professor also advised him to defer advanced science courses and concentrate for now on his English. Deo thanked him, thinking there was no way he was going to slow down. At midterm, he was summoned by the dean, who told him he was on the verge of academic probation and gave him the same advice as the chemistry professor. Deo didn't take it. He botched his physics final because every question had to do with the motion of a "carousel." He didn't know the word, and, out of old habit, didn't dare ask the instructor for its meaning. At the end of the spring term, however, Deo had made the dean's list.

Sophomore year began with a struggle, too. He sat down at his desk in the Black Hole, opened his text to the beginning page of his assignment in the English literature survey course, and saw "Whan that Aprille with hise shoures soote . . ."

"Wah!" He reached for his English dictionary. There was no "whan" or "hise" or "shoures" or "soote."

"What is this, Chinese?"

His teacher calmed him down, his professor in African-American literature gave him a modern English translation of

Chaucer, and he finished that course with an A. He had begun to find his way around the curriculum, thanks mainly to a graduate student who befriended him. Deo was majoring in biochemistry and, for reasons that were clearly not practical, in philosophy.

He loved his course in American literature, and most of all W.E.B. DuBois's *The Souls of Black Folk*. He read and then reread it until very late in Butler Library, a favorite place at Columbia where he often spent half the night before heading home to SoHo. There was a homeless man camped out in the subway station. Deo could smell him from a distance, but went over to his campsite anyway, and talked to the man until the train arrived. The car was all but empty. Deo sat and began reciting his favorite passage from DuBois: "To be a poor man is hard, but to be a poor race in a land of dollars is the very bottom of hardships." He felt DuBois might have been speaking to him, back when he'd been lugging groceries into penthouses, feeling that he would be better off in a peaceful Burundi among people as poor as he—if Burundi were peaceful. Deo went on reciting, not realizing he was murmuring aloud: "He felt the weight of his ignorance, —not simply of letters, but of life, of business, of the humanities; the accumulated sloth and shirking and awkwardness of decades and centuries shackled his hands and feet." There was just one other passenger in the car, a young man. He got up and walked quickly away.

Deo hadn't made many friends among his classmates at Columbia, but he had many now among graduate students and faculty. With difficulty—for a while it looked as if he might be deported—James O'Malley had argued a judge into granting Deo refugee status, but he was still waiting for permanent residency, for his green card. Nevertheless, he had joined a protest in front of city hall—it had to do with MetroCard transfers, and being a daily bus and subway rider, he was an interested party. This had felt like a significant act, something he'd never have thought or dared to do three years before, a New Yorker's act, another investment in this place.

One of his lives would remain forever unfinished. That was simply a fact. He was resigned to it. Another life now lay before him, with new friends, a new education, new parents.

But he still listened many nights for news of Burundi on the French broadcast, and once in a while he still made streetcorner calls. On a day in his sophomore year he was riding the subway home from Columbia and remembered that he hadn't talked to Claude for weeks. He got off at 125th Street. He went through the usual drill with the men who hawked long-distance calls at the pay phones. He dialed the house full of internal refugees in Bujumbura, as usual, and the voice of a bus driver named Pierre answered.

"Is Claude there?" Deo asked in Kirundi.

"No."

"This is Deo calling."

"Oh, Deo. I have some news for you," said Pierre. "Some of your family are alive. Your parents also."

———

Weeks of phone calls followed, to Bujumbura from the sidewalks of Harlem, from Nancy and Charlie's loft to the Office of the United Nations High Commissioner on Refugees. There were searches for relatives. It was a time of reunions by phone and of *gusimbura*. Many aunts and uncles and cousins had died. His sister and two youngest brothers, one adopted, had been living in forests and had ended up in a military camp. Two brothers had been killed, victims of the civil war. Part of the body of one of them had been found in a swimming pool in Bujumbura. The other had died when rebel militia had attacked his high school. Deo didn't ask after Lonjino. No one spoke the old man's name to him over the phone, a silence that amounted to a death certificate. He had mourned Lonjino and the rest of his family already. He mourned the dead again. But his parents really were alive, in a refugee camp in Tanzania. There were months of phone calls, and many arrangements fell through, before he was notified that his mother and father were back in Burundi, re-settled not in Butanza, but in Kayanza. There were no telephones there, but his favorite uncle would bring them to his house in Bu-jumbura so that Deo could speak to them. He made the call from Nancy and Charlie's. They insisted, and never mind the cost.

When you greet someone in Kirundi, you usually say, *"Ama-horo,"* "Peace." When you repeat *Amahoro* many times, as Deo did when he heard his father's voice, it means that you are overjoyed. "Father, this is Deo!"

"Oh, okay," said his father. "So it's good to hear your voice." Then his father asked, "Are you you?"

Yes, he was Deo!

"Hunh," said his father, as if he were puzzled. "I expected your voice to be changed."

"Why?" Deo asked.

"Oh, okay," his father said. "So where are you?"

Deo said he was in America, the United States.

"Oh, in Iburaya," said his father.

The voice Deo heard over the line lacked the authoritative, peremptory tone that had always been part of the memory he'd car-ried of his father. But maybe his father was simply shocked to hear his son's living voice, as Deo was shocked to hear his father's. He wasn't sure what else his father said, if anything. His father really was alive. And what must his father be thinking? "Where is Deo right now as I speak to him? Where could he be?" But Deo had no words to describe where he was, none that could be assembled into terms his father would understand.

Then his mother's voice was on the line.

"Mother, this is Deo!"

"No. It's not you," he heard her declare. "This is a voice in my head." There was a click on the line, and then silence.

Deo placed the call again, and got her on the phone once more. She didn't hang up this time, but there was no way to settle into conversation with her. She was guarded, as if she felt he were trying to sell her something that she wanted but knew she couldn't have. Besides, his mind was wandering again. It was wonderful to hear his mother's voice, more than he had dared to hope for, and it was frightening to hear it. What exactly had happened to his mother and his father? They were old by Burundian standards. He imagined them trekking to Tanzania. He could picture the mountains they must have crossed, bent under what they'd taken of their possessions. What had they endured on the way, and in the camps? Could his mother have been raped? What if his mother began to tell him? He was trying to think how he could reconcile his feelings, all this joy and dread, into the old feelings for his parents that simply had to be preserved, and at the same time he was trying, at five of Nancy and Charlie's dollars a minute, to think of words to convince his mother that this voice she heard was really Deo's—she must acknowledge his existence!—all the while knowing he was going to fail.

He had believed that his family was lost forever. His greatest burden was gone, and a new burden received. There were moments when he wished he was back on his own. Now and then he imagined leaving everything behind and slipping back at night into Central Park. But then he thought of his parents trying to rebuild their burned house in Kayanza, of his widowed grandmother in Butanza, of his siblings hiding in the forest. And here he was living off Nancy and Charlie and going to an Ivy League school where he had been mistaken for the son of a king, studying organic chemistry and philosophy. The words that came into his mind were "useless," "selfish," "parasite." It would take years to become a doctor with a real salary. He should study for a practical career, so he could help his family sooner. He enrolled in a basic economics course. The class was interesting enough, but every moment he was in it felt like a betrayal of his dreams. After a week, he dropped the course, feeling ashamed.

He thought of going back to Burundi to visit, but this was impossible. He had only narrowly won refugee status. As his lawyer, James, pointed out, the immigration service might well refuse to readmit a refugee who went back to the place he had supposedly fled.

One thing he could do was send money.

He often stopped to see Sharon at the rectory. He'd learned through Nancy and Charlie that she used to be a nun. He didn't ask her about this. He didn't want to know more about her than she wanted him to know. He could tell she was always glad to see him. She'd say, "Tell me the latest." When he delivered good news, that he had been admitted to Columbia for instance, she would give him a hug, saying, "I'm so proud of you." She had suffered with him through the search for his parents, and for a time afterward he had asked her for money to send them. She gave him what still seemed like large sums—a hundred dollars here and there. But then he and Nancy and Charlie helped Sharon move, from the rectory to a small apartment that belonged to a rather addled lady, where Sharon occupied a tiny alcove. After seeing her lodgings and few possessions, Deo realized she was living almost like a homeless person. He didn't want to ask her for donations after that.

He took odd jobs, tutoring high school students in math, bartending now and then. He could always save a little from his college loans, and from the weekly envelopes labeled "Deo" that Charlie left on the kitchen counter every Monday morning.

Charlie did this, Deo knew, to make it easy for him to accept spending money. One hundred dollars every week. From the first morning the envelope appeared, Deo hated taking it. He had spent as little as he could, hiding the remainder in the Black Hole because he thought that if he tried to give it back, Nancy and Charlie would be hurt. Now he started to save more, so as to send it to Burundi.

He figured he needed only twenty dollars a week for subways to and from Columbia, and sometimes he could save part of that by walking from lower Manhattan to the campus up in Harlem. He began skipping lunch. In a biochemistry class, he and his fellow students were learning about the mechanics of starvation, how in the early stages the reactions of the liver often produce bad breath. A fellow student in that class, an acquaintance, not a friend, actually said to him, "Man, you need to eat." Deo modified his regimen, but only by eating more during the evening meals with Nancy and Charlie.

Getting the money to his family was harder than saving it. His family didn't have bank accounts. He figured he had to send cash. He made a package out of postcards, gluing two cards together with money inside. He sent one of these to Antoine, then learned via Claude that the glued-together postcards had arrived, but without the money.

Most likely the theft had happened in Burundi. But maybe, he thought, someone rifled the packet at the post office he used in New York. Maybe he should try another post office. One time he went with Nancy and Charlie to visit friends of theirs in Cambridge, Massachusetts. He was taking a walk alone through a residential part of the town, with money for home in his pocket. Seeing a house with an American flag on a pole out front, he went up the walk and knocked on the door. A man appeared. Deo said he wanted to send a letter. "Are you all right?" asked the man, and Deo hurried away. A national flag in Burundi meant a government building. Evidently, flags had other meanings here.

Through a chance encounter outside the United Nations in New York, he met a Burundian expatriate who was driving a cab in the city. The man introduced Deo to friends in the Burundian consulate. Attempts at making peace in Burundi had begun. Deo volunteered to show New York to Burundian dignitaries who came to the United Nations. He did this gratis. He'd show them around, then ask them to carry money back to his relatives, usually to Antoine, who would distribute it. Deo would call Claude and ask him to tell

Antoine that he had sent money. Once in a while, Deo would hear in a subsequent call that Antoine found the courier, the person whom Deo had shown around New York, and the courier claimed that he'd lost his wallet or that her suitcase had been stolen. But this procedure usually worked.

When Deo had started giving tours, he had hoped they would make him feel connected to Burundi. He went about the job with some missionary zeal at first. He'd take his fellow Burundians to the World Trade Center, and pointing up, he'd say, "Look. Look at how people built and constructed a country, as opposed to us." But many seemed less interested in the sights than in shopping—usually for sheets; he never asked why. After a while Deo came to think that most didn't want to see New York so much as they wanted to be able to say they had seen it. Deo continued giving tours until he couldn't stand it anymore.

Anyone who has been far away from home has felt the oddness of its seeming at once very close and very far away. Home as he'd known it was right there in the light of dawn at the windows in Nancy and Charlie's front room, in the thoughts that arose as he bent over the radio in the Black Hole late at night, listening for news of Burundi. But he was conscious—it felt like grief—of the great physical distance and the impossibility of actually being home. Nancy must have sensed all this. When Deo's uncle sent a photograph of himself, she had it framed and hung it over Deo's desk.

He tried to return to his studies. When he had first heard his parents were alive, everything else had fallen aside for him, including Columbia. Bad news from home could still overwhelm him. During junior year, he missed weeks of school and didn't fully realize it, until he returned to the class in organic chemistry, long the crucible of pre-med students, and found he understood almost nothing of the lecture. He explained what had happened to the professor, who urged him to drop the course and take it again the next semester. Deo said he couldn't do that, the professor offered to tutor him weekly, and after the course ended the professor wrote a letter for Deo's file, saying that Deo's C plus in the course was not a true reflection of his abilities.

———

Americans, Deo thought, seemed to look forward to evening. He dreaded it. Not that he never slept, but he still found himself awake many nights, wishing for perpetual daylight as he sat over his textbooks in the Black Hole. At the urging of a friend he went to see a psychiatrist. In the midst of telling his story, he sensed that the psychiatrist was shocked. The doctor said he had no experience with Deo's sort of trauma. Maybe Deo could find someone from a culture that had been obliged to deal with injuries like his. It was the first time that Deo had tried to tell his story out loud, really tell it in full. He left reproaching himself. What was he thinking, talking like that, pitying himself? He could handle his own problems.

Early in his sophomore year, on October 10, 1996, he had found this message in his email. It was written in Kirundi, in lowercase and without punctuation. He translated it later for the authorities. It read:

> i found you are my classmate at columbia but you would never be able to know me because i look like other black people i've learned that you are a dog from the tutsi we palipehutu people will wipe you out and i just want you to know that any time we want any moment we can get you around columbia we will see you but keep in mind that we watch you everywhere you go

The email was signed "committee of palipehutu in new york." PALIPEHUTU, along with other rebel groups, continued to wage war against the shaky Tutsi-dominated government in Burundi. Deo mentioned the email to a classmate, who told him to take it to the dean of students. The dean had the email traced, but to no avail. The writer had used a public computer, most likely at an Internet café. The dean told Deo not to worry. New York was safe, he said. Deo should stay among friends and avoid being alone with people he didn't know.

Deo hung a printout of the email on the wall by his desk in the Black Hole, not very far from his uncle's photograph. He told himself, "You better get used to this." Keeping the threat in plain sight, he imagined, might be a way of taming it.

But the smallest coincidence could draw him back. Simply opening a text to T. S. Eliot's *The Waste Land* and seeing the word "April" did the trick, because that was the month in which Rwanda's genocide had begun. The familiar cycle would start again, the whirlpool of nightmares and waking visions and sleeplessness to avoid nightmares and ensuing exhaustion that seemed to leave him still more vulnerable to nightmares. He would come down with immobilizing headaches. As a medical student in Burundi, Deo had seen people pushed away from hospitals, not only when they had no money, but sometimes just because they were dirty and smelled bad. Now news that a relative was ill would keep him worrying for days, imagining that his mother or a sibling might even now be receiving such treatment.

His grades suffered more or less in cadence with his nightmares and with troubling news from Burundi. Then he would recover and do well for stretches, more than well enough in the end to make it through Columbia.

He graduated in a spring rainstorm, especially memorable because the ceremony went on outdoors without a tent. Nancy and Charlie and Sharon came, of course, and Lelia and James, who was still trying to get Deo his green card, and half a dozen others, all part of the Wolfs' wide cast of friends, Deo's support group.

The email from sophomore year, the warning from the supposed member of PALIPEHUTU, still hung over his desk in the Black Hole. The paper had grown brittle. Nothing had come of the threat. It was like the noise one hears lying in bed at night, a noise outside the house. As time goes by you doubt the noise was real, and then again you don't.

NINE

Burundi–Rwanda–Burundi,
1993–94

On October 22, 1993, Deo was working as an intern in a rural hospital, deep in the countryside of northern Burundi. It was in a town called Mutaho. He had finished his third year of medical school, and had chosen to do his first internship here, in part to get away from the clamor of Bujumbura and back to the country. And Mutaho's hospital had recently been improved. It was a very large hospital by Burundian standards—three hundred beds—with a first-rate staff.

In retrospect, Deo thought he might have foreseen what was about to happen to the country. There had been omens: the killings of 1988, the Hutu Ten Commandments, the postelection protests, his angry classmate's comparing him to the tail of a beheaded snake. But the election of a Hutu president, Ndadaye, had not affected Deo in any way so far. In order to go on with our lives, we are always capable of making the ominous into the merely strange.

He had been assigned a room in a wing of Mutaho's hospital, a little room with a window and door that he could lock and a narrow bed and a small table on which he kept his one change of clothes. He didn't have much money. When he got some time off, he took a walk or went for a run on the red dirt road that ran roughly north and south past the hospital. More often, he hung out with the nurses, and especially with patients. When he was with patients, he never felt lonely.

His workday began at seven-thirty, when he'd begin rounds with a doctor and nurse, checking on patients and taking notes. On the morning of October 22, 1993, he came out of his room ready for work, but he couldn't find either the doctor or the nurse he was supposed to accompany. In fact, walking around the hospital, he couldn't find any doctors at all. He saw only a couple of nurses, at the opposite end of one of the hospital's many corridors. The nurses looked as if they were in a hurry. He wouldn't bother them. But why so few nurses and no doctors? Maybe they'd gone on vacation, and no one had bothered to tell him: he was just a lowly student. Maybe this part of Burundi celebrated a holiday he didn't know about. The hospital gave him a weird feeling this morning. Then again, it was a disorienting place—a large, concrete, single-story complex of buildings joined by open-air corridors and crisscrossed by hallways. Mutaho was out in the middle of nowhere. He knew no one in the town. Something could easily have happened to the medical staff without his knowing. Something bad, even. "Oh, it's probably just me," he thought. "Imagining things."

Deo went off on rounds by himself, visiting the patients for whom he shared responsibility. The eerie feeling grew as he made his first visits. Several times as he approached a room he heard the voices of the patients inside, but the moment he opened the door, the talking stopped. After a while he decided to go to the room of a malaria patient, a young man whose family lived nearby. Deo sat down on the edge of the bed, a small bed with a rusty metal frame like his own. From previous visits, Deo had surmised that the young man was mildly depressed. "You look fine," Deo said cheerily, and the man smiled weakly up at him. Deo checked his notes. He was still sitting there, chatting idly, when the patient's brother arrived. Deo had met him a few days before, a university student. He came in without knocking. He seemed to be in a hurry.

Deo stood up to greet him. "Your brother's doing fine," Deo said. Then, knowing that the family was local, Deo remarked, "It's a really strange day. It's a slow day. What's happening?"

The brother shifted on his feet, looked one way, then another, and said, "Actually, I want to take my brother home."

"Home?" said Deo. "He hasn't been discharged."

"Deogratias, don't you know what's going on?"

"No. What's going on?"

"President Ndadaye's been killed, and they say he was killed by some Tutsis in the army, and now the war is going on, the Hutus are retaliating and killing every Tutsi all over the country."

This news had urgent meanings, and one of them seemed to be that there was no time to think them through. Deo blurted out his first thought, a protest. Hadn't Ndadaye been president for all Burundians, both Hutu and Tutsi? Just because Ndadaye was a Hutu and his killers were Tutsis didn't mean all Tutsis were guilty. Deo hadn't killed the president.

"I have nothing to do with that." The young man was helping the patient get dressed. "I really think you should get out of here." Clearly, he now knew that Deo was a Tutsi, if he hadn't guessed before.

"Please help me," said Deo. "I don't know anyone around here."

That was impossible, said the patient's brother. Some of his relatives were even now at work killing Tutsis, he said. "I just hope you don't get killed in front of me. That's all I hope," he said, as he helped his brother get his shoes on.

The patient spoke up. There must be a way they could help Deo.

The patient and his brother argued. "I'm leaving!" the brother yelled. "If you don't want me to help you get out of here, then stay!"

The sick boy rose. His brother helped him to the door.

"Where should I go?" Deo asked.

His patient turned. "Oh, Deogratias! I know you're not going to survive. I always enjoyed seeing you. You were very helpful to me. May God bless you."

All of that Deo remembered clearly, indelibly. But then his mind grew "messy," as he liked to say. He remembered loud noises coming from outside and remembered running out of the patient's room and looking frantically around for an exit from the building, and throwing open a door only to find himself facing a toilet. He thought he must have resembled the rats that would come out of the bush onto a road, running this way and that. The next thing he knew, he was running back toward his room, less out of forethought than by reflex.

The route was direct, down a long hallway and then along one of those pasages that connected the buildings. It opened onto a part of the hospital's dirt parking lot. He heard trucks. He heard whistles and drums. He had crossed the open area when he heard a truck pulling in. It sounded as if it was right behind him, chasing him. Inside the next enclosed hallway there was pandemonium—weeping and wailing, the metal doors of rooms slamming, the sound of shoes and flip-flops slapping the concrete floor, the sound of his own footfalls. As he ran, he had to dodge other people, relatives trying to get their sick family members out of that place—young women with babies in their arms, elderly men and women being carried and half carried down the halls by frantic-looking relatives.

He rushed into his room and crawled under his bed. He wanted to shrink. He wanted to dig a hole in the concrete floor. What if someone looked under his bed? He rolled onto his back and grabbed the rusty springs and tried to pull himself up flat against the springs. Impossible. He rolled onto his side. From under his bed, he could see across the floor to his doorway, and he realized he had forgotten to close and lock his door. He couldn't make himself move. He curled up, burying his head in his arms, trying to bury himself in himself, trying not to breathe.

In the following months, Deo had no room for reflection, only reaction. When he was able to think clearly about his long last day in the hospital at Mutaho, he was left mostly with questions and suppositions. As near as he could tell, both patients and staff had been a mixture of Hutus and Tutsis. All of the doctors and most of the nurses must have heard of the president's assassination on the radio the night before, or learned about it from people who had heard the news on the radio. But why had the radicals, the militiamen, attacked the hospital? Maybe their leaders had reasoned, "There are Tutsis in that hospital and Hutus who aren't going to help us." But how had the militiamen managed to mobilize so quickly? Later, he would wonder if it was true, as some people claimed, that all this had been planned far in advance. And he'd think about the capriciousness of fate: he heard stories of other people who had escaped by hiding above ceilings or immersing themselves in rivers or latrines, whereas he had merely panicked and forgotten to close and lock his door.

He had lain under his bed, covering his ears with his hands, but he could not shut out the noise that was reverberating down the tall narrow hallways outside. At one moment he thought, "Oh, God, where do I go? Should I get up and close my door?" But he was too scared to move. He heard metallic crashes, and realized these must be the sounds of militiamen throwing their shoulders against doors that were closed and locked. The sounds of smashing glass had to be militiamen bursting into rooms from outside.

Noise seemed to be coming from everywhere, and then he heard loud voices right nearby, just outside his doorway. He uncovered his eyes for a moment. Two pairs of ragged trouser legs and bare feet stood in his doorway. A voice said, "The cockroach is gone. He ran away." Then the trouser legs and feet vanished.

He heard drums and whistles. He heard male voices chanting what sounded almost like a song, one he'd never heard before. But some of the words and phrases were completely familiar. *"Susuruka!"* "Warm them up!" And a phrase that meant, "Get them soaked and toss them in the fire!" And *"Inivo nu gutwi!"* "At the level of the ear!" There was singing and laughter echoing from all directions in the narrow concrete hallways, and screams accompanying them. He peeked toward the doorway and saw a small child run past, back and forth, several times, making frantic cries.

Then a commanding voice yelled, "Clean up!" The child's cries ceased.

There were loud curses and shouts. "No! I'm not going!" He heard voices begging, "Please don't kill me!" And voices yelling, "Are you a Tutsi or a Hutu?" There was no way of knowing how many militia were there. He imagined dozens. Once or twice, he heard a gunshot. He began to smell gasoline, then smoke. The smell reminded him of cow skins being burned. He held his breath for as long as he could, for fear of taking in that smell. Then he lay panting, afraid of the sound he was making. Hiding was like running in place, a repetitive motionless motion. It went on and on.

Gradually he became aware of silence, which frightened him, differently but as much as the sounds it had replaced. It sounded as if the world were dead and he were alone in it, a graveyard of sound. He lay in it for hours, until he realized that the light was fading around him. He peeked from under his bed toward his window. It was a darkening rectangle. All the daylight would be gone in a moment.

When he crawled out from under his bed, he had only one thought in his mind: "Go. Get out of here. Run." He wore the same clothes he'd put on that morning—he didn't wear a uniform, just cotton pants and shirt, a light cloth jacket, and sneakers he'd bought some time ago at the central market in Bujumbura, the least expensive he'd been able to find.

The stench of burned flesh was thick in the hallway. Already he could hear dogs barking and growling, fighting over the bodies no doubt. He groped his way by memory, out of the building into a grassy courtyard with a tree in the middle. He started across what had been grass. There was no moon, but he could make out the shapes on the ground. He picked his way among the bodies, slipping and sliding, stifling the yelling in his mind. From the edge of the parking lot he could make out the hospital driveway. He couldn't see anyone out there. He ran down the drive to the main road, the orange dirt road he'd walked and jogged along in the weeks before. On the other side of the road, he knew, lay a valley, the valley of the Mubarazi River. The choice was easy. There might be snakes in the brush and grasses and trees, but the road meant people. He sprinted across the road, and scrambled down the embankment into the dark fields.

He stopped running once he reached the valley floor. He was standing in tall grass when he thought, "It's kind of wet." Then he realized it was spitting rain. There had been rain on and off the last few days. The rainy season was just beginning. It occurred to him— this was a thought cast up from memory, out of the many cross-country treks of his childhood—that the rain was a good thing, because it would soften the grasses, which could be like needles when dry. Besides, in the rainy season one encountered fewer people outdoors, and he'd always liked to run in the rain; rain had seemed to lend him energy.

Hidden in darkness, Deo tried to think. The main thing was to get away from Mutaho. Looking back in the direction of the hospital, he could see the road, some distance away and above him. Parts of the hospital seemed to be on fire, and fires were burning on the road in both directions. For now, he must stay away from the road. He thought, "Where should I go? I don't really know this place.

Where should I go?" He remembered that on long walks in previous weeks he had passed through a little town with a Catholic church. It was about five kilometers south of the hospital. "God, maybe I should go to church," he said to himself. If he made it safely away from Mutaho, he would go into the church and pray, to give thanks for deliverance from Mutaho and to ask for safe passage somewhere.

It was a long night. Deo waded through grass and thickets of thornbushes and among stands of tall trees. Whenever he heard a noise, a cry or a yell, he would veer away from it. He moved parallel to the main road, stopping often to listen and look. He could make out the road from the silhouettes of the towering eucalyptus trees at its shoulders, and from the lights of what he took to be oil lamps scattered along it. Occasionally he saw bonfires up on the road and the figures of people clustered around them. Very late that night, thinking he was near the little town with the church, he turned toward the road and moved gingerly until he heard voices close by, many voices. It sounded like a market. To go up on the road and try to find the church would be a bad move. No, suicidal.

He went on through the brush, heading south, toward the next big town, Bugendena. He crossed a river in the dark: it had to be the Mubarazi. His clothes were soaked, but the rain was warm. To travel long distances and quickly, cross-country in the dark, wasn't just a matter of stamina, but also of experience. He'd had years of experience. What he had to concentrate on was his own mind, to keep himself from running and letting out the panic that was like a sound behind a door inside him. In the first gray light of morning, he saw a huge pile of trees up on the main road, where it intersected the smaller road to Bugendena, and across the main road he could make out the hillside rising toward Bugendena and the figures of people, lots of people, on that hillside. Were they running toward the town for safety? Or were victims being taken there? He had no way of knowing. But the pile of trees and the sight of the crowd on the hillside meant that the roads directly south from Bugendena were probably blocked. He had thought for a moment of trying to get back home, to Butanza or Kayanza, far to the southwest. He had thought of his family there—one reason for having thought he should go to church. But the region was much too far away. The whole country must be on fire. He would try to get back to Bujumbura.

Birds were beginning to sing, as they always did an hour or so before *samoya*. The fields were lifting up around him out of the dark, the whole world covered in gray light, and gradually, up ahead, rose the outlines of a bunch of houses, small traditional houses of mud walls and thatched roofs. A village. The air had the sour smell of wet ashes. He crept a little closer to the houses, bending low to keep himself hidden. There was no need. The houses were smoking, their thatched roofs smoldering in the rain, and there was no one in sight. He crept up to the first of the houses. It was small, little more than a hut, with a window in one wall—a typical crude little window opening that the inhabitants would cover with banana leaves or old clothes. He looked in. Bodies lay on the dirt floor inside. As his eyes adjusted to the fainter interior light, he saw them individually. Three children, a man, and a woman. She was lying on her back, and some fleshy stuff filled her opened mouth. Male genitalia. Deo turned away and ran back the way he'd come. He didn't encounter anyone living. No one was out working the fields that morning.

He was too exhausted to run anymore by the time he got back to the Mubarazi. He walked along the river, looking for a place to cross, here and there sinking into mud almost up to his knees. Perhaps he only imagined that the river's water was red, but there were bodies floating in it and bodies that had fetched up on snags. He found a narrow spot and tried to leap across, but didn't quite make it. He had to haul himself up onto the far bank, clutching handfuls of grass, frantically. He didn't care that his clothes and body were filthy, he only wanted to get out of that river.

Over the next four days, or maybe more, Deo traveled about seventy kilometers. He drank from streams and rivers, reluctantly at first, knowing the pathogens he must be swallowing. Those first few days, the cultivated fields he passed were empty. He'd dart into one and break off a piece of sugarcane or a stalk of corn to chew on—he knew his plants; each of those contains liquid and sugar. Or he would pull up a root vegetable, a cassava or a sweet potato, and eat it raw, holding it up, tilting his head back, taking it down in only one or two bites; soon he hardly bothered to wipe off the dirt. He had no map and he didn't know the countryside. But one time he had ridden in a bus from Mutaho to a town called Kibimba, to visit his cousin Geneviève at her high school. Kibimba was on the way to Bujumbura. Maybe he would be safe there. Maybe he'd find refuge at his cousin's school.

He headed to the southwest, along the valley of the Mubarazi, keeping to woods and brush and tall grass and avoiding all roads. In places, the river's shallow waters seemed all but dammed with bodies, and the valley was littered with them, the corpses and feasting dogs thickening as he approached Kibimba, where just before sunset he saw smoke rising from a building on a hilltop. It was his cousin's school. So much for any notion of finding Geneviève. He turned to the west with the river and then to the north-northwest, skirting the city of Muramvya, the ancient capital of the kingdom of Burundi, the mountains growing steeper, until he reached a paved main road. He and some medical school friends had once driven on it. The road ran north from Bujumbura and across the border into Rwanda, and then, he knew from maps in geography class, right through Rwanda, all the way to Uganda.

This was the place where he had planned to turn south toward Bujumbura. He knew he must be only about thirty kilometers from the capital. But he also knew something of the countryside he would have to cross on the way, a mountainous area, packed with houses, and, by reputation, a stronghold of rebel Hutu militia. He scouted the road a little, and from his hiding places he saw people in peasant clothes—local farmers, most likely—carrying logs on their shoulders down that road in the direction of Bujumbura. He saw one group of people cutting trees, with a huge, gasoline-powered saw. They were making roadblocks, that seemed obvious. And they were doing so, he reasoned, in order to impede the army. He hadn't seen any soldiers or military trucks. The little he knew about the army didn't inspire confidence. It seemed possible that it had already been defeated by the Hutu militias and that Bujumbura was even now a graveyard of Tutsis. And if people who lived along that road were making roadblocks, they were probably also going off into the mountains beside the road and killing any Tutsis they could find.

Deo didn't exactly decide where to go. Mainly he decided not to go toward Bujumbura. He crept up to the road, then ran as fast as he could across it. Reaching the other side, he looked down the road. In the near distance, he saw a group of people sitting on the pavement. He imagined they had established a checkpoint and would grab anyone they suspected of being Tutsi. They didn't appear to have seen him. He headed in the other direction, away from Bujumbura.

He moved in stages, pausing to sit under the cover of grasses or in a thicket, and listening for a while. Now and then he had seen people with machetes seated on the edges of roads—and, he imagined, some would be sitting in the bushes beside roads. He assumed these were militiamen, waiting like cats for prey. Several times he would be sitting and listening, surrounded by utter silence, and then quite suddenly he would hear a cry or a yell, and he felt certain this meant that someone was being slaughtered. Then utter silence would follow.

He passed around Teza, with its large tea plantations, and entered the national park, Kibira. Simply and aptly enough, the name means "Forest." For days, he kept to the eastern edge of Kibira, moving in and out from under its immense green canopy, climbing and descending mountains six and seven thousand feet high, loping across open forest floor and wading through thick undergrowth.

Deo knew that he was heading generally north, toward Rwanda. He had visited the country on that one trip with friends from medical school, and they hadn't run into trouble. They'd gone to visit Rwanda's national university, in Butare, a lovely place with its own medical school—though not as good a school as Burundi's, he felt. He knew, of course, that Rwanda had a troubled history, and he had heard the rumors of war. But according to those, the fighting was confined to the far north. Southern Rwanda would be safe, he imagined. Or safer than Burundi now. Any country would be safer than Burundi now, he thought. He had no way of knowing that Rwanda, in a little more than five months, would become safer than nowhere. Then again, it wasn't as though he was thinking that he had to get to Rwanda. Mainly he was just going, because stopping in any one place for long seemed equivalent to waiting for a killer to find him, and moving seemed like the only way to keep down thoughts of what he'd seen.

It was impossible to plan, because he never knew where the dangers lay until he got close to them. The signs were obvious by now. Rising smoke meant burning houses up ahead, and wheeling birds a place full of corpses. Swarms of flies meant killings nearby. Sometimes he saw a dog trotting past with a severed head or an arm in its mouth. The main thing to avoid was other living human beings. It was just as Lonjino liked to say: safer with a wild animal than a human being. Deo remembered how as a child he'd hear Lonjino say this and he'd think, "What's Grandfather talking about?"

So far he had seen other living people only from a distance—men at roadblocks and frightened unarmed people running, most vividly women, their colorful, saronglike Burundian dresses flapping as they ran. His first face-to-face encounter came somewhere in Kibira. He was making his way through woods. He was startled by the sound of coughing, not at a distance but directly overhead. He was startled, frightened, and at the same time the coughing made him think, "That sounds like pneumonia." Looking up, he saw a boy clinging to a branch very near the treetop, like a big bird. "Keep going!" the boy whispered harshly.

There must be militiamen nearby. That must be what the boy was telling him. Looking up, Deo said silently, "God, I'm sorry." Then he hurried on, weaving his way among tree trunks. Soon he couldn't hear the coughing anymore. Not that he could have done anything for the boy. But any thought of trying to help hadn't stood up, even for a minute or two, to fear. It was as if the sights and sounds and smells of the past few days—screams, corpses, burning flesh—were all collecting into something like another version of himself, another skin growing over him.

He was walking wearily through a patch of open forest floor in mountains north of Teza when from around the tall trees on the slope above him a group of men appeared, brandishing spears. There were perhaps six men and on the slope behind them he saw some women and children. The men yelled angrily at him. "Are you following us? What are you looking for?"

Deo raised his hands. Militiamen wouldn't behave like that. Militiamen wouldn't be traveling with women and children. These men sounded as frightened of him as he was of them and their spears. "No, no, I'm sorry," he called up the slope. "I'm running away. I'm innocent."

He camped with them for a day and a night in that spot. They were Tutsi farmers on the run. They had decided to stop in this piece of forest and wait for the war to be over. It couldn't go on much longer, they said. The army would be coming. In the morning Deo awoke to find himself among a forlorn little group, wet and cold and hungry, the women and children all silent, the men talking softly about what they should do. He felt refreshed himself, with hopeful thoughts. Maybe it really was all over. He said he'd go down the mountainside and see if he could find a farm and take some cassava. Four of the men went with him. They were talking as they went, confident that their hopes were real, and militiamen in the valley must have heard their voices, because when he and the others came out of the forest, they saw men with machetes running toward them, up the steep slope, maybe two hundred meters away. Fortunately, that group didn't have guns, or arrows—he had seen bodies of people shot by arrows. Deo turned back toward the forest and ran. He didn't see the little band of refugees again.

On the next day or the day after or the day after that, he was wading through brush along the bottom of a ravine. He heard dogs barking, and voices yelling, "Get out!" Were people being hunted, or were the militiamen simply yelling into the forest, saying in effect to people who might be hiding there, "We see you. Come on out." An exhausted person might be stupid enough to obey. Deo crawled under a bush, facedown on dark muddy ground. The barking and yells were coming from the ridge above. He heard small crashes in the brush around him. The men must be throwing stones at random down into the ravine. He felt a sharp pain in the small of his back. He lay writhing, clenching his teeth so as not to cry out. After a while he heard the dogs and men moving away, and he got up and went on, reaching back now and then to examine the wound on his back with his fingers. It might get infected, he thought. What did it matter?

When he thought about what was going on, he thought the massacres must have been planned. He knew from the smells in the hospital at Mutaho that the killers had jerry cans full of petrol, and he knew from sounds he'd heard that some had guns and grenades, and clearly the killers had systems for signaling each other, by beating sticks on their jerry cans or by blowing on whistles. From time to time in his hiding places, he heard loud whining sounds, then the thunder of trees crashing down. And the sources of that noise were those large, gas-powered saws. Where had such things come from, in a part of the country where many people couldn't afford to buy salt and only a very few owned anything that ran on gasoline?

It had been raining off and on ever since Mutaho. A lot of the countryside had turned to mud. Deo had thrown away his socks. His sneakers, the no-brand-name pair he had bought at the central market in Bujumbura, had held up so far, though they had long since turned from white to brown and the laces had broken—he'd thrown those away, too. From time to time he had to stop and clean the mud out of his sneakers. He had slept now and then, during daylight when it didn't seem safe to move. He would pick out a hiding spot, not a spot that seemed safe, because no place seemed safe, but a spot that had cover and looked comfortable. Then he'd sit or lie down and sometimes fall asleep, but never for long.

He had paused in his trek only to rest or to hide or to find food and water. From time to time he had gotten entangled in thickets of thornbushes in the dark. He had scratches everywhere, any one of which could become infected. He could feel an infection brewing in the wound in the small of his back. He had diarrhea, too. What had revolted him at first no longer bothered him. Repelled at first by the thought of drinking dirty water or eating a muddy sweet potato, he had told himself he had to be flexible. By now the counsel was irrelevant. He couldn't taste anything anymore.

He had been weaving his way north, moving in and out of the forest, Kibira. One rainy afternoon he found himself outside the forest in a field of banana trees. The rain was heavy. He couldn't stop shivering. He was stumbling along, hugging himself. He saw swarms of flies and smelled putrefaction before he saw the bodies. The thick grass among the banana trees was full of them. In what seemed like only moments, he couldn't smell them anymore. He didn't feel like running away from bodies as he had four or five days ago. He didn't feel much of anything except weariness. He sat down with his back against a bunch of banana trees. Then he saw the baby.

Just a little distance away, the figure of a woman was slumped against another bunch of banana trees. There was dried blood on her face. She must have collapsed there and died, but the baby was alive. It was in her lap, its little hands groping at its mother's bared breast. And it was looking right at Deo. He stared back at it for a long moment.

The baby wasn't crying. "It must be wondering where it is," he thought. It must be terrified like him. But he couldn't help the baby. He couldn't even help himself.

He got to his feet and staggered off among the clumps of banana trees, deeper into the grove. He sat down again with his back against another tangle of spindly trunks. The fronds overhead gave a little shelter from the rain. Nothing was important anymore, not the flies or the bodies. All that mattered was that he couldn't see the baby.

———

He had no idea how long he slept. Maybe only that night and part of the next day, or maybe through two nights. He woke up to gray daylight and rain. He didn't move. Maybe he was dreaming. He heard voices, and then a line of people appeared, trudging through the banana grove. About thirty people, all women and children, walking sticks in their hands, baskets and bundles on their heads.

One of the women left the line. She had spotted him, clearly. She was coming toward him with her walking stick. He wanted to run, but he couldn't even make himself get up. He wanted to vanish, imagining that with an effort of will he could do this—squeeze into this banana tree.

She seemed to be a little older than his mother, forty-five or fifty, but it was hard to tell. She had a farmer's weathered skin, missing teeth, and sinewy strength. She was carrying a baby on her back and a huge bundle on her head. Hardly a terrifying vision, but all people were terrifying. The sight of dogs devouring corpses was nothing to him anymore, compared to the sight of this woman.

"Are you alive?" she asked him in Kirundi.

"Yes," he said. "But please don't kill me."

"No, no, no, no," she said. "I want to help you. I don't want to kill you."

He had begun to cry, warm tears on his cheeks mixing with rainwater. "Please, if you really want to kill me, I just hope that I'm not going to be tortured. Don't torture me."

Her voice sounded sad. She said she knew what he was thinking. He was thinking she was a Hutu, and in fact she was. Then her voice turned, not fierce, but declarative: "But I'm a woman and I'm a mother." That, she said, was her *ubwoko,* her ethnicity.

A woman and a mother. Maybe she wasn't going to kill him after all.

She said she wanted to help. She wanted to get him out of this place. But Deo had entered the country of despair. It was not uncomfortable. There was no way he could extract himself from this time and this place. He didn't even want to be extracted. He just didn't want to die painfully. And he didn't want to move from his spot beneath the banana trees. He seemed to be content where he was. It was peaceful right here, even though he was surrounded by bodies.

"I'm too tired," he told the woman. "I'm just going to stay here."

"No, no," she said. "The border, it's nearby." Then she said, "Get up!"

He couldn't trust anyone. He didn't fully believe in her. But he obeyed her, mainly because she was so persistent, leaning over and pulling at his upper arm, saying, "Come on, come on, please come on."

They walked together through a mixed landscape, under tall eucalyptus, through banana groves, across cultivated fields. Sometimes when the path was narrow, he followed behind her. Other times they walked side by side, and she talked to him. She told him that she knew what he was going through, because she had many Tutsi friends who had been killed and many Hutu friends, too, who had been murdered by the army and even by militant Hutus because they had refused to join the killing or because the militants wanted their land. One of her own grown sons had been killed by militiamen, she said. She had been married to a Tutsi who had been killed years ago, and she had been vilified as a traitor by radicals on her hill. She had remarried, to a Hutu; she didn't say where he was now, and Deo didn't ask. She and most of the women and children of her village were fleeing both from the Hutu militiamen and from the Tutsi army's retaliation, which was certain to come.

He knew they must be nearing the Rwandan border. Other groups of fleeing people were joining their procession, and the Hutu woman was getting nervous. She told him he must not tell anyone he was a Tutsi. He must not show fear the way he had back in the banana grove. He should say he was her son.

It didn't occur to him that he might turn back. Everything he'd witnessed told him he had to get away from Burundi, and this was the nearest way out. He was sick to his stomach, he was beyond thought, it was easier just to go on. As they waded across the stream that marked the border, she pulled him close to her, an arm around his shoulders. By then it was too late to turn back. Up ahead stood bunches of armed men, some in blue uniforms, some in brown uniforms, some in civilian clothes. They were questioning everyone. He was aware of their Rwandan accents. "You go. You go. You! What's your name?" He noticed their equipment—portable radios, policeman's nightsticks, pistols, and rifles. He felt vomit rising. He had experienced fear before this. But this was fear in the extreme. He felt his hands shaking. He couldn't stop them. Several men with fierce faces were peering into his from all sides. "You look like a cockroach," said one. "What are you doing here?" said another. The Hutu woman tightened her arm around his shoulder. Without realizing it, he had placed his hands on either side of his head, covering his temples. So many of the corpses he had seen were cut at the temples, *inivo nu gutwi.*

"Open your eyes!" A sneering face was pressing very close to his. "You look like you are afraid."

Clearly the men on the riverbank were looking for Tutsis among the refugees. But physical stereotypes were all they had to go on, since Burundian IDs no longer revealed ethnicity. One of the interrogators raised a bayoneted rifle, so that the blade of the bayonet touched the tip of Deo's nose. He flicked Deo's nose back and forth without cutting into it, and said something about its being too thin for a Hutu nose. Then he lifted the point of the blade to Deo's hairline—Deo was only twenty-one, but he had a widow's peak, not a straight hairline across the forehead. "Look at this," said the man with the bayonet.

The Hutu woman still had her arm around Deo. She pulled him half behind her, away from the bayonet. "Don't torture my son. He's been so sick."

"What? Sick?" said one of the interrogators.

"He can't handle it, he's not useful," said another.

"You need to die anyway," said a third, peering in at Deo's face.

"No, no, no. This is my son!" said the woman.

There were a lot of people crossing the little river. The interrogators couldn't spend all day on him. One of them grabbed Deo's left wrist and tied a piece of black cloth around it. "Go over there to that group. We'll question you later."

"No, I'm telling you, he's my son," said the woman.

"If you want to go with him, go with him," said one of the men.

Beyond the interrogators lay a wide field, full of people milling around. Many voices were talking all at once. Some were shouting. People were hurrying this way and that. The woman walked Deo a little distance toward the group of suspected Tutsis, all clustered together in a corner of the field. Then she stopped and made as if to adjust her clothing. She was dressed in the traditional Burundian way, in layers—first a shirt and skirt, then a wrapping of brightly colored cloth, and finally another colorful wrapping that wound around her back and held the baby in place. She loosened the cloth of the outer dress, and then as she began to refasten it, she dropped a fold over Deo's left forearm and hand and quickly untied the piece of black cloth. Then she put her arm around Deo again, and walked on with him a little way.

Another group of militiamen passed by. They stopped her and Deo. For a moment Deo thought they must have seen her remove the cloth. "What are you doing? You belong over this way." They pointed toward the main group of refugees, milling about in the field.

"Oh, I just want to find a seat," said the woman. "My son is sick."

"Are you Hutus?"

"Yes. Of course."

"Over there." They pointed toward that main group and turned away.

The woman walked Deo a little farther on, then whispered to him, *"Genda!"* "Run!"

He obeyed. He ran to the crowd, the human forest, the only hiding place in sight. It was the last time he saw her.

In Rwanda, moments were the only time he knew. He spent nearly every moment worrying about the next. Six months felt like a minute, and moments when it seemed as though there was no time in front of him felt like eternity.

The Burundian refugees were herded, loosely, into fields and woods, not camps with tents or any other kind of shelter, though occasionally someone would construct a traditional lean-to. There were, later reports would say, more than 300,000 Burundians in makeshift camps near the border. The great majority had to be Hutus, fleeing the Tutsi army's retaliation. Periodically there were distributions of food and clothing. The stuff would come on trucks with the logo UNHCR on their doors and canvas tops. The initials stood for "United Nations High Commissioner on Refugees." Deo heard some young Rwandans who were distributing food remark, "Oh, yeah, we are helping. We are volunteers." And he thought to himself, "How many people volunteer in Africa?" He felt sure that

they were at least fellow travelers of the people who seemed to supervise everything, the Hutu militiamen.

He heard them call themselves "Interahamwe." The name meant
"Those Who Work Together." Many walked around holding portable radios to their ears. From time to time, he saw them training.
He could tell they weren't policemen or regular soldiers, because
they wore ragged civilian clothes and many were barefoot. Most
were young. Sometimes they seemed like just a bunch of peasants
running around with make-believe weapons. They would try to
make it look as though they were just playing games, but to Deo
their games looked much more like practice in the arts of clubbing
and bayoneting and chopping. Once in a while men in blue and
brown uniforms arrived in vehicles and supervised these exercises.
"Oh no, this is not how you do it," these uniformed men would say,
laughing at the trainees. Sometimes he saw larger exercises from a
distance—a crowd of men running in ragged formation across a
field, carrying pieces of wood roughly shaped like rifles. Sometimes
he heard them singing songs or having songs sung to them. The one
he heard most often went like this: "God is just. God is never unjust. And we will finish them soon. Keep working, keep working.
We will finish them, we will finish them soon. They are about to
vanish! They are about to vanish! Don't get tired! You are about to
be done!"

He couldn't tell for sure which, if any, of his fellow refugees were
Tutsis. He knew most must be Hutus, and it was safest to assume
that all were. Occasionally, Interahamwe would hang around with
groups of refugees, around a campfire or a tree. Often these seemed
like recruiting sessions. Keeping to the peripheries, never saying a
word, he'd hear militiamen tell the refugees that the RPF, that army
of Tutsi cockroaches from Uganda, was moving close, slaughtering
Hutus. They said that the RPF had spies among them, right here, in
these very refugee camps. They should be on the lookout for spies.
Deo doubted all this. The last time he'd heard anything about the

RPF, they were far away in the north. Indeed, the last he'd heard, a peace agreement had been made between the RPF and the Rwandan government. He figured the militiamen were trying to scare the Burundian Hutu refugees, many of whom were already bitter and militant, judging from their talk. The talk about the RPF certainly scared him, because "RPF" was clearly the equivalent of "Tutsi." Some of the refugees would sit around angrily denouncing the "cockroaches," and one or another of the Rwandan militiamen would say, "Someday things will be fine. Someday they'll be over, and things will be fine." And in every group like that, he noticed that some refugees, usually older people, sat silently with their heads bowed or made small movements—a slight shift of posture, a pursing of the lips—which he took as signs they disapproved. He would not allow himself any such liberties.

From time to time he asked himself, "Why did I come to Rwanda?" But his thoughts rarely strayed that far into the past, and almost never into the future. When the United Nations trucks arrived with food, the refugees would get in lines, and sometimes they would fight, and sometimes Rwandan militiamen would intervene. Sometimes the militiamen would inspect people in line. Usually it was the muscular young men they'd approach and pull out of line, saying, "You don't need to be here. You need to go to work." One time early on, he saw a group of militiamen surround a man in line. They led him some distance away, into a nearby woods, and not long afterward there was a scream, then silence. And sometimes Deo saw them pull a young woman out of the line and walk with her toward the woods. Deo would turn away and pretend not to notice. Later, he would see the same young woman coming out from among the trees, head bowed, face averted, and then three or four men would come sauntering out of the woods behind her, smiling and laughing.

He never ate during the days, for fear that while standing in line he might get caught up in one of the arguments over food and be noticed, then scrutinized. It wasn't impossible that he might come face-to-face with a Hutu who knew him from Burundi. He ate only at the evening distributions. Once in a while, when there were a lot of militiamen nearby, he avoided even those, and went hungry. Stomach cramps and diarrhea had long since become companions, and his feet itched with what he knew was fungus. The wound on his back became a hot abscess. If he had been his own patient, he would have drained it and administered antibiotics, but his immune system would have to deal with it unaided. Occasionally he would find a place to sleep by himself, a thicket of brush, a stand of ferns in the woods, but usually he slept on the ground among others, because it was dangerous to be seen alone. For the moment, it was safer to be in a crowd, and if it seemed appropriate to talk at all, safe only to talk about the weather: "Yes, it's cold," and "Wet again." He would wonder sometimes whether a fellow refugee was a Tutsi or Hutu, but it didn't feel safe even to think about that, and life seemed even more miserable when he did. "Just forget about it," he'd tell himself.

He moved four times among the impromptu, open-air camps. Twice it was other refugees who initiated the moves, saying the place where they were camped had grown too crowded. Another time it was militiamen who suggested that some of them relocate. To Deo, another place was always better. After a month or so in a camp, he'd worry that his face was becoming too familiar. He'd imagine he had caught a glimpse of someone he knew in a crowd, or he would dream that someone had recognized him. Several times he sensed that some of the other refugees were eyeing him. It helped that he was often sick and therefore someone whom others tended to avoid. One time a militiaman called to him, "Hey. Come here and clean up this shit on the ground." It was literal shit.

"Oh, okay," Deo called back. "I'm coming. Just let me get a tool." But he couldn't risk being exposed, alone, in front of Interahamwe. He turned and disappeared into the crowd.

So when a group of refugees decided to move, he'd insinuate himself among them. He didn't dare ask anyone, "Where are we ex-

actly?" or "Where are we going?" But listening in on the talk at
night, he gathered that he was still near the Burundian border and
not very far from Butare, the Rwandan university town. Sometimes
he thought of finding his way to Butare. He imagined he'd be safe
there. Maybe he would find refuge at the medical school, or just
someplace to stay out of the rain, someplace where there might be
someone he could trust enough to talk to. But how to get there
without exposing himself to soldiers or police or militiamen, and
without being seen by farmers who would alert the authorities?
There was no way he could get to Butare on his own.

At the third camp, an aid worker appeared, a young man, who
began dispensing medicine to the sick, who were arrayed in a long
line. Deo watched him. The aid worker had to teach every person
how to take a pill. Deo could tell he wasn't a militiaman. The languages of Burundi and Rwanda, though differently named, are
identical for all practical purposes, but the two main accents are dis-
tinctive. This man spoke Kinyarwanda/Kirundi with a funny accent,
an accent Deo had never heard before, so he figured the man was
neither Burundian nor Rwandan. *Médecins Sans Frontières,* "Doctors Without Borders," was painted on his pickup truck. Deo had
heard of the organization in medical school.

Deo wanted aspirin, but he didn't dare stand in the line. He approached the young man from the side. The aid worker was saying
to the next person in line, "Okay, first put the pill in your mouth,
then drink this water."

Deo whispered in French, "I know how to do this."

The man turned to him, and asked in French, "How do you
know?"

"I'm a medical student," Deo said. He felt panic rising. He could
feel the people in line staring at him, probably because of the
French. He could speak openly in French, because people who had
never taken a pill wouldn't understand the language, but for that
same reason he was now marked as different. "It is not safe for me.

I'm afraid," he said hurriedly to the young man. "Can you help me get out?"

"Stay here with me," said the young man.

When he had finished his work at that camp, the young man drove Deo away in his pickup. Deo asked if he could take him to Bujumbura or to Butare. The young man said he wished he could. In fact, he sometimes drove to Bujumbura to pick up medicines. Burundi was a mess, but the killing had died down, he said. The problem was Rwanda. Every road had checkpoints, where every passenger had to produce an ID. It would be too dangerous to run that gauntlet with Deo on board, too dangerous for him, too dangerous for Deo. Instead of taking Deo toward Burundi, he drove north and dropped Deo off at another makeshift outdoor refugee camp, not far from a paved road. He told Deo to stay there, and he would try to figure something out.

Some time later—days or weeks, perhaps—Deo was sleeping with other refugees in yet another open field, in utter darkness, under a drizzling sky. Suddenly, the night erupted, like a thunderstorm, a man-made thunderstorm. Flames rose on the horizon. The lights of trucks went racing past. He could hear people shouting, not in the camp, but in the settlements nearby, and choruses of voices just outside the camp, voices lifted in song: "It's the beginning of the work. . . . Before the end of the night, the cockroaches are not going to wake up again." Through a loudspeaker somewhere, he heard that chanting song: "God is just. God is never unjust. And we will finish them soon. Keep working, keep working. We will finish them, we will finish them soon. They are about to vanish! They are about to vanish! Don't get tired! You are about to be done!" All the voices lifted in song sounded jubilant, as if they were singing the Hallelujah Chorus in the church in Sangaza at Christmastime.

For five months, Deo had been living with a stomachache, which

he attributed to worms and dread. It had long been obvious that
something very violent was coming in Rwanda and that it was
going to be aimed at Tutsis. That had been clear since the day he'd
crossed the border, and from the training of militiamen he'd witnessed and from the songs he'd heard. Over the next days he heard
people say that the plane of Rwanda's president had been shot
down in Kigali the other night, the night of the fireworks. They said
that Burundi's appointed president had also been on board. Deo
guessed that the event for which the militiamen had been training
was now under way.

The refugee camp started to scatter. He hid among the remnant,
for how long he couldn't have said at the time; in fact, it was for several more weeks. For a while, there were still some extremists
around, angry Burundian Hutus. Now and then they'd gang up on
someone, saying, "You look like a cockroach." A few people were
taken away and no doubt killed. But soon the most militant had left
the group. Many of the young ones, Deo later presumed, had volunteered or been forced to join the Interahamwe. Now the people
left in his camp were mostly the women and children and elderly.
From the accents, Deo knew that most were Burundians. Some, he
guessed, were Congolese who had fled their homeland for Burundi
and now were on the run again. He was now among a safer class of
people, not people he could trust, but peaceful people. Many, he
imagined, were Hutus who didn't want to participate in what was
going on here. Maybe there were some Burundian Tutsis hiding
among them, as he was.

Around fires at night in the diminished camp, small groups
would sit and speak softly to each other, as if they were friends.
Maybe they were friends. Deo sometimes sat among them. No one
seemed afraid of him—probably because he was so quiet and skinny
and sick. He heard them tell stories that marked them as peaceful,
stories told in low voices that would be dangerous to tell in a militiaman's earshot. He heard one about a Rwandan militiaman toss-
ing a baby into a campfire with one hand while munching on an ear

of corn with the other, and many tales about the tricks militiamen would employ. One woman told how her husband had been murdered by militiamen simply because his last name was the same as that of a leader of the RPF—and, as it happened, her husband was a Hutu. Someone in the group had a transistor radio. Over it one day, Deo heard a Rwandan official declaring that displaced people should go to a town called Murambi. They would be safe there, he said.

A day or two later, a fleet of Toyota trucks drove by, men standing in the beds blowing whistles, shouting through bullhorns, saying that displaced people should go to the school in Murambi. If they were hungry, if they wanted to get out of the rain, they should go to Murambi. It seemed as though many of the people around Deo believed this. He did not. He suspected the message was meant for Tutsis, that a trap was being prepared; but when his group started walking north, he went along, because the group was his only hiding place. When more men in trucks came by offering the refugees rides to Murambi, Deo made himself scarce. His group walked on together for several days. They numbered about two hundred. Probably, he later thought, most were Burundian Hutus who didn't know the score, who didn't know why people were being urged to go to Murambi. Soon his group had left the vicinity of the road and were hiking through countryside, and the militiamen no longer visited them.

The region was all hills and narrow valleys. It was still light when he got a glimpse of what he figured must be "Murambi," a large school set on a hilltop plateau and made up of many narrow single-story buildings, each about the size of his old elementary school. From the distance he saw crowds milling around the buildings.

The next thing Deo knew, the next thing he would remember being aware of, his little crowd of refugees had disappeared, and he was on a hillside, and all around him people were running, propelled, it seemed, by screams from the town to the east. He heard voices around him saying, "If we can make it to the school we'll be safe." He stayed among the hustling, panicky crowds, until he found himself in a little wood, at a crossroads of sorts. Here streams of people were coming from several directions, women and children and men with frightened eyes and contorted faces, all running down this hillside to the valley, and up the next hillside toward the school. From their accents, he knew that most of the crowd streaming by was Rwandan, and since they were fleeing, most must be Tutsis.

Deo felt weak, for the moment too weak and sick to walk any farther, and also too frightened. He sat down by the crossroads. Then he got up and walked a few feet down the trail, and sat again. Someone stopped and said to him, "Come on, you can make it." Deo shook his head without even looking up.

He was vaguely aware of the people passing by him, and of the cries of children, the angry shouts of men who were yelling at their wives and children for not running fast enough. But he was busy with his own thoughts. He kept hearing himself say silently, "This is dangerous." Images of the fields of corpses near Kibimba, of his cousin's high school burning on its hilltop, had been filling the landscape of his mind for months, particularly at night, no matter how hard he had tried to stop them. Large groups had been his refuge, but they were dangerous now, and this was a huge group gathering at the school on the next hilltop. He wasn't going there.

Deo sat down a little distance off the trail. He waited until the sky was growing dark. Then he made his way slowly along the hillside, until he was well past the village that lay to the east of the school. For what must have been hours, he crept through tall grass, down the hillside to the edge of the valley. It curved around the base of the plateau, like a moat. The grasses were soft and as tall as his shoulders. He walked on very slowly in the pitch dark, for another half kilometer or so. Then he climbed partway back up the hillside, and stood looking across the valley toward the school on the plateau.

He could see fires there and, he later thought, headlights. He knew he heard screams and voices amplified by megaphones, echoing across the valley. Did he hear snatches of that song—"God is just. God is never unjust. And we will finish them soon"—or did he just hear the words in his mind, having heard that song so often? After maybe an hour, he heard occasional pops of gunfire and some dull explosions, which he took to be grenades. Was it before then or later on that he heard the Interahamwe had been instructed to conserve bullets? He fell asleep in the tall grass.

In his conscious mind, Deo was aware of being afraid, not of dying, but of dying the way his uncle the doctor had, or the family in the house in Bugendena. Not that he wanted to die. Not that he wanted desperately to live. Survival simply had its own momentum. And to survive, it was clear, he had to get out of Rwanda.

Burundi lay to the south, and south was to the left of the wet, gray dawn. He moved mostly by night and only cautiously during the day, running when he thought he saw or heard another person or when it seemed as if the drums and whistles of the militia were closing in. He struggled up hills and all but rolled down them, unable to brake. Sometimes he saw other people from a distance. Usually they were running along the same trail or skirting the same hillside as he was. He would wait until they were out of sight and then wait a little longer, remembering stories he'd heard, in his last refugee camp, of militiamen pretending to flee so as to lure Tutsis out of hiding.

When he thought, it was of things like birds. Watching them from some hiding place—flocks coming and going from some spot nearby, a sure sign of a killing site—he'd wish for reincarnation as a bird. He'd study a fly on a leaf and think, "How lucky you are not to be a human being." Back on the first part of his journey, Deo had wept at the sight of corpses. Now when he found himself hiding near bodies, he was more likely to feel laughter coming up, and he would sit there with his chest heaving, trying not to laugh out loud and give his position away.

He had been trying to keep his body clean, at least a little, by washing in streams when he could. In the camps, he had made himself rub his teeth and clean between them with twigs of eucalyptus. Nevertheless, a back tooth had become infected and had come loose. It took some time and all the hand strength he could muster to yank it out.

From the time when he had gone with friends to visit Butare, he knew that if he headed a little east of south he would pick up the paved road to the Burundian border, the road that ran on to Bujumbura. He aimed in that direction. So it wasn't entirely by luck that after many days he saw headlights through the trees. From then on, he followed the road at night, keeping a safe distance from it, as he had followed roads when he'd been fleeing Burundi. There was a lot of traffic, and there were roadblocks, and he could hear the joyous singing of the militiamen, almost as terrible as the actual killing it euphemistically described. More terrible, maybe. The songs and chants made it seem as if in the world there were only insanity and the silence of corpses. When headlights and roadblocks ceased, and he came to the banks of a small fast-moving river, which had to be the Akanyaru, the border river, he saw the road was filled with soldiers in Burundian uniforms and army trucks. Clearly, the Tutsi army had heard that Tutsis were being slaughtered wholesale in Rwanda, and had known that refugees would be flocking to the border. Evidently, they had come in force to keep the Rwandan army from blocking the Tutsi refugees: to help people like him. He had been on the run forever, it seemed—for six months, in fact. Now running was over. He felt a moment of exhilaration. It didn't last. Soldiers were pulling bodies out of the border river. There were crowds of wounded everywhere.

When he crossed the bridge, a soldier approached him and asked where he wanted to go. The truck Deo rode in to Bujumbura was packed with refugees. "Packed like meats," he would say. "In Burundi we don't have sardines. So we say 'like meats.' 'Like peas.'"

The truck was large, with an open back. The refugees were

pressed together in the middle and nervous teenage soldiers surrounded them, their rifles pointing out at the thickly wooded mountainsides. It was a long ride to Bujumbura, and tense, especially when the truck slowed down and bumped along over makeshift detours. He didn't count the mountain bridges that had been blown up. There were several at least, and when he stood up in the crowded truck for a change of position, he saw corpses of cows and human beings by the sides of the road, more numerous, it seemed, on the last descent toward Bujumbura. The soldiers helped him down to the street in front of the Coca-Cola stand in the border district between Kamenge and Ngagara, across from the medical school and a half mile or so from his dormitory.

The school had closed. The campus had been a killing ground, he was later told by the classmates he ran into. Some were still around because they had nowhere else to go; Bujumbura wasn't safe, but it was safer than most other places. His dorm, when he first walked up to it, looked abandoned. Grass had grown up high around it. He slept in his old room on a bare mattress. The next day he came outside and ran into one of his closest friends, just by chance: Claude.

Claude looked at Deo and did a double take. "Deo! Are you still alive?"

Deo said he'd just returned from Rwanda. He sketched the story.

Claude told him that he had managed to go back to the area of Butanza a while ago and had found that all of his own family had been killed. He said he'd heard that Deo's family was gone, too.

Deo had imagined this, but to hear it was different, of course. "God. Okay. Okay." Deo started walking. He walked around and around the dormitory building, not knowing what to do or where to go. He felt as though he were cramping up from diarrhea again. He felt as though he might faint. Claude walked beside him, saying, "Hey, we can kill too. They also bleed."

Deo thought his friend was only speaking out of grief and anger. Deo couldn't imagine Claude killing anyone. But who knew what had happened to Claude's mind over the past six months? Deo avoided his friend for a while after that. He wanted no part of that kind of talk, and he didn't want to hear about his own family again.

Before they parted that day, Claude did give Deo some good news. Claude said he had been out at Prince Regent Hospital, not far from Bujumbura, and some of the students from the high school in Kibimba were there.

"Yeah, okay," said Deo.

"Your cousin's there!"

Deo took a bus to the hospital the next morning. He thought it was dangerous to travel inside the city, and no doubt more dangerous to travel outside it. He told himself he didn't care.

Geneviève was disfigured. Beneath her bandages, one eye was gone, and part of her nose. Gauze covered burns on her arms and legs. But she recognized him at once. "How did you survive?" she asked.

"No," he said. "Tell me how you survived. I'm fine."

She said, as he later remembered her words: "Well, I went through a window when we were suffocating, in this thick smoke. The auditorium was locked, and the militia had all these clubs and they were smashing things, and everyone was trying to break through the windows and get away. But the thugs got so busy stealing clothes of these kids and their shoes, that they forgot about some of us, and we got away while they were fighting over the clothes and shoes, and I was able to squeeze through this window, and I ran, and this guy threw a spear right in my eye and I fell down and they left me for dead. But I was not dead."

Riding back to Bujumbura in the bus, Deo thought, "Okay, the rest of my family is gone. They are dead." He could not live on here alone, with only a cousin for family.

He spent the night in his dorm room. The next day his old friend Jean appeared, looking for him. He'd heard Deo was back. Jean said it wasn't safe here at the university. Deo should come and stay with him in his apartment. It was situated on the way to the airport, in an area the army had so far managed to secure.

When he had left for his internship in Mutaho, Bujumbura had seemed loud and disorderly just because it was a city, full of vehicles and strangers and mysterious energies. Now it was a chaos. Everywhere he looked he saw cows. Farmers fleeing to the city had brought their cows. Of course they had. He understood the impulse. Bujumbura had become a city of refugee cows, pastured in impromptu United Nations camps for the internally displaced, and also lowing on streetcorners, trudging along on sidewalks, herded into narrow vacant lots behind gas stations. Propriety had been abandoned. There were people squatting in public. There was manure and human excrement on the pavements, and in the mornings there were also fresh bodies—on the streets and in the river, the Ntahangwa, that flowed through town. He didn't see nearly as many corpses as he had on his long escape, but the supply seemed steady. Usually one day's bodies would be gone by nightfall, but every morning there were new ones. It rained every day, heat and humidity following. The city steamed. On the run, he had mostly lost the ability to smell, and at moments he regretted its return.

In the imposing, once green hills above the city, the forests burned. The smoke was so thick at times you couldn't even see the hills. There was war up there, and something like war down here. Gangs roamed the streets, urban youth gangs essentially, some Tutsi and some Hutu. Most of the city had been divided up, into sections where a Hutu would be hunted down and sections where a Tutsi would be crazy to go, but it wasn't as if ethnicity, so hard to determine anyway among strangers, guaranteed anything. Kids and adults walked around carrying guns and grenades. He tried to avoid both them and the occasional corpses. Many killings, he thought in retrospect, were probably the result of armed robberies.

Deo's friends said that everyone was trying to leave the country or saying they wished they could leave. His friends from school said

that most of the faculty was gone or about to be evacuated on special flights, on Air France or Sabena. Jean and his parents would be
flying to Paris, but Jean didn't see how they could take Deo with
them. Everyone who knew anything about politics—and Jean was
nothing if not worldly—knew that France was the staunch ally of
the Hutu regime in Rwanda. If Deo went to France, if Jean could
somehow manage to get him on the plane, he'd probably be deported. They talked about other options. The Congo wasn't far, just
across Lake Tanganyika, but how would Deo get there, and what
would he do then? Deo even wondered about going overland to
Uganda, but it was a very long way, with a third of Burundi and all
of Rwanda in between, and he'd never make it. No, said Jean, Deo
should leave Africa. He should go to the United States, to America.

Sometimes it is better not to know what is impossible. To Deo,
the name meant vast wealth, a country that probably looked like
Kiriri, the tree-lined part of Bujumbura where the ambassadors' res-
idences were situated, mansions behind tall stone walls. Why not
America?

Jean knew some of the ropes. Deo would have to get a visa. First
he'd have to go to a municipal office and get a new identity card,
then to the U.S. embassy, for a business-visitor visa. Jean's father
would provide the letter that said Deo was going to America to sell
coffee. "I don't know anything about coffee," said Deo. The little library he liked was still open. Deo spent the better part of a week
there, reading about coffee beans.

For days the smell of cooked food sickened him. There was still
running water occasionally in Jean's apartment. Deo was able to
bathe. His generic sneakers had made it all the way back, but they
were full of holes and stank. He was notorious among his friends
for pinching pennies and never throwing anything away. Jean
chucked out those sneakers, and bought him another pair. The abscess on Deo's back had resolved, leaving just a scar. His feet were a
fungal nightmare, and there was nowhere to buy medicine for them.
He could brush his teeth properly now, but he knew he had cavities,

because it was painful to put anything hot or cold in his mouth. He had scars on his arms and legs. Also a scar on one cheek. He hardly recognized himself in the mirror. He had always been thin, but wiry, farm-boy thin. Now he was emaciated. The clothes he'd retrieved from his dorm room were at least one size too big. He made himself as presentable as he could. Jean walked with him to the American embassy downtown. Jean was a *muzungu*. The gangs didn't mess with *muzungu* as a rule—from fear of the unknown, Deo guessed.

A woman received him at the embassy, a middle-aged woman. She spoke to him in French. He gave her the letter from Jean's father and delivered his lines about selling coffee, but she didn't ask him any questions about that. She gazed at him from behind her desk, and asked, not unsympathetically but in the way a worried aunt might, "Where have you *been*?"

The woman behind the desk was reading him, he felt, and he thought he was reading her. She didn't press him for an answer to her question. He sensed that she already knew the answer generally: that he was a person on the run.

"How much money do you have in your bank account?" she asked.

He'd never had a bank account, but Jean had known that Deo would be asked this question and had told him the right response. "Two thousand dollars," said Deo.

She presented him with his visa the next day. Then she stood up and offered her hand, and as he took it, she said, "Good luck in New York."

PART TWO

GUSIMBURA

TEN

Boston,
2003

I first met Deo in Boston, about a decade after he had fled Rwanda and Burundi. The moment I was introduced to him, I knew he wasn't American. It wasn't his accent; I hadn't yet heard him speak. And there was nothing foreign about his clothing, which was merely colorful—he wore, I recall, an orange sweater. I think I sensed something missing: the protective opaqueness that many Americans, maybe especially black Americans, learn to put on for strangers, certainly by the time they are thirty. Deo's face jumped out at me. It was a night sky full of lights, a picture of eager, trusting friendliness. He seemed younger than he turned out to be. This impression of innocence lingered, even after I knew that it was mostly inaccurate.

A mutual friend introduced my wife and me to Deo. Our friend told Deo he should talk to my wife, because she was interested in refugees, and just like that, Deo began to tell a fragment of his story.

Afterward, my wife told that fragment to me. It lingered in my mind, the secondhand memory of someone else's memories, as strange and unresolved as the memory of a dream. Three years later, I saw Deo again. I had arranged to meet him at a coffee shop in Hanover, New Hampshire, and I asked him for the story of his escape. He told it briefly at first. His six months on the run, with all their horrors, went by in only minutes. But then, once he was safely out of Africa and had arrived at JFK, his accounting grew detailed. As he went on, telling me how he had stood alone in line at Immigration, I began to sense he was no longer in the coffee shop with me. He was describing the moment when he understood that the Russian journalist wasn't going to help him. His voice was steady. He didn't seem to realize that tears were rolling down his cheeks.

Deo told me details of his story gradually, over the next two years. I'm sure that the account of his escape suffered here and there from memory's usual additions and subtractions, and there was no direct way to verify a lot of it—no way to find the Hutu woman who had saved him at the border, for instance; he never even knew her name. But his story was consistent—and sometimes slightly, reassuringly inconsistent—with the facts that I could find. The story of his escape seemed the most difficult for him to repossess. He told it to me in bits and pieces. The memories seemed to come at him that way. Some returned repeatedly, such as the rainy day in the banana grove when he had seen the baby at its dead mother's breast, staring at him. He had lived long enough, he would say, to have committed sins that might have warranted punishment. But what had that baby done? It was a memory, he seemed to say, that challenged the belief of his childhood, not in the existence of God, but in a God who practiced comprehensible, human justice. And it was a memory, clearly, that challenged his belief in himself, as once again he staggered away from the baby, so as to avoid its eyes, knowing the baby would die.

Deo said that when that memory sneaked up on him, he would

try to reason with himself, to think, as he put it, "in a political way." He would tell himself, "Oh, well, it was not my fault." He'd speak to himself as he remembered doing at the moment, in the corpse-strewn banana grove: "I just can't help that baby. I can't." All this was futile, he said. "It's there anyways. You can try to make yourself feel comfortable, but it's there."

We often speak of moments we will always remember, in order to keep them. Deo would say, of walking away from the baby, "It is one of those things I will never be able to forget." The words didn't sound self-pitying, just realistic. A third of his life had passed since that moment. If he hadn't shed the memory by now, he probably wasn't going to.

But he had found antidotes. Mainly, he had found a purposeful community.

Deo had graduated from Columbia without permanent residency, without a green card. His lawyer, James, had been trying ardently to get him one, but the waiting list seemed interminable. And without a green card, it was all but impossible for him to apply to medical school. He tried several times anyway, filling out the forms on his computer, each time reaching the same dead end: the question that asked for his permanent residency number.

But Deo refused to give up. In the two years after graduation, he stayed as close as he could to medicine. He took a course at Columbia in biochemistry, and corrected his grade in that subject from his sophomore year's C to an A. He worked at a hospice unit in a New York hospital. And, in the summer of 2001, he enrolled at the Harvard School of Public Health, and moved to Boston.

Near the end of his time at Columbia, prowling the stacks in Butler Library, Deo had come across a book called *Infections and Inequalities*. He later learned, after recommending this book to a dozen friends, that the title alone could turn some people away. Deo took it off the shelf and as he read the first sentence, he felt, he would later say, "This is all about me!"

> Early on the morning of her death Annette Jean was feeling well enough to fetch a heavy bucket of water from a spring not far from her family's hut.

The case study that followed told of a Haitian peasant who had died from tuberculosis. Similar stories followed, about poor people suffering and dying unnecessarily, from curable diseases like TB and newly treatable diseases like AIDS—from diseases, indeed, that most of those patients wouldn't have contracted in the first place if they hadn't been desperately poor. The stories were set in the slums of Lima, Peru, in the prisons of post-Soviet Siberia, in the famished and deforested central plateau of Haiti. But Deo felt that the author could just as easily have been describing deaths from intestinal parasites and malaria in Butanza or Sangaza or Kayanza or the slums of Bujumbura. The author could have been writing about Clovis. And the analyses of the cases read like Bishop Bududira's discourses on the ways that poverty gets into the bodies of people. But this was a vastly expanded discourse, on the maldistribution of all the good fruits of modernity, especially of medicine and public health, a discourse that was both scholarly and passionate.

Could anything be done to redress these inequities? Of course! the author said. And he wasn't merely talking. The author and others had an organization, called Partners In Health, which wasn't just trying to build a little clinic as Deo once had in Sangaza, but had actual projects in a Peruvian slum and in a Russian prison, projects that aimed to stanch epidemics of drug-resistant tuberculosis—to prove to the world that this could be done, and to teach the world how to do it. The organization also had a big hospital in Haiti, which was bringing modern medicine and decent public health to some of the poorest people in the world.

There are degrees of loneliness, Deo once told me. The worst he knew was to be a poor person "oppressed by diseases." He said, "You can't afford to see a doctor. You can't even talk about 'This is how I feel,' because you may be called a weak person. So you make your pain your friends." And there was the loneliness he'd often felt in New York, the loneliness of feeling that only he understood the plight of the indigent sick back where he came from, the loneliness of feeling that he understood something vital that no one else around him could fully understand. But the author of this book understood. As he read, Deo paused every few paragraphs to think: "Okay, I know that someone is writing about this. I don't know him, but somewhere there is a circle of friends that I wish I could talk to." The book's author was named Dr. Paul Farmer. The dust jacket identified him as "a physician-anthropologist with more than fifteen years in the field."

Deo resolved to meet the man.

He got his chance about a year and a half later, after he had moved to Boston. One day, heading to class at the Harvard School of Public Health, he saw an advertisement on a bulletin board for a lecture by Dr. Farmer. By then Deo knew a lot about the man: Farmer was an infectious disease specialist at the Brigham and Women's Hospital, a professor at Harvard Medical School, the principal founder of Partners In Health, and the author of several books, all of which Deo had read. On his way to the auditorium, he bought another copy of *Infections and Inequalities*—an unusual extravagance for him, but he had left his own copy at Nancy and Charlie's in New York. After the lecture, after waiting his turn in the crowd around Farmer, Deo got his book signed and also Farmer's email address, which Deo used only about fifteen minutes later, composing an email and to his astonishment receiving a reply within the hour. Soon after that, he was sitting with Farmer in the doctor's apartment at Harvard. There were interruptions—phone calls, other visitors—but Dr. Farmer turned out to be able to answer emails while he talked. They stayed up all night talking, while Farmer worked. They spoke to each other in French. Evidently, Paul Farmer didn't sleep much either. But he had a choice, Deo figured. He imagined that Farmer's sleeplessness, unlike his own, was self-imposed and purposeful, and therefore admirable.

Deo went to work at Partners In Health, becoming, in the organization's vernacular, a PIH-er. Actually, they didn't have a slot for him at the time, but Farmer and the organization's medical director—a doctor named Joia Mukherjee—created one. "He needed a job, any job," Paul Farmer remembered. "And we needed someone who could speak French and wade through documents in that language, and by then we knew he was plenty smart." They kept him busy, looking after Haitians whom PIH brought to Boston for surgeries, and performing whatever other jobs needed doing to support the work in Haiti.

Deo liked all his jobs, and he relished being around Paul Farmer, listening in on his conversations, listening to him talk while answering email. At the moment, in the high councils of international health, there was great debate as to how the world should address the AIDS pandemic, not in the United States and Western Europe, where the disease seemed more or less under control, but in places like Haiti and sub-Saharan Africa, where it was still growing with terrifying velocity. On one side were those who argued it was best to spend all the available resources, which were still meager, on strategies to prevent the further spread of the disease—that is, on prevention. On the other were people like Paul Farmer, insisting that the distinction between prevention and treatment of AIDS was artificial, that the world now had a lot of drugs to treat the disease effectively and must begin to employ those drugs everywhere, along with measures for prevention, especially in the places with the greatest burdens of AIDS. This was what PIH was trying to do in Haiti. At the school of public health, Deo had heard the term "prevention" used repeatedly. But if there was someone who really understood prevention, he thought, it was Paul Farmer, and prevention not just of dis-

ease but of catastrophes like genocide. In his mind, Deo distilled the
PIH message this way: "By all means, let's do prevention! Prevent
people from suffering! Don't wait for people to feel like their lives
are not worth living. Once they feel that way, how are they going to
feel about another person's life?"

Paul was always going somewhere. Sometimes at the end of a
long day and night, Deo would drive with him to the airport. The
first time Deo did this, he sat beside Paul in the backseat of the car.
He noticed Paul was dozing off. Then he felt Paul's head fall onto
his shoulder. Deo shifted slightly, trying to make his shoulder a
more accommodating pillow. He thought, "This is a wonderful, unusual person. I'm so lucky to be with him at this moment." He told
himself, "I am responsible for protecting him. If I had the power, I
would have the obligation to keep him alive forever." The only
feeling he knew that resembled this was the feeling of falling in
love. When they got to the airport, Deo sprang into action, not on
Farmer's orders, but all on his own. He took control of Farmer's
passport. When they found that the flight to Haiti was delayed, Deo
hurried off and bought Paul a sandwich and a bottle of water. Paul
said to him, "I wish you could fly with me to Haiti." But, Farmer
added, this would be a bad idea, because Deo didn't have a green
card.

Deo soon was given a more substantial job, as Joia Mukherjee's
research assistant. But unlike many of the other young PIH-ers, he
wasn't sent to Haiti. There was the matter of his immigration status,
and besides, Joia thought that sending Deo would be risky. Some
people visited the PIH hospital there and spent most of their time in
tears. The experience might be hard on Deo, and if so, he might add
to the burdens of the Haitian staff. In retrospect, Joia felt she had
been unfair to Deo. "We underestimated him," she'd say. They had
their reasons.

As soon as Deo started working as Joia's research assistant, she
began receiving emails from him. Many were full of information
he'd found on the Internet about dreadful events, past and current,

in Burundi and Rwanda, and, rather alarmingly, she'd see that he had sent them at two or three or four o'clock in the morning.

Joia was working on a scholarly paper to show that treatment and prevention were a single indivisible strategy for dealing with the AIDS pandemic. Deo was supposed to be collecting data and reviewing the scholarly literature for Joia, but he routinely became incensed at the papers arguing against treatment and would send Joia long diatribes, backed up not just with facts, but also with material from the websites of conspiracy theorists. She'd say to him, "Let's think of concrete ways to make our argument, for the world, and make it less sort of swirling." He listened, and with her help figured out how to identify reliable websites and journals. When she put him to work on the pharmaceutical industry, much the same thing happened. To Joia, the problem wasn't that Deo got upset at the way patents on drugs, for instance, left the indigent sick of black Africa bereft of modern medicine. These things upset Joia, too. And it wasn't as if Deo didn't seem to realize that anger and indignation were no substitute for fact and reasoned argument. Rather, anger and indignation seemed to take control of him, at least for a while. "Offensive things are so offensive to him. Understandably," Joia said. "It's just like he has no skin. Everything just penetrates so much."

When she was alone with him and there was time to talk, it seemed as though he was compelled to tell her about the genocide, and to recite parts of his own story. There seemed to be no end to this. It was as though he were trying to purge himself of his story, again and again. Joia asked him several times if he would like to see a psychiatrist. He would politely decline, or change the subject, not mentioning that he'd tried that once.

"It was not because I wanted to get out of listening to him," Joia told me. "But I just was very worried about him. It seemed like he never slept, it seemed like the genocide was such a part of his every day. Not that any of this defied understanding, of course, but I didn't know how a person could possibly cope with it." She thought about her own father: she grew up knowing that he had narrowly survived the massacres during the partition of India, events just as cruel and bloody as most other ethnic and religious wars, and for body count even bloodier than the Rwandan genocide. But her father had never talked about his experiences. His way of dealing with his memories had seemed to be hypochondria. Joia told me: "He had been sick and dying my entire childhood, and I always thought that he was just strange until I met Deo, and when I saw how much pain Deo had incorporated into his every day, I thought, 'What are your options if you see that kind of tragedy?' Your options are pretty much to let it spew out all the time like Deo, or try to suppress it, which is what my dad did, and I think it came out in his hypochondriasis, thinking he was dying all the time."

Paul Farmer was the only other person to whom Deo told his story in detail. And, as he did with Joia, he told it to Farmer repeatedly. "The first time we spoke privately, he broke like a distressed dam," Farmer remembered. "I was worried about him, but I never recommended that he see a shrink. It was hard to imagine an American psychiatrist medicating him for having survived genocide in two countries."

Farmer soon came to think of Deo not as a patient or charity case, but as a friend and colleague in lingering distress. And the best remedy for Deo, he thought, would be a return to medicine.

Deo vividly remembered the hospice in New York where he had worked. That had been a place, of course, where everyone was dying. He had sat beside the patients and talked with them. In his mind, he placed himself in their deathbeds, remembering times when he was fleeing and had felt as they must now: "I probably have maybe a minute for the rest of my life, to be alive, and then I'll be gone." He'd sit down beside a patient's bed and say, "Tell me about your life. Tell me something you enjoyed." Talking to them so that they could die the good death, he imagined. Many burst into tears. Mostly, they said they felt guilty, for having accomplished nothing compared with what they had planned, or for getting divorced, something they regretted now when they could no longer even try to repair the break.

After that time of hearing deathbed stories, to walk into the offices of PIH felt like one of those transitions he'd read about in Greek myth, when the mortal consigned to the underworld is granted a parole to return to the light. And it also felt, as one said in Burundi to describe a feeling of special warmth and liberty, "like going to Grandmom's." Deo said, "Walking into that building was like a whole world opening for me. It was like opening my own house and just *right there*. I had such an unusual feeling. A great feeling. You enter, you know that you are not just going to work. It's like you're going home, and everyone there is so nice and friendly." Sometimes he stayed all night with the other young PIH-ers, assembling documents and facts for papers that the higher-ups had to present within days in Geneva, in Barcelona, in Moscow. They'd buy pizza and beers, put on some music, and work until dawn. "Oh, my God. It was great," Deo said. "I actually loved those days." He liked to go to the meetings where the director of PIH, Ophelia Dahl, and her staff would talk about what PIH was accomplishing in Haiti, a place that Deo imagined to be very like Burundi. In Haiti PIH was building houses and schools for the poorest families and cleaning up water supplies and bringing in doctors to do heart surgeries and constructing new clinics. He would glance around the conference room. It looked so small and organized compared with all the big and messy work PIH was doing outside those walls. "It's a really tiny place that is changing a great big environment," he remembered thinking. Then he'd exclaim in his mind, "No group of people is really too small to change the situation!"

He loved all of it, from going to the airport to pick up a jar that contained a Haitian patient's severed breast and taking it for a biopsy at one of the Harvard teaching hospitals, to pounding computer keys all night so that Farmer or Joia or Jim Kim, another big figure in the organization, would be fully supplied with ammunition to argue the rights and needs of poor patients at high-level meetings that week.

"To be part of that meant a lot, a lot, to me, and made me feel that I was really being productive and participating in the good cause," he told me. Sometimes he would look up from his computer and around his little janitor's closet of an office and wonder, "Am I really here?" He remembered thinking, "Finally, finally, this is who I am. This kind of work is not just work. It's part of me, my life, me. There is no way of separating that and me. It feels so good!"

After some months at PIH, Deo was invited to give the weekly lunchtime talk to the office staff. He had not yet told these colleagues his story in full. He hadn't tried to do this with anyone except abortively with the psychiatrist and with Paul and Joia. As he began to speak, he felt tears well up—embarrassingly, then not. He couldn't have dissected all he felt, one feeling from another. Maybe relief was uppermost. It was as if something in him had to compensate for the years of silence. Deo talked on and on, long after the lunch hour, long after the time when everyone had to get back to work. But PIH was the right place for this to happen. Ophelia Dahl remembered sitting there, watching Deo and thinking, "If anyone gets up and walks out now, I'm going to kill 'em." No one did.

He had been lucky again. He'd found a group of people equipped and willing to understand him, and models for himself, and a vision. He'd made many new friends, including a girlfriend, a medical student. She had since become just a friend, but a close one. James O'Malley had finally got him permanent residency in the United States. And, with a lot of help from Paul Farmer, he'd enrolled in medical school at last, at Dartmouth.

I was once introduced to an old, dying man who had spent his late adolescence at Auschwitz and had refused to speak about it afterward, for nearly forty years. If an acquaintance happened to ask about the provenance of the pale blue numerals tattooed on his forearm, the survivor would say, "I've always had great difficulty remembering my phone number." In old age, though, he had finally begun to tell his story. He told me, "The problem is, once you start talking it's very difficult to stop. It's almost impossible to stop."

By the time I met Deo, he had told pieces of his story to various people and he had been telling all of it repeatedly to Farmer and Joia for about two years. I think he had gone through most of his time of finding it impossible to stop. When I next saw him, two years after we first met, he had grown much more reticent. His story wasn't pleasant. "It isn't time for tea. It is not," he would say. He didn't want to burden his friends with it anymore. Once, I listened to Deo deliver a rather scholarly public-health talk about Rwanda, and a person in the audience asked him what had happened to him during the genocide. Deo took a deep breath, then delivered a three-minute précis of his escape. By the time he finished, the room was hushed. Deo made a small, pained smile and said to the gathering, "Maybe you are wondering, 'Why did I ask?'"

Now and then one friend or another would urge him again to visit a psychiatrist. I asked him why he continued to refuse. He said, "It's true that I really had, I still do have all these problems. There's no way that they will go away from me. But I deal with them the way I can." He lifted his chin. "And I'm very happy with the way I deal with them."

ELEVEN

New York City,
2006

I felt uncomfortable at times, during the two years or so when I was asking Deo my questions. Sometimes I felt that to remind him of the past was to traumatize him all over again. On several occasions, I offered to stop my search for his story and let his memories die, if they would. Once or twice, I hoped he would accept my offer. But he always declined. He'd say, "No, it's all right." In retrospect, I feel as though we went on a journey together, moving backward through his past, sometimes on tiptoes, as it were. I don't know what useful purpose, if any, this trip served for him. For me, Deo was the attraction, Deo and his story. First of all, there was New York.

A young man arrives in the big city with two hundred dollars in his pocket, no English at all, and memories of horror so fresh that he sometimes confuses past and present. When Deo first told me about his beginnings in New York, I had a simple thought: "I would not have survived." And then, two years later, he enrolls in an Ivy

League university. How did this happen? Where did he find the strength, and how had he won the beneficence of strangers? How had it felt to be him? I asked him to show me some of his New York.

We started in Harlem. Deo hadn't been there in five years, and as we walked up Malcolm X Boulevard past rank after rank of renovated brownstones and gutted brownstones covered with scaffolding and clusters of new chain stores and banks, he made exclamations. "Look at these buildings! They used to have wood on their windows. This is unbelievable! This used to be the worst place here, people peeing, yelling. Gosh, that building is brand-new." He wondered what had become of his old neighbors. He said, "This is not good news for the poor."

He'd never seen joggers in Harlem before, he said, let alone white joggers. Actually, back when he lived here, the only white people he saw were cops, always angry because—so he surmised—always scared. The pay phones, once his only way back to Burundi, were gone. By the time we reached 124th Street, it wasn't changes in the landscape but the sight of something familiar that astonished him. "Oh my God! Look! 'PEN'!" The windows and doorways of the abandoned tenement were bricked up, but the graffito was still there, high on a wall. "This was a door right here. There were many entrances. And people used to hang around on these fire escapes."

Out front there was a bent metal awning with this written on it: "All Cure Health Variety Patties, Natural Juice, Newspaper, Magazine And Lot More." The awning must have been there back then, already a relic of a defunct store, but Deo said he didn't remember it. "You know there are a lot of things that I didn't even look at, things I don't remember." What he seemed to recall most clearly from his month or so in this place was his state of mind. He had escaped physical danger. Here the problem had been to escape the torment of memory.

As he looked around, he was laughing one moment, pensive the next. I wondered whether he was feeling a touch of perverse nostalgia for a place where he'd known so much pain and confusion. He pointed at the staircase for the 125th Street subway station. "This is where I tried to bargain for a token, for less."

"Oh, you tried to bargain for tokens?" I said. "You didn't succeed."

"No."

I laughed. "You actually tried to bargain for tokens?"

"Yes," he said, rather stiffly.

It hadn't occurred to me that he might be annoyed by my laughing over what an innocent he'd been a decade ago. Hoping that I would seem to be laughing at someone else, I told him I was thinking of my grandmother, who once managed to pay a New York City bus driver with postage stamps. He chuckled politely. I had the feeling that to Deo my grandmother's behavior wasn't all that peculiar either.

We descended to the subway station, the same from which Deo had departed on his long, long ride of years ago. We went to the end of the line in the Bronx, then all the way to the other end in Brooklyn. One round trip took about two hours, and he had made several round trips on that day twelve years ago. As we rode along, Deo remembered how, worry overcoming pride, he had attempted to ask other riders for help, in French. "Some people would walk away, some would curse at me." After he'd stopped asking, he had begun to sense, in the background of his loneliness, changes in the human landscape of the cars. When the trains had passed through what he now knew to be Midtown, he had been struck by the whiteness and the purposeful haste of the riders, their fancy dress, the perfume of the women. Then everything had changed. After a couple of round trips, he told me, he had begun to understand: "The farther you go uptown, the blacker and poorer the people, and also when you go downtown. And I realized I didn't fit anywhere."

I thought I could picture him as he was then, a skinny, worried-looking youth, moving from panic to exhaustion and finally giving up all hope of escaping the subway. He remembered the moment when he had told himself, "No one is in control of his own life," as he'd dozed off on the screeching, roaring trains. For a moment when we came above ground, I found it hard to reconcile that picture of Deo with Deo as he had become.

I had two images of him in New York's SoHo district. In the first it was evening twelve years back and he was being led by Sharon—led by the hand, so to speak—out of the subway station on Prince Street, past the lighted windows of chain stores, art galleries, and boutiques, toward the Wolfs' apartment. In the second, the apartment was his home, and he was lounging on the sofa, laughing uproariously as Charlie, for my benefit, reminisced about those contentious dinner-table lessons in American idioms. What lay between those two images was an extraordinary act. A perfectly sane, reasonable couple had taken in a needy stranger from Africa who didn't speak their language, who had no means of support, who might become their dependent for the rest of their lives. What sort of people would do that? Who were Nancy and Charlie?

I went to see them alone. I rode up to their loft, as Deo and Sharon had done on the night when they had first come for dinner, in the small old-fashioned elevator, with unpainted wooden walls and a metal gate. You rang for a ride and Nancy or Charlie would bring the machine down. It was Charlie who came for me. I remarked on the apparent age of the elevator, and Charlie began—in a deep and measured voice, which wasn't a drawl but carried traces of the South, like phrases of an old song: "The original passenger elevator was installed across the street. In the Haughwout Building. Built by old man Elisha Otis, in 1857. Without which, of course, the high-rise would not be possible. That and structural steel. Cast iron was the last-generation technology. . . ."

The elevator opened right into the living area, itself open to the kitchen. The furniture was plain. Everything in the tidy kitchen seemed to have been there for years. I didn't see a single gleaming culinary gadget. There was no TV in the living room. Books covered most of the walls. I noticed some small African objects—carvings, bowls—on a shelf and a table, but most of all I noticed the wall that faced the street. It was all windows, large, old-fashioned double-hung windows that looked out on a grand geometric collage of rooftops and round wooden rooftop water towers and restored, imitation-Renaissance façades across the street. From Nancy and Charlie's windows on a summer day, it was possible to imagine a Venetian canal.

At the rear of the loft, in Nancy's studio, the floor was rough unfinished wood. Several works in progress stood on the easels and hung on the walls, large and meticulous drawings that made me think of dreams, familiar as if I'd just remembered them—troubling dreams of cityscapes, where human beings had shrunk beneath monolithic architecture or been consigned to old, abandoned buildings. I thought of the building PEN, of course.

Between the living room and studio lay the Black Hole, still intact, as if awaiting Deo's return, as it always did await him. The photograph of his uncle still hung above the bed. The threatening email from the self-proclaimed member of PALIPEHUTU was still taped to the wall above the desk.

Nancy and Charlie had moved into their loft back in the 1970s, when the building still reeked of printer's ink from the factory below and SoHo was still block after block of derelict buildings and machine shops. A friend of theirs had told me that, unlike the neighborhood, their apartment hadn't really changed at all: "It's a time capsule, a mid-seventies SoHo artist's time capsule." Not that there was anything outlandish about them, but out on the streets in their evening clothes they seemed to me a little like time capsules themselves: blond, long-legged Nancy dressed like an art student, in sandals and worn corduroys, interesting earrings (with Russian constructivist designs on them), and a floppy Renaissance beret; and Charlie with a trimmed beard, and a plain Parisian beret perched on his gray hair. Convention, of course, has everything to do with children. For a married American couple of their era, not to have children was in itself a rather unconventional act, yielding ample freedom for other unconventional acts. And the lives they had led before Deo arrived had been unusual, even adventurous.

Deo had told me Charlie was modest about his accomplishments. "You ask him, 'What do you do?' And he will say, 'I wish I could know.'" Charlie got his Ph.D. in sociology at Princeton. He had taught at Brown University, Dalhousie University, the City University of New York Graduate Center, the University of Wisconsin, the University of Illinois, Carleton College, the Polytechnic University of New York University, and the University of North Carolina at Chapel Hill, his alma mater. He had been the president or organizer, and on occasion the reorganizer, of various sociological associations. He specialized in what is called "social impact assessment," the side of environmental impact assessment that worries about the effects of technology on human beings. Among many other things, he was a fellow of the American Association for the Advancement of Science, and had directed research or consulted on various projects for the states of Mississippi and Washington, for the United Nations, for the Army Corps of Engineers, for Congress's Office of Technology Assessment, and for the presidential commission that investigated the accident at Three Mile Island.

Nowadays, Charlie worked mainly as a consultant, quite often in African countries. He called himself "a reformed academic." I think by way of trying to tell me something about his adoptive father, Deo had given me an article Charlie wrote many years before. The paper was about Athens, Ohio, where Charlie had attended a conference called "Engineering and Society." Charlie found events in Athens more interesting once he discovered that the town was in the process of diverting its river. He tried to interest his fellow conferees in the matter, with limited success. Undeterred, he conducted his own sociological investigation, reading documents, interviewing officials and citizens. He concluded his paper as follows:

> Did I, as instructed, "get the whole story"? There is no "the whole story." What is the story in Athens, anyway? The short detour of a sorry river? Not at all. It is the college and the town, the river and the road, man and nature, truth and beauty. Palpable though writ small, the story in Athens is the story everywhere, always: the human condition. If that is pretentious I do not apologize.

When he and Nancy had first moved to New York, in 1977, Charlie had volunteered to take care of pruning all the publicly owned trees south of Forty-second Street. "I'm a country boy in my heart, and a country boy in my soul," he explained. A bad bicycle accident had put him out of commission for a time, but he'd given up tree work only after Deo had arrived and had insisted that it wasn't good for Charlie's injured arm.

The Wolfs had traveled. While at Brown, Charlie had taught a course called "Technology and the Moral Order." His favorite student had been Ethelbert Chukwu, Sharon's old family friend from Nigeria, now a professor of applied mathematics. Chukwu had invited Nancy and Charlie to help him get a new technological university started in Nigeria. They had accepted at once. They had lived in Nigeria, in the town of Yola, for two years in the early 1980s, and the experience had affected both of them strongly. Nancy remembered being driven for the first time into the remote northern part of the country. She had gazed out the car windows at the passing towns: open sewers, houses and stores with cinderblock walls and corrugated-zinc roofs, old tires and innards of automobiles scattered everywhere. She was reminded of the landscape she had known as a child when walking beside Route 1 in New Jersey. Off in the distance, though, she'd caught glimpses of traditional villages—round houses, smoke rising through the holes in thatched roofs. These seemed beautiful to her. Her first impression, of a society torn between tradition and modernity, lingered and grew over the next two years.

In Yola, Charlie helped Chukwu get the new university organized and taught Nigerian students his "Technology and the Moral Order." And Nancy taught art, feeling as though she learned more than she taught. "It struck me very forcefully in Nigeria that art wasn't just something out there, a commodity that people bought. It was a part of everyday life, it was a basic necessity," she later said. She got to know a lot of Nigerians. Their traditional crafts, it seemed to her, were providing the people with "a sense of order in times of chaos." She told an art critic some years later, "I believe it is human to hope to find order and a connection between one's soul and the world outside."

Clearly, they were a couple disposed to take chances and to look kindly on a young African. Deo's neediness had been obvious. Nancy remembered, from that first time they'd met him, at dinner here in the loft, suffering through Deo's attempts to speak English, suffering the way one suffers inwardly for a person afflicted with a stutter. On that occasion, she and Charlie hadn't tried to tell him about their own experiences in Africa. Deo's story was more interesting to them; besides, communication was difficult and, for Nancy, nerve-racking. She said that during the whole meal she kept thinking, "This man is so skinny! This man needs to eat!"

At that dinner, Charlie said, he had sized Deo up as a "serious" person. From the way Deo had talked about his tortured country, Charlie had concluded that he had "depth."

Charlie had been in his sixties then, Nancy in her fifties. They weren't young, and their loft, which wasn't large, served as both Charlie's office and Nancy's studio. Years before, when Charlie was away teaching for six months, Nancy had shared the apartment with Lelia, later James O'Malley's wife. Lelia had planned to look for another place once Charlie returned, but they all got along so well there seemed no point in this. "Stay on!" Charlie had declared. Lelia, helping out with expenses, had ended up staying parts of four years in the loft. So when it came to sharing their lives, the Wolfs had a precedent.

Then again, Charlie told me, speaking of Nancy, "Worry is her natural state." And when he said this, Nancy replied, "But it's true!" Every argument for sheltering a stranger would have come with at least two worries about the consequences. One thing at least seemed clear, though: the Wolfs didn't regret what they'd done.

In their living room, we sat and talked about the time just before they'd first met Deo, when the genocide in Rwanda had been all over the newspapers and TV. The news had struck Nancy all the more forcefully because of the time they had spent in Nigeria. She thought of those years as the most important of her life. The troubled thoughts and feelings about the modern world that she'd been striving to express in her American pictures had all been magnified in Nigeria. For about a month, she and Charlie had been obliged to stay in safe houses, because of eruptions of factional violence near the university in Yola: some two thousand people had been killed. That memory had made the news of the Rwandan genocide seem near.

"You had paid attention to what was happening in Rwanda," I said.

"Oh my God!" said Nancy.

"Paid attention?" said Charlie. "After the fact, like everybody else."

"There was this footage on television," said Nancy. "I'll never forget seeing that."

"I was in Zambia, Tanzania, and Kenya in April 1994," said Charlie. "And we didn't hear the first thing. I never heard anything until I got back to New York."

By that time, Nancy said, she'd had her fill of hearing about slaughter on the radio and staring at footage of bodies floating down Rwandan rivers. "I had been watching it and listening to it, and I couldn't even talk about it, I was so upset. I couldn't even read about it. And so anyway, when Sharon called us about Deo, and then it turned out he was from Burundi, I of course didn't know that Rwanda and Burundi had anything to do with each other."

Nancy hadn't known that this young man had escaped a civil war and a genocide, until Sharon brought him to dinner: "She explained for Deo that it was the same process, that he'd been caught in all that. And then the other thing that was so interesting was that he said, or Sharon translated, that he was a third-year medical student in Burundi, but his father ran cows. And we knew cows from Nigeria, from the Fulani. We would watch the cows and the young boys and the shepherds go up and down the hills. So we knew that scene, and that seemed like a long way from medical school."

"But to look at the boys at the back end of a cow, directing traffic, and one of them could have been Deo," said Charlie. "In Burundi instead of Nigeria. Just like on the street in New York today. I look at the delivery people, at the people working in the supermarkets. Almost all of them seem to be Africans."

"And you think, 'Where did this person come from?'" I suggested.

"And what kind of human potential does he have?" Charlie said. "Potential that is not going to be discovered, is not going to be expressed, is not going to be shared. So I think it really was . . . Well, we wouldn't have stopped just anyone, or even Deo, on the street and said, 'You look like a bright young chap, a likely fellow, why don't you come around for dinner.' No. No."

After meeting Deo, Nancy and Charlie had kept track of Sharon's quest to find a place for him. On one occasion, the failures mounting up, they had told Sharon they would take Deo in, then called her back to say they couldn't after all. Weeks had passed. Finally, Sharon had called to say she'd found a place for Deo—in a halfway house for recovering drug addicts and alcoholics. Deo could stay there so long as he went to group therapy, for problems that he didn't have. "That was too much for us," Charlie remembered. He had told Sharon, "Bring him down."

"Sharon was very, *very* persistent," said Nancy. "She's a very persistent woman."

When I first went to see Sharon at St. Thomas More, she told me she'd recently spoken to Nancy and Charlie. "They said that they had realized that Deo was the best thing that ever happened to them. They had realized this together, that this is the best thing that ever happened to them. Without children, you know, to have a real focus, I guess."

The phrasing interested me. Maybe taking Deo in hadn't been entirely an act of volition. Maybe part of the truth was that Deo had happened to Nancy and Charlie. If so, what happened to them first was Sharon.

It was raining the day I first went to see her, at the rectory. Sharon arrived draped in a plastic raincoat, her shoulders bent forward under a backpack that was lodged under the raincoat. This image of her stuck with me—the raincoat especially, the cheapest kind one can buy. She was still a beautiful-looking woman, as she had been when Deo first met her, but now at a different stage of beauty, her skin still porcelain, her blond hair gone more decidedly white. A beautiful, spiritual-looking woman, utterly without pretense.

She showed me around the rectory: the kitchen where Deo had deposited the groceries the first day they'd met, the mail slot where she'd found his letter asking for help, the basement room where she had sometimes shared her lunch with him and helped him find the clothes he hadn't wanted to wear to the party that he hadn't wanted to attend. When we went into the church proper, a voice called out, "You're the best!"

Sharon turned. A man was sitting in the shadows, in a pew at the back of the church. "I'm fine, thanks," Sharon called to him. "Good to see you."

"She's the best!" called the man—to me, I guessed.

"He's a drunk, kind of homeless, but he doesn't want to talk about it," Sharon whispered to me. We turned toward the altar. Sharon bought and arranged the flowers for St. Thomas More. Her latest arrangements reposed in giant vases on either side of the steps leading up toward the altar.

I stared at the arrangements. I told her they were beautiful, and I meant it. "And you're self-taught," I said.

"Well, actually as a child I started arranging flowers," she said. "I would pick wildflowers. We had a list of chores. My brother would get to choose first because he was the elder. But I always wanted to go get some flowers for the kitchen table. And color, I used to see people as color, a person's personality."

"You did?" I was struck by a thought. "What color is Deo?"

"I don't do it anymore," said Sharon. When she was a teenager, a psychiatrist heard about her gift of color transference and arranged for an interview. "And I just clammed up," she said.

"I think it's wonderful that you associate people with colors," I said.

"I used to."

"You don't anymore. Okay."

"Maybe it's subconscious now. I don't know."

"Well," I said, "if you still did it, what color would Deo be?"

Sharon didn't answer for a while. She gazed toward the altar. She gave a long exhalation. "I think a kind of magenta," she said.

Sharon grew up in Norwich, Vermont, in an Irish Catholic family, a little strapped for cash, and frugal. Her parents managed to send her to Wellesley College, where she would have been in the class of 1960, but once she discovered her vocation, she transferred to the Catholic school Manhattanville. She traveled some, in Europe and the Middle East. In late 1960, she entered a Benedictine convent in Connecticut. Speaking of that convent, she told me, "I always say that, just for me, that was not the right place." She said this without a trace of irony, I noticed, even though it had taken her thirty years of cloistered life to decide the place wasn't right.

Sharon began to think of leaving the convent when the abbess launched the construction of an elegant building to replace their rather makeshift quarters. She remembered thinking, "Gee, I thought we were supposed to be living simply, the way we all should. Let's share with people who have nothing."

Her parents had subscribed to *The Catholic Worker*, a dangerous organ of left-wing Catholicism to some, and to others an extension of the ideas in the Sermon on the Mount. Sharon grew up reading it. She didn't regret her years at the convent. She had learned a great deal. Among other things, she seemed to say, she'd found that she yearned to play a little part in the affairs of the world. She had received dispensation to resign as a nun, but still wore her ring from consecration. She had come to New York without a job or even many clothes and had found her way to St. Thomas More. She was paid a small salary to do various jobs at the church—taking care of flowers for the sanctuary, helping at wedding rehearsals. She also taught Sunday school to the four- and five-year-olds.

Sharon believed her job in life was to discover the abilities she had received and to use them "in a deep, giving spirit," for the glory of God. She threw herself into all her jobs, but she spent at least as much time in her self-appointed role, which was receiving people who came to the church in distress. The supply was abundant even on the Upper East Side. "I feel this is just being a Benedictine in another situation," she said. The prescriptions for receiving guests were laid out in chapter 66 of the sixth-century Rule of St. Benedict. The basic instruction was simple: "Receive all as Christ." The porter, the doorkeeper, should respond to visitors with "all the gentleness of the fear of God." I took it that, at least in part, Sharon had left her Benedictine convent in order to become a Benedictine doorkeeper.

The job entailed a certain amount of potential embarrassment, and I had the feeling that, for her, embarrassment was sometimes a temptation. She told me that not long ago a well-to-do friend, a parishioner, had seen her pushing a shopping cart full of used clothes for the needy toward the church, and had told her that this just wasn't done. Respectable people just didn't push shopping carts down the sidewalks of Fifth or Madison Avenue. "Well, maybe *they* don't," Sharon told me she had replied. "But I do. I don't care." Not long ago, she told me, a man had staggered into the sanctuary in the pangs of drug withdrawal and collapsed writhing on the floor, and as she knelt over him, first kneading his shoulders and legs, then pounding on them to try to loosen his cramps, she was thinking, "If someone comes into the church right now and sees this, they'll wonder, 'What the heck is going on?' But I don't care."

She didn't discriminate among the needy people who arrived at the door, she said. Whatever troubles they brought, she took them on, if she could, and none of the people bored her. Not, for instance, the retarded lady with whom she lived for several years after the pastor at St. Thomas More decided he no longer wanted women living in the rectory. The retarded woman didn't bathe, her apartment was crammed with garbage and junk, and it took about six months for Sharon to get the woman and her place cleaned up, but she didn't mind any of it, she insisted. She'd tell herself, "Hey, this is some adventure here. What kind of headway can we make here?" She thought of what she did as offering "undifferentiated help to anybody." "It boils down to whoever walks into my life." There were the "druggies," who were afraid to come into the rectory. And the woman who hadn't been in a church for twenty years but told Sharon she was aching now to go to confession. And the homeless lady, a paranoid schizophrenic, who would lie down on a pew as if on a park bench—the church authorities had finally decided they had to throw her out.

Sharon still befriended her and all the others, and felt glad to see them when they arrived. But not glad, she allowed, in quite the same way she felt on seeing a select few. She had her favorites. Deo was one, of course, and had been, she thought, right from their first meeting.

I asked her why. She said maybe it was the remark he'd made about being "very interested" when she had told him that, yes, this was a church. This had made him seem like "someone who could see beyond his own nose." But beyond that, she didn't have an explanation. Her description of Deo back then was in itself more convincing.

She remembered that he was very skinny and that he had buck teeth (later straightened at the NYU dental school). Also that his breath smelled dreadful—so she wasn't surprised when she received his letter asking for help in finding a doctor. She had been in New York for several years when Deo arrived in her life. In the places where she'd lived before, up in Vermont and in the convent, one gathered asparagus and picked cherries early, but one had to wait for potatoes. Here in the city, though, every imaginable foodstuff came in from all over the world every day. It was easy here to forget how to "appreciate the moment," how to "wait for the right time." And this applied to the development of people. One shouldn't expect anyone to be complete at any given moment. Everyone was "on a pilgrimage." She had wanted to understand Deo's and to help him on his way.

"He was grateful for everything," she told me. Of course she had been aware of times when he seemed withdrawn, and of periods when he didn't come to see her. But she knew from experience that people often resent the help they've asked for, often in direct proportion to their neediness. She had imagined it must be hard for Deo to be a man both physically and mentally and yet need so much. She was having some heart problems when Deo entered her life, but she felt Deo's case was far more urgent than her own. "It's hard to generalize," she told me. "But the few Africans that I know have such great openness to other people and a warmth and a desire to connect, and I just felt that had been shattered for Deo, and somehow there wasn't much I could do except just try to let him know I really cared in whatever way."

She remembered that first dinner at the Wolfs' loft. She remembered trying to interpret Deo's French for Nancy and Charlie, but having a hard time because she was paying less attention to the conversation than to her hopes for it—her notion that the answer to Deo's material and spiritual needs might well be sitting right across the dining table from her, in the persons of Nancy and Charlie. She remembered worrying over every lapse in the talk, issuing silent instructions to the others, "cheering them on silently." She remembered looking at Nancy and Charlie and thinking, "You have to love him right away!"

In a phone call soon afterward, Charlie asked her, "What do you think he needs?"

"Well, he needs a family," Sharon said. "*That's* what he needs."

And of course she remembered the phone call in which Nancy and Charlie at last informed her that they would take Deo in. She said she was delighted, overjoyed. I had the feeling, though, that it would be too much to say she was surprised. What surprised and disappointed her, I thought, were the many failures.

Deo never knew the half of Sharon's attempts to find him a home. She later gave me documents and notes she'd saved from that time. On many slips of paper and old envelopes and on the backs of old bookmarks and church announcements, I found the names of dozens of agencies and programs that she'd contacted, among them "the Manhattan Valley St. John the Divine Youth Project," "Grenadier Realty Corp. Milagrosa Houses," "Oxfam," "Red Cross homeless services," "Travelers Aid NY," "World Council of Churches," "Emmaus House," "Family and Children's Services Catholic Charities," "St. Vincent de Paul," "St. John the Divine Crisis Center," "City Shelters," "UN Quaker mission," "Hope House," "Trinity Retreat House in Larchmont." There were notes with the names of priests and nuns for her to call, some with the notation "Very caring." One note read, "A doctor from Zaire will lend books." One note was the name of a woman, beside which Sharon had written "widowed." A prospect, evidently. Beside the name of another woman, Sharon had written "divorced."

She was an unusual person, obviously, and for Deo to have run into her on his grocery delivery rounds was a great piece of luck, maybe even—in Sharon's presence, I was tempted into thinking this—providential.

In *Survival in Auschwitz,* Primo Levi writes, "Today I think that if for no other reason than that an Auschwitz existed, no one in our age should speak of Providence." But for all the horror visited on Deo, the list of strangers who had saved him seemed remarkable: the Hutu woman in the banana grove, Muhammad the baggage handler, Chukwu and James O'Malley and above all Nancy and Charlie and Sharon. It wasn't as though there was some sort of outreach program in place for people like Deo. I thought of the door he had left open in Mutaho. No doubt because I was in Sharon's presence, I found myself thinking, "Something must have been looking out for Deo." And I disliked hearing the words in my mind.

I said to Sharon, "One of the things I've noticed about some of the genocide narratives I've read, people will say, 'God spared me.' The problem I have with that is then you think, 'Well, what about all the people who got their heads chopped off? Did God not like them?'" I added, "So I'm not quite sure that's the way to look at it."

"I have a theory," she replied. "I remember thinking long ago, 'We're loved infinitely for however little bit of time we have.' And it's not ultimately tragic to die at any age. Whether we're talking about being blown into little pieces or what is ultimate tragedy, I just think there isn't ultimate tragedy except for evil, and God doesn't will *any* evil. And we're surrounded by—I tell the little kids about the Good Shepherd, I think it's a great image for them, but the vine and the branches is great, too—but whether we feel it or not, we are surrounded by this tremendously loving presence, and that covers every second of every day. Of *everybody.*"

TWELVE

New York City,
2006

On Central Park South, as usual, limousines were idling on one side of the street while on the other side, adjacent to the park—on what Deo called "the other shore"—a homeless man was sleeping on a bench with a cardboard box over his head. The homeless man was what Deo noticed. He laughed about the box on the man's head, after we'd passed by. He said, "It's sad." He told me, "It's hard when you don't have any hope. You just hope to get to the next meal. Bread and milk and cookies." But then he laughed again, and as if to explain, recited a Burundian saying: "When too much is too much or too bad is too bad, we laugh as if it was too good. You just laugh instead of crying. Accidents of birth."

At my request, Deo was taking me on a tour of his former homelessness. An unusual sort of tour, devoted to what would have been hidden, or at least far in the background, for most people walking through that landscape. It was those things, the things meant to be unnoticed, that jumped out at Deo. Not the awninged and carpeted

entrances to the buildings, but the little signs that read "Service Entrance" and the wrought-iron gates and the stairs leading down to
basements. This building wasn't a nice example of early-twentieth-
century architecture; rather, it was a building with a bad service entrance, and that building next to it had a doorman who claimed the
tips that by rights should have gone to deliverymen. Deo took me
on the routes he has traveled with his grocery cart and past the grocery stores where he had labored. One of the stores had vanished, to
his consternation. I thought I could read his feelings. This had been
a part of his painful little world. How could it have vanished? How
could it be so insubstantial?

We walked into the park, to look at the various bedrooms he'd
found there for himself twelve years before.

It was impossible, at least for me, to know the story of Deo's lost
year, of his long escape and his sojourn in crack houses and Central
Park, and not imagine lingering costs. He had told me that he felt he
was overly sensitive: "When someone says something really bad, or
I realize I said something ridiculous or did something bad to someone, it really takes me days to recover, and I just don't know why
I'm such a weak guy." Once, when I told him he was still young,
only in his thirties, he replied, "But I feel I am a hundred and
thirty." He still had bouts of insomnia and dreams that involved im-
mobility and appalling quantities of blood. But the most obvious effect of his ordeal—or what I took to be an effect—was the
ungovernable quality of his memories.

For now, as we walked through the park, it was clear that he was
merely repossessing memories. He was not possessed by them, for
the moment. "I will show you how I made progress," he said, smiling, as he led the way to what had been his last campsite in the park.
It was a cozy-looking spot, like a niche in a cathedral, a group of
benches surrounding the monumental statue of a sculptor named
Albert Bertel Thorvaldsen, all under the canopy of grand old trees,
and shielded from the roadways by smaller trees and bushes. There
was a little garden off to one side. Deo looked up at the bronze

image of the once famous Danish sculptor; he was clad in a belted tunic, a mallet in one hand, a chisel in the other. "He has a hammer," Deo said. "Too bad he was not around. He could have built a shelter for me." Deo smiled, surveying the spot. "This was big progress. I'm telling you, it really was great." He pointed to a grassy space shielded by bushes. "This is where I got my mattress stolen. Right here. This was my biggest progress. I preferred sleeping in the park. Because I could see stars, and . . ." He didn't finish the sentence.

"It was like being in Butanza?"

"Yah. And then that was cool, but it was trouble at the same time. To bring back all those memories. Come back to be intimate with nature, and the sky." His voice growing soft, he talked about seeing the shape of the rabbit on the face of the moon and being reminded by this of his grandfather.

"You didn't know he was dead then, but you assumed he was?" I asked. It was the perfectly wrong thing to say.

"Yah, I assumed," he answered, and he turned and walked on. I walked with him. He murmured that his stomach was bothering him. He didn't speak again for a while.

I thought that he wasn't walking through Central Park recalling a bad memory now; he was really back in that time. Even the stomachache was probably the same, I imagined.

I apologized for mentioning his grandfather's death. He didn't respond. I didn't think he was ignoring me. He just didn't seem to know I was there. He walked on, toward the Reservoir. He stood at the fence gazing out at the water, squads of joggers passing behind us. Gradually, he seemed to return. "This was . . ." He paused. "Very relaxing to me."

He had found a better place to recover, of course. I wanted to visit it with him. We took the subway uptown to Columbia. As we walked through the gates, Deo's mood changed utterly. He might have been a student again, conducting a campus tour. "The gym is right here. It's huge! It is *a*-mazing. . . . Every student here after freshman year, you have your own mailbox. It's really cool. . . . You see this building here, this is physics. You go down, there are nine floors down. It blows my mind. This one here is astronomy. . . . Oh, this is the math department. Oh my God, I made a lot of money from that department. Teaching children. And this is chemistry. The chemistry department is quite famous, it competes with Berkeley. . . . I loved it here."

Deo stopped on the steps of Low Library and pointed across the quadrangle at another monumental building, a product of the Italian Renaissance Revival, one of many all around us. This one advertised itself with names carved in the granite frieze above its broad front: HOMER, HERODOTUS, SOPHOCLES, PLATO, ARISTOTLE, DEMOSTHENES, CICERO, VERGIL. "That is the Butler Library. It's such a beautiful library. I love it. It's the library in my heart." He was laughing softly. "I loved that library. I like to be back here, actually."

"This was a happy place," I suggested.

"Oh my God yes!" He was smiling. "Gosh, I really miss being here." He added, "The sad thing was I didn't make many friends with students my age. It's such a lost opportunity, you know. These are people, they intellectually grow up with you."

He remembered a classmate, a woman, who had seemed to take a great interest in him, even giving him presents.

"Was she pretty?" I asked.

"Very pretty girl," he said.

I laughed. "What's the matter with you?"

"She said, 'Always when I study with you I do so well.' She was always, you know, saying, 'When we go to medical school we can apply together.'"

"Where did she go?"

"I have no idea. I never kept in touch, I never . . . I'm terrible."

I wondered whether the problem was that most of his classmates were wealthy and he wasn't.

"Well, actually I was," he replied. "I had Nancy and Charlie. I mean here." He tapped the left side of his chest.

We walked on. Inside this building was where he'd studied Chaucer. "Oh, boy. That was not easy."

And here was Philosophy Hall, an official National Historic Landmark, where John Dewey, among other luminaries, once kept an office. A casting of Rodin's *Thinker* sat on a granite pedestal out front, bronze chin on hand.

The *Thinker* bears about the same relation to sculpture as the *Mona Lisa* does to painting, or "Stopping by Woods on a Snowy Evening" to poetry—a great work of art that has become hard to see for itself, buried under banal associations and dumb jokes. But for the moment at least, the sculpture seemed renewed, a monument to the attempt at answering the kinds of questions Deo had brought through the arched doorway and up the marble stairs of Philosophy Hall. And it felt odd to be standing with Deo in front of such a monument, because the thing itself and everything it represented seemed so far removed from the source of those questions of his.

Deo's course of study had puzzled me. You'd expect a penniless immigrant to major in something marketable, like computer science. But he had taken as many philosophy courses as he could fit alongside his biochemistry major, and he'd gone on taking philosophy courses all his four years here. Some time ago I had asked him why. He had said, "I wanted to understand what had happened to me."

Since coming to the United States, Deo had read some of the history that underlay what he'd endured. But when he had arrived here at Columbia, his main interest hadn't been historical. To me, his quest sounded spiritual. How to reckon with the fact that, unlike some other genocides, the slaughters he had witnessed had been mainly low-tech mayhem, committed mostly with machetes, spears, bows and arrows? This had been true in Rwanda especially. It had been possible to kill many hundreds of thousands with hand tools only because large minorities of the population had participated. "The Belgians made a big mess, yes," Deo said to me. "But what kind of a human being are you, if you can take a machete and kill your neighbors?"

This was the kind of question he'd been hoping to get answered here in his philosophy classes, questions about the nature of good and evil, humanity and God. They arose in him, insistently, because of his continuing discomfort in the world. He had told me, for instance, "Mutaho terrorized me. Before the genocide, I probably was naïve in terms of believing people, trusting people. Now I am always trying to be very careful. We are talking about teachers killing their students, priests killing their parishioners. Who is left to trust, really? God? God the most powerful, who let everything happen?" And people here on this campus, people he did trust not to harm him, couldn't imagine what he'd witnessed. Deo had felt like a stranger, he said, among his classmates. One time, he'd told a fellow student that he'd grown up tending cows, and the other student had asked earnestly, "Did you keep the milk in the refrigerator?" He'd had experiences his classmates couldn't possibly relate to their own. He had walked around the campus wearing a pleasant smile to cover up feelings that he knew no one else could share. And on the occasions when the few close friends who knew he'd witnessed genocide asked him about what he'd been through, he didn't know how to explain. He had not yet met Paul Farmer and Joia. He had not yet told his story in full. He had thought, "There are no words." But he had begun to look for words here at Columbia.

I imagined him sitting late at night in one of Butler Library's twenty-four-hour study rooms, poring over the likes of Kant and Hume and Plato, his favorite of all the philosophers he read, looking for a means to close the gap between what he'd experienced and what he was able to say, looking for something reliable in a world that had become untrustworthy, looking for some sort of structured belief, some grand encyclopedia with an index in which he could look up "genocide" and learn where it fit in the universe. He was, I imagined, looking for an antidote to loneliness, both cosmic and personal. And needless to say, he hadn't quite found it.

I liked to think of Deo here on this lovely campus, safe and far away from horror after all that he'd endured. But that distance and safety must also, inevitably, have stood like a wall between his memories and his attempts to make sense of them. What Deo had experienced made Deo mysterious, especially here. I tried to picture him with his books on his way to philosophy classes, hurrying past the *Thinker,* several tons of gravitas that might have said to a less experienced undergraduate, "This is what thinking looks like." We didn't go inside the building. I asked him what the rooms were like.

"Very beautiful rooms," he said. He described big tables and heavy chairs and large windows.

Deo had some authority to speak about evil—far more than other undergraduates. He must have been tempted to do what he'd ended up doing at Partners In Health—to get up in a philosophy class and tell his story. This, I imagined, would have quieted the room. But he'd never done that. The closest he'd come was in the introductory course in moral philosophy.

"The instructor was a pretty young guy, pretty intense guy," Deo remembered. "He said to the class, 'Animals are not rational, only human beings are rational.' That was very interesting to me. I said, 'Well, can you explain to me how we are rational, and animals are not rational?' And the instructor said, 'Animals kill for food. They act on instinct, that's it.'"

Deo had tried to digest this. He had known cows and he had known militiamen, and for rationality he thought he'd take cows any day. All the instincts bred into him at Burundian schools warned against disputing a teacher's statements, but he couldn't help himself. He said to the instructor that his family used to have dozens of cows, each of which had a name. You could call

Yaruyange and only Yaruyange would come. How could it be said that a cow didn't think, when every cow he'd grown up with not only knew her own name but recognized her babies among all the others and knew how to take care of hers? Cows did all sorts of interesting things, and not all could be explained with a word like "instinct." How could the instructor say that all animals were stupid, that they didn't think, that they had no free will? Maybe we human beings simply didn't understand their languages. Maybe we hadn't evolved that far. Maybe animals were laughing at us. If animals killed only for food—as they usually but not always did—then they were more rational than people. What about Rwanda? What did that say about human rationality?

Rwanda was an extreme example, said the instructor, a special case.

There were about forty students in the class, all silent. "Probably they were thinking I was a little annoying," Deo said. But he couldn't stop. He kept on arguing, the class ended, he cornered the instructor in the doorway, and he went on arguing with him for another half hour. When the instructor finally said he had to catch a subway, Deo said he was going to the subway, too. "I followed him because I felt like there was no way he could convince me, because Rwanda is not a special case. It's not. Armenians, Jews, American Indians . . ."

It was a cheerful memory. In Burundi in high school, if you asked your teacher a question he couldn't answer, he was apt to make you stand outside in the rain for an hour, if not for the rest of the day. "I've been so blessed and lucky in spite of all these tragedies," Deo said. "I don't know what I would be in Burundi, even without a war, if I hadn't been exposed to this environment. I got so much here. To be able to sit in a class where people have access to so much and having teachers who love teaching, who enjoy seeing the result of their energies and their students making progress, it's not something I was used to. And that opened up my mind. At Columbia University the teachers were like colleagues."

The next time he met up with his instructor in moral philosophy, the man suggested he read Hannah Arendt on the Holocaust. As instructed, Deo read *Eichmann in Jerusalem: A Report on the Banality of Evil*. He was left asking himself, "What if the German people had said no to Hitler?" It was a question many people had asked, of course, the same he'd asked about his own people. Reading Greek mythology had left him, he told me, with a sense of the antiquity of murder and mayhem, but no real explanations. Like many other students before him, he had ended his career in philosophy feeling that he hadn't gotten answers but only more questions. The journey had been absorbing, though. "Just walking around here, you know, it keeps your mind busy, just thinking. I loved it," he said.

Before we left, Deo wanted to visit some of his favorite extracurricular spots: the benches overlooking Harlem on Morningside Drive and the Riverside Church and finally St. John the Divine, the immense unfinished Gothic cathedral in Morningside Heights, just a short walk from the campus. We sat down in a pew some distance back from the grand altar. There seemed to be a service in progress up there, but we were seated too far away to hear it. "It really blows my mind," said Deo. "The first time I was here I was taking art, and I said, 'God, if the Sistine Chapel in the Vatican is better than this . . .'" He laughed. "I mean, just look at it."

We were surrounded by towering columns. The place was vast, dark, and mysterious. We talked quietly. I had the impression it was in this place and in his other sanctuaries that Deo had reconciled his experience of genocide with his belief in God. He liked to frame his solution jocularly: "I do believe in God. I do believe in God. I think God has given so much power to people, and intelligence, and said, 'Well, you are on your own. Maybe I'm tired, I need a nap. You are mature. Why don't you look after yourselves?'" Deo would pause, then say, "And I think He's been sleeping too much."

Deo had spent a lot of time, in the classrooms and cathedrals of this rarefied piece of Manhattan, thinking about the catastrophic violence in Burundi and Rwanda. He had left Columbia believing that misery had been not the sole cause of the mayhem, but a primary cause, a precondition too often neglected by scholars: little or no education for most and, for those who did get it, lessons in brutality; toil and deprivation, hunger and disease and untimely death, including rampant infant mortality, which justified all-but-perpetual pregnancy for women until menopause. He told me, "Women get so exhausted that by the time they are thirty they walk like, you know, old ladies. And they are the ones most of the time who do the farming. At sunset, go down the hill, get water to cook. And women are not allowed to own property. . . ." He went on: "Almost everyone has got worms. They are *there* since they were born, and worms will be their friends until they die. Can you imagine that kind of life? It's terrible. How are you going to think right? With pain everywhere. So it's been really hard to blame the people who have been slaughtering each other, though I do blame people all the time. They were not themselves. They were something else."

Some histories had seemed unreal to him—for instance, the way some writers described Burundi's kings, as if they had lived like European kings, in palaces instead of wooden buildings with grass roofs. Some accounts of the violence infuriated him, in part because he thought they laid too much blame on Tutsis. Of course he saw the nightmares as he'd lived them, as a Tutsi being pursued. But he wanted to believe that most Hutus and Tutsis in both Rwanda and Burundi had been like him, "wholly innocent," and that the rest had been misled by selfish elites. And even the leaders, he imagined, were probably deeply unhappy, exercising power that had no basis except guns and machetes, so as not to become victims of power themselves, so as to survive.

Deo's stance seemed remarkable. How many people in his place would have divided up the world into good guys and bad guys,

Hutus and Tutsis, and left it at that? Not just philosophy but all his studies here had helped him find a way around self-poisoning hatred.

"Really, I trained my mind to be flexible," Deo said. "Some of the stuff I learned was, be willing to know that even when you think you know for sure, always leave room for uncertainty. And someone who always agrees with you is not necessarily your friend. You can always learn something good in a hard time, if you survive it. And there is really no mathematical formula you can follow to achieve what you want. Just trial and error."

These were truisms, things everyone should learn in college, and I liked hearing Deo say them. He had been able to bring himself back from a world gone irrational, back from militiamen to cows. It was pleasant to feel this about him in the cathedral, and pleasant to think of him sitting here alone with his thoughts in the years of his recovery. This place must have been another refuge, I thought, from that catalogue of memories and fears, especially fears for his family, which back then and even now seemed apt to open at random and all by itself in his mind.

"I can't tell you how many times I came to this St. John the Divine," he said.

"Just to sit and look and think and try to make sense of things?" I asked.

"Yes. It is so peaceful. Your mind is so open. You know, I really have been successful in finding my own peaceful corners. On my own."

THIRTEEN

Burundi,
June 2006

Deo had spent the summer of 2005 working in Rwanda, at a district hospital rebuilt by Partners In Health. While there, he had thought repeatedly, "Burundi needs hospitals like this." He had brought a couple of PIH doctors to Burundi, to visit Kayanza, where his parents had resettled, and he had begun to see how a clinic and public health system might be created in the village. Now, in June 2006, Deo was going home again. He had agreed to have me come along. He would spend most of July and August working on the underpinnings of his clinic. He and I would go a few weeks early, so he could show me the stations of his life in East Central Africa.

I had known Deo for several years by now, and had spent a large part of the past six months in his company. I had begun to know him well enough to realize there were things about him that I couldn't know. But I hoped I could get closer to an understanding by seeing Burundi and Rwanda with him.

I picked him up at his apartment in New Hampshire. Nancy and Charlie were there to see him off, Nancy making a visible effort to keep her hands still and not help Deo pack his bags. I felt a little nervous myself. Burundi's civil war had ended, but only recently. Tourist guides were still warning against travel there, and so was the State Department. A while back, Deo had sent me an article from Amnesty International with this headline: "Burundian Police Attack Journalists." I had sent him a worried email. He had written in reply, "It is very safe for us to go to Burundi." But then, in the car to Logan Airport in Boston, Deo told me this story, about the first trip he took back to Burundi, seven years after his escape:

It was late December 2001. Burundi's war still wasn't over. Friends and family, in the United States and in Burundi, urged him not to go. His lawyer, James O'Malley, was especially worried because Deo still didn't have permanent residency. But Deo had to see his parents. He would never forgive himself if they died while he was waiting for his green card. He flew from New York and arrived in Brussels on Christmas Eve. His next plane left the following morning, so he spent the night wandering around the airport, agitated and all alone except for a few security guards. French Christmas music and security announcements played over and over again. He finally took shelter in the airport chapel. It was divided into four separate chambers—Catholic, Protestant, Jewish, Muslim. He went into each and said prayers, for his family and his friends and himself. Afterward, he felt better. "So really my spirit is still alive," he remembered thinking, as if he had realized only then that his conversation with God could continue and that something important remained of the part of himself that had been grown in Burundi.

About a year before his trip, in 2000, a militia group had fired at a Belgian plane as it was landing in Bujumbura, and most long-haul flights had been discontinued. So Deo couldn't fly directly home. First he had to go from Brussels to Kigali, the capital of Rwanda. On that long plane ride he met a fellow Burundian, also on his way home, also for the first time in years. Deo had planned to fly on from Kigali to Bujumbura in a small commercial plane. His new friend planned to take the bus and wanted Deo to go with him. The bus was safer than the plane, Deo's new friend said, and from the bus they'd get a close look at their homeland. Deo was persuaded, but he couldn't get a refund for his plane ticket, and his frugality prevailed.

"I flew, he took the bus, and guess what," Deo said to me in the car. "Around three o'clock in the afternoon, the bus was attacked."

The bus had been owned by the weirdly, prophetically named Titanic Express. A Hutu militia group called FNL, a branch of PALIPEHUTU, had waylaid it. They'd ordered everyone off, sorted them out, and murdered anyone they thought was a Tutsi, twenty-one people in all, including Deo's new friend. Deo got word of the massacre at his uncle's house, in Bujumbura.

"For that whole time in Burundi I had diarrhea, fear, I threw up. I remembered how I tried hard to get a refund for the ticket, and I thought that 'God, I am in your hands.' The parents. It turns out that this guy who was killed, his parents were good friends of my uncle, and they knew that I was coming, and they called my uncle and they said, 'What happened to your nephew?' And he said, 'Well, he flew and he saw your son before.' They came to my uncle's house. All these people crying. His mom came and said, 'Which hand did you use to say goodbye?' Just smelling my hand, thinking that she could smell her son, asking me how he had seemed, what he was wearing."

I had packed a bottle of antianxiety pills, for the flights. Pretending to look for something else in my briefcase, I retrieved a tablet.

I needn't have worried. Deo and I flew that night from Boston to London. In the middle of the next night, on the leg from London to Nairobi, Deo remarked that we were passing over Khartoum. "Sudan," he said to me. "Darfur. Isn't that really crazy? People down below us now, being burned, slaughtered." Mostly, he spent the time telling me about the Burundi of his youth and about his hopes and plans for a clinic. The flights were long, one was delayed for hours, but all were uneventful. After two and a half days we were walking across the tarmac of little Bujumbura International.

Deo later told me that exhaustion from our flights had left him so addled that he was having hallucinations, imagining that he recognized terrifying faces in the airport crowd, faces of killers. But the rush of fearfulness he felt didn't show. He strode into the terminal, back into Burundi again, wearing his dark glasses and his hat—the black hat with a chin strap, the brims curved up on either side, like an Australian bush hat. He scolded a woman who cut the line at the passport control booth. In the baggage claim room, he greeted his tall, lanky, soft-spoken uncle cheerily, in a booming voice—they exchanged what I took to be the customary greeting among the men of his family, each placing hands on the other's waist and shoulder, as if they were about to hug but then thought better of it. Then Deo took charge of finding our baggage, barking orders right and left.

The comfort one gets from being with a person who knows his way around a place—I hadn't anticipated feeling this with Deo. I had known him only in his American roles, as an assistant at PIH and a medical student, and I think my first impression of him, of youth and neediness and damage, hadn't entirely worn off. Not until then. Blearily watching this slender young man in his rakish hat and sunglasses, who was carrying himself with what seemed like just the right amount of swagger—not too much to give offense but enough to get things done—I had the feeling that somewhere between the United States and East Central Africa he had become a size larger.

I slept a little at our hotel in the city, and was awakened by the sounds of an evangelist preaching through a bullhorn outside on the street. The evangelist woke up Deo, too, but I was simply puzzled by the noise, whereas Deo imagined for a moment that war had broken out again. After breakfast, he took me on a tour of the capital.

Gashes of red earth spread across the hills above Bujumbura. It looked like a city of walls. In residential areas especially, sheets of corrugated roofing metal had been placed on end to make provisional-looking barriers, all high enough to block direct gunfire, which I imagined was their purpose. The stately trees that Deo remembered on the margins of the city's grandest avenue had been cut down and replaced by billboards. In a little grassy square where one would have expected the statue of a national hero—such as the beloved Prince Rwagasore, the champion of independence who died too soon—there stood instead a giant plastic bottle of Heineken beer. Apropos of which, and of a pair of stumbling-drunk, armed policemen we'd recently passed, Deo said, "This is a country of alcoholics now."

A lot about Bujumbura felt familiar, common to the capitals of impoverished countries: the potholes, the dust and noise, the hydrocarbon haze, the close calls between pedestrians and vehicles traveling too fast—"If you drove like this in the States, you would lose your license," Deo said. "Even in New Jersey." But much was strange to me, especially the bicyclists with sheaves of fresh-cut grass heaped on their backs, processions of them bringing fodder for the herds of cows that milled around the tents and makeshift huts in the urban camps of the internally displaced. "This is so pitiful," said Deo. "I mean, cows in the city. All these are internally displaced cows. Most of the people here just say, 'Our land has been taken,' or 'We can't live next to people who killed our families.'" Here was the teeming market. "It's still a chaos. Look at this, look at all these people waiting for something, and people really cross the street without looking. This is mental retardation, right here. People simply don't care. Oh, see this cow?" The animal, being led down the street on a rope, had one long horn, but the other was missing. It must have been knocked off by a taxi, Deo said. "I mean, this is the heart of disorganization, right here."

Deo remembered, from a previous trip, taking a walk here in Bujumbura with his beloved older brother, Antoine, and coming upon a corpse. This was back during the war. The body was laid out on top of a heap of garbage. Deo had yelled at the sight, frightened and appalled. His brother had looked at the corpse and said, "What's strange here?" Then he'd looked at Deo and said, "You've been away too long."

In Bujumbura, Deo told me now, the dreadful had become normal. Just as in some troubled dreams.

His litany of passing sights went on and on: young men racing barefoot down the sidewalks in hopes of getting a little job unloading a truck; men and women and children washing themselves in the dirty water of open storm drains. Goats around gas stations; half-destroyed buildings; children playing in trash heaps; dump pickers. "All these are people who are in misery. This is another abandoned health center. It's big, totally abandoned. Public. Of course. Now it's trash. Look at the destruction. Abandoned abandoned abandoned."

He had never liked Bujumbura. Now, he said, he loathed it. The ostentatious corpulence of the well-to-do, the huge gold cross he saw hanging from the neck of a priest—"God knows how many people are dying in Congo in a bloody war for diamonds, for gold." A woman with a baby at her breast came up to our vehicle, begging. He shooed her away, she wouldn't leave, and he said angrily to her, "Next time I'll bring a stick." It is possible to hate people for their weakness. They can excite your fears about yourself. I thought that for Deo the begging woman personified the problems of his country, and his fears for it. He said, as the woman walked away, "I hate these people!" I gathered he was speaking about all his people. He paused and looked at me and said, "And of course I love them."

———

Deo had given me two cautions before our trip. He had said it would be best if I didn't take notes openly. And he had told me I

must never use the word "genocide" or the terms "Hutu" and
"Tutsi" in public.

I had done some reading on the history of those fatal names in
Rwanda and Burundi. Who were the Tutsis, the people who, most
scholars write, made up about 14 percent of the populations of both
countries? Who were the roughly 85 percent called Hutus?

There are no simple answers. For decades, ideologues of Hutu or
Tutsi supremacy have borrowed or invented myths about the origins of their ethnic groups. The real history remains uncertain,
mainly because of a lack of records. Even the composition of the
two countries' populations is, as historians say, "contested." But
there are scholarly hypotheses on the origins of the two groups, and
a great deal is known about their evolution, about how the difference between Hutus and Tutsis became lethal in Burundi and
Rwanda. These, it seemed to me as I read, are the essential facts:

Hutus and Tutsis might once have been separate peoples, maybe
several separate peoples, back in unrecorded days. By the time the
European colonists arrived, late in the nineteenth century, Hutus
and Tutsis had a great deal in common: language, religion, and for
the most part culture. (Later, they would come to look much alike
as well, at least in general.) There were many exceptions but, very
broadly speaking, the aristocracies of the kingdoms were drawn
from the populations of cow-owning Tutsis, and their inferiors or
dependents were predominantly Hutu farmers. (There was a third
group in both kingdoms, called the Twa, usually described as pyg-
mies, who made up about one percent of the populations and had
very low status.) Not all scholars agree that Hutus and Tutsis have
ever constituted "ethnic groups," but some use the term—to describe two groups that are different because they have been treated
differently and because they believe they are different.

It was the colonizers—first the Germans, then the Belgians—
who simplified what had been complex societies and made the
Hutu-Tutsi difference a paramount and rigid fact of life for Rwandans and, to a lesser degree, for Burundians. The colonizers intro-

duced a racist myth: Tutsis were Caucasians with black skin who had come from somewhere else—Ethiopia, perhaps—and civilized the native blacks, the Hutus. In effect, the Europeans altered the societies to fit that myth and to suit their main purpose, which was to make profits for themselves. The Europeans never occupied Rwanda and Burundi in large numbers. They kept their expenses down by governing indirectly. They made Tutsis (and in Burundi, both Tutsis and a small princely class) into their intermediaries. Most Tutsis didn't benefit, and no doubt many suffered. As one historian puts it, 90 percent of "ordinary Tutsis" were all but invisible to the colonists. But Hutus suffered most. Colonial administrative changes made them powerless. They were completely vulnerable to the demands of the colonizer and to the demands and depredations of the Tutsi chiefs. They were subject, among many other things, to onerous taxes, to the forced planting of certain crops, to involuntary, unpaid labor on projects designed by the Belgians and Tutsi chiefs, and to whippings for disobedience. One result of all this appears to have been periodic famines, and, in Rwanda, great resentment among Hutus, easily generalized to all Tutsis.

Burundi and Rwanda became independent again in 1962. In both countries, political struggles accompanied independence, old and new elites vying for control of the state. Ultimately, in both countries, the contests were organized around ethnicity. But the results were roughly opposite, mirrorlike. What one scholar calls a "vicious dynamic" was established, "with events in each country presenting to the other, in a kind of distorted mirror, the proof of its worst fears, its worst nightmare." In short, Rwanda and Burundi accentuated each other's path toward mass violence.

In Rwanda, Hutus took power. The "Hutu Revolution" grew increasingly bloody. Small attacks by Tutsis in exile led to larger and larger reprisals by the new Hutu authorities. Thousands of Tutsis were killed. By the middle 1960s, something like 140,000 Rwandan Tutsis had fled to neighboring countries. Ethnic violence lent strength both to Tutsi supremacists in exile and to ideologues of Hutu power, ascendant inside Rwanda. Ironically enough, each side adopted parts of the European colonists' racist myth. To the Tutsi supremacists, God and nature had chosen them to rule the inferior race of Hutus. To the ideologues of Hutu power, Tutsis were an alien race that had conquered the Hutus, stolen their lands, and held them in bondage. After a coup in 1973, a new Rwandan military government allowed Tutsis a small role in politics. Some Tutsis prospered economically. But they remained potential scapegoats, available when needed.

In Burundi, by contrast, the postcolonial political struggles weren't ethnic. Not at first. In Burundi, social divisions had long been more complex and the barriers among them more permeable than in Rwanda. In Burundi, it was mainly the small princely class, called the *ganwa,* whose members fought each other for power when the Belgians left. But that fight led to the assassination of Prince Rwagasore, the newly elected prime minister, immensely popular with both Tutsis and Hutus. In his absence, politics devolved into struggles among the old and a new elite, among ganwa and Hutu and Tutsi, and the struggles gradually became infected by events in Rwanda. During the Hutu Revolution, many Rwandan Tutsis fled across the border into northern Burundi. The refugees and the example of the new Rwandan state terrified Tutsi elites. They feared the loss of power and privilege at best, pogroms and exile at worst. And the Rwandan example whetted the appetites of some of Burundi's Hutu elites.

The terms of Burundi's political competition became simplified into Hutu versus Tutsi. Attempted coups and killings were perpetrated by both sides. Eventually, a faction of Tutsis deposed the king and took control. Over the next twenty-seven years, from 1966 to 1993, three Tutsi military governments ruled Burundi. Power changed hands, through coups, but its geography remained the same. All three of Burundi's unelected presidents came from the same town. Two of them were cousins.

Rwanda and Burundi had a lot in common, linguistically, histori-
cally, culturally. And from the early 1970s until the early 1990s,
their governments also looked similar. Both were military dictator-
ships. Both were dominated by cliques from a small region. Each
clique ruled for its own benefit, mainly, and used repression and violence and forms of ethnic politics to hold on to power. That is,
both countries looked like versions of the colonial state.

But they also differed, fundamentally. Indeed, they could stand
as a textbook case against the notion that countries are shaped by
the intrinsic qualities of their people. In these two cases at least, the
shaping was done by the competition for power and privilege
among a relative few.

In Rwanda, it was competition among Hutus. The winners practiced self-serving government while claiming to represent the majority. For this, anti-Tutsi prejudice was essential. The government
portrayed itself as a bulwark against the return of alien, Tutsi hege-
mony, the ever-present threat, which events in Burundi made entirely plausible.

Burundi's Tutsi military rulers couldn't claim to represent the
ethnic majority, of course. So they found it expedient to claim that
ethnicity was a colonial invention, that all Burundians were just Burundians, equal in the eyes of the law. An enlightened-sounding position, completely at odds with the fact that discrimination against
Hutus—and indeed against many Tutsis—was the rule, in education
and business, in the army and the institutions of government. To
maintain their power, the various military governments resorted
to violence, considerably more violence than in Rwanda, until the
1990s. The pattern of bloody Hutu uprisings and even bloodier repressions by the army reached its height in the slaughter of 1972. This
was much more than a reprisal. It was, as one historian writes, a
state-sponsored "selective genocide," clearly designed to eliminate all
potential Hutu leaders, even including children in secondary school.

The massacre lasted two months. At least 100,000 Hutus were murdered, not a few, it seems, in ingeniously horrible ways. About 150,000 fled, many across the border to Rwanda. The mass killings of Hutus in Burundi reaffirmed long-standing fears and anti-Tutsi prejudice among Rwandan Hutus, further strengthened the position of the ruling faction, and inspired massacres of Rwandan Tutsis and more flights of Tutsi refugees into Burundi. This in turn justified, for some Burundian Tutsis, both the slaughter of '72 and continuing discrimination against Hutus. Meanwhile, Hutu and Tutsi refugees outside Burundi and Rwanda became some of the principal and angriest keepers of the memories of massacre and injustice, and their camps became staging areas for opposition movements—most consequentially, settlements of Rwandan Tutsis in Uganda and of Burundian Hutus in Tanzania. Each group's fear of the other ethnic group had long since become a justified reality for everyone in both countries and, in both, a tool for those in power.

From 1972 until 1988, the years of Deo's childhood and adolescence, Burundi looked fairly calm on the surface. The military government and its supporters referred to the bloodbath of '72 as "the events." International donors seemed content with the euphemism and continued sending development aid, crucial to the very existence of the government and, of course, a principal source of wealth for the few. But the apparent calmness rested on fear. For years, it is said, "the events" had left many Hutu families afraid even to send their children to school. As for the top dogs in the government, it may be axiomatic that those who rule by fear also rule in fear. The government tightened its control over every aspect of the country's life. It also made a shambles of the economy, among other ways by creating a bunch of new state-owned enterprises and with them new opportunities for cronyism and corruption.

The seeming calm ended in 1988, with the revolt and army repression that caused Deo and his family to spend a week or so hiding in the woods. For once, international donor nations responded. Facing losses of foreign aid, among many other problems, Burundi's president instituted reforms, bringing a number of Hutus into the government. The elections five years later, in 1993, were widely praised by outside observers, but they also represented a grave threat to Burundian Tutsis with positions in the middle and lower levels of the government. Many lost their jobs soon after Ndadaye took power, and the loss of a job often meant rejoining the impoverished masses. For many Tutsis, and many in the military, an end to Tutsi control of the army seemed imminent, and to them this represented an even more dire threat. What followed, of course, was the assassination of President Ndadaye (and of the president and vice president of the National Assembly), the beginning of Deo's long flight, and Burundi's civil war.

According to rough estimates, about fifty thousand Burundians died in the violence of 1993, Hutus and Tutsis in roughly equal numbers, most of them civilians. After a period of maneuvering, Tutsi politicians reclaimed power, and the war went on, growing wider. For the most part it was waged between the Tutsi army and various Hutu militias, with most of the population caught in the crossfire. Burundians, it seems important to say, are no more or less inclined to violence than other human beings. Only 3 percent of the country's young men joined armed movements during the war.

A virtual library of treatises on the Rwandan genocide has been published, and a relative handful on Burundi. As I read, I felt drawn especially to the work of Peter Uvin, a scholar with long experience in both countries. In several articles and in separate books about each country, he attempts a synthesis not just of the events that led up to catastrophic violence, but also of the political, social, and economic forces at work. While careful to say that no single factor can explain each country's violence, he tries to depict the essential settings of the slaughters—that is, the lives of the peasant majorities.

For this, Uvin borrows the term "structural violence." Violence, that is, of the quotidian kind, the physical and psychological violence of poverty, the type of violence that had surrounded Deo all through his childhood and adolescence. Hunger and disease and untimely death. Exclusion from the means to a better life, especially exclusion from secondary school and college. And examples of what the peasant majority was being excluded from—portly men in suits, foreign development workers and their privileged Burundian and Rwandan counterparts riding through dirt towns in suvs. I thought of Deo's descriptions of easy arrogance among fellow high school and university students. There was the violence of widespread unemployment, the plight of many young men who were prime recruits for armies and militias. There was rampant and blatant corruption, and complete impunity for those who practiced it—and impunity also for the soldiers who killed and the officers who gave them their orders.

In his book about Burundi, Uvin describes what he calls "the micro-politics" of the country's long war, not just the competition for power among national elites, but the facts of life in urban neighborhoods and on rural hills. The justified grievances of the Hutu majority. The increasing segregation of the two ethnicities, and the ever-growing fear between them, which made violence, especially preemptive violence, a rational strategy for self-defense. The ability and willingness of local elites to organize and foment violence. Uvin writes: "In societies where the rule of law is close to nonexistent and security forces are neither effective nor trusted, small groups of people willing to use violence can create enough chaos and fear to force everyone into making violent choices."

The Rwandan genocide was a carefully planned case of scapegoating, launched by a government of the majority against a powerless minority. Burundi's mass violence was an ethnic civil war between a minority government and rebels drawn from the majority, a war between two equally powerful armed factions. In Rwanda, ordinary people killed mainly out of prejudice. In Burundi, it was mainly out of fear. These were different catastrophes, Uvin insists, not to be conflated. But they had essential ingredients

in common: "Social exclusion and the ethnicization of politics . . . are the two central elements to violent conflict in Burundi
and Rwanda that, like electrons, spin around a core of massive
poverty and institutional weakness."

———

Rwanda's genocide began in April 1994, and ended about four
months later, in July, after the Rwandan Patriotic Front had conquered most of the country. Estimates of the dead vary, from
around 500,000 to a million; most split the difference and put the
number at around 800,000. Some two million Hutus fled the country. Many of the killers went with them, carrying their weapons. By
2006, most of the refugees had returned, forced back by the government of Tanzania and by civil war in what was then called Zaire.
Since the end of the genocide, leaders of the RPF had ruled Rwanda.
The RPF's former commanding general, Paul Kagame, was now
Rwanda's president. Criticism, indeed condemnation, of Kagame's
government was widespread, but far from universal. By the time I
set out with Deo, Rwanda was said to have achieved a stable
peace—or, as the critics might have said, an absence of war.

Burundi's tragedy was less notorious but much more prolonged.
It continued through the 1990s and into the new millennium.
Rather early on, a host of African and Western countries initiated
peace negotiations. After four years, an agreement was signed, but
the fighting went on. Actually, it may have increased, because the
principal Hutu rebel groups weren't included in the talks. It took
another three years for the largest rebel organization to sign on.
Wrangling over the fine points and negotiations with the second
largest group, the PALIPEHUTU/FNL, were still dragging on when
Deo flew home to Burundi for a visit, his fourth trip back, in 2004.

He went via Nairobi. During his layover there, he ran across half
a dozen of the Burundian peace negotiators. He recognized many of
them from photographs. Following at a distance, he watched the
group go en masse into the airport liquor store, laughing and slap-

ping each other on the back—a bunch of men in suits, Hutu and
Tutsi, who seemed like the very best of friends. Deo flew to Bujumbura on the same plane as the negotiators, and he watched those
men transform themselves into stage enemies when they entered the
airport and faced the press. "They arrived and everyone was arguing. It was, 'No, we didn't agree on that,'" Deo remembered. "And
they are fighting with each other like desperate pigs." He had felt indignant at the spectacle. He described it indignantly to me, and I
thought this was remarkable, that politics as usual could still sur-
prise and disappoint him. In spite of all he'd been through, I
thought, he still hadn't acquired the reflex of cynicism.

But Burundi's transition to peace had succeeded in spite of extraordinary obstacles. In 2005 a new constitution was ratified. It
provided for multiethnic government. The largest of the Hutu rebel
groups won the elections that followed, but it had by then become
a multiethnic party, and the new president, a former Hutu militia
leader, had pledged an end to ethnic war. When Deo and I arrived in
Bujumbura, curfews were still observed, and there were reports of
sporadic fighting between the government and the PALIPEHUTU/FNL,
which still hadn't agreed to terms. But there were reasons for optimism. Most important, all militias except the FNL had been demo-
bilized and the army and police had been fully integrated. Each was
half Hutu and half Tutsi, a great measure of security for all Burundians.

International diplomatic efforts at peacemaking had been inge-
nious, even daring. Attempts at rebuilding the country had been less
impressive so far. According to Peter Uvin, international aid work
had fallen back into its old uncoordinated patterns. The total
amount of foreign assistance came to about $300 million a year.
This was considerably less than Rwanda was receiving. It represented most of Burundi's national budget, and a lot of the money
wasn't going to ordinary people but, as Uvin writes, to "experts,
consultants, managers."

Since the onset of civil war, Burundi's per capita gross domestic product had fallen from roughly $180 per year to about $80, the lowest in the world, and of course that paltry figure understated the general penury. In 2003 a United Nations agency had attempted to rank countries by the suffering of their women and children; Burundi was among the bottom five. More recently, Burundi had been designated one of the world's three worst countries in which to do business.

This last conclusion seemed unfair to the general population, famously diligent and hungry for jobs. Burundians, Deo believed, were also hungry for peace—a notion borne out emphatically in Uvin's book. Reading Uvin's postwar research, I felt that in many ways Deo embodied the general feeling of Burundians: far from declaring despair for the future, but also far from being able to forget. According to some estimates, 100,000 had died in the war. Another said 200,000, still another 300,000. If you read too many numbers like those, they begin to take on a pornographic quality—all those lives turned into integers, the bigger the more titillating, and the more abstract.

FOURTEEN

Burundi,
June 2006

We left Bujumbura for several days and drove into the high country, where we stopped again and again so Deo could gaze at the yellow top of Ganza and snap at least one hundred pictures of it. And then one morning we drove farther into the country, toward Deo's birthplace. The roads went up and up through the mountains of his childhood, and the day grew sunnier, windier, cooler. Vistas widened. Now and then we had to stop to let herds of cows go by, their long horns nearly scraping the windows of our vehicle, Deo and our driver declaring like old codgers that cow horns weren't what they used to be. We passed a hut with a Coca-Cola sign on a wall. "Coca-Cola can reach here, but not medicines," said Deo. He laughed. Several American friends of his—three medical students, a young PIH doctor—had arrived to help with Deo's clinic project and had joined us on this side trip. One of them wondered if the World Health Organization might not enlist the services of Coke. After that, Deo grew increasingly quiet.

It was on the last ascent, on a single-lane dirt road, that I first heard the word *gusimbura*. When Deo warned me not to speak the name of his dead friend Clovis, I heard the more general warning that *gusimbura* implied: that reviving painful memories was worse than inconsiderate. Deo had stayed away from his "hill," from his hometown and its neighborhood, for almost fourteen years. Maybe he was also warning himself, or trying to brace himself for what he knew was coming.

We stopped first in Sangaza, the town where he had gone to elementary school. We walked toward the schoolhouse, across what had been the cemetery of his childhood. I wondered if we were walking over Clovis's grave, but Deo couldn't remember its location, and all the wooden crosses had vanished. It was just a lumpy pasture now—owned, Deo said, by someone from Bujumbura— which meant that people from around here had to carry their dead a great distance now.

We walked slowly on toward the schoolhouse. Classes were over for the year, the place deserted. The building looked shabbier than he remembered, but otherwise much the same. He pointed through an open window of the fourth-grade classroom, at a sheaf of eucalyptus switches, standing upright in the corner beside the teacher's desk.

Then we headed toward Butanza. It had been thirteen years since his parents had abandoned the place, but many relatives still lived there, including his grandmother, whom he planned to see, of course. We went on foot, Deo leading the way along the paths he had taken as a schoolboy, the paths and scenery largely unchanged, except that the bald hilltop had been replanted in pine trees, and there were no chimps or monkeys anymore.

His grandmother's appearance was a little delayed. She'd grown wary of visitors, Deo had been warned. "Every time she sees someone coming, she's afraid he's bringing bad news. She will say, 'Go and ask what he's bringing,' before she'll meet a person entering the compound." But in a moment, on the arm of a young girl, she came tottering out, a tiny woman covered from head to toe in colorful cloth so that only her weathered face was visible. She had bright, observant eyes. She hugged her grandson and asked him why it had taken him so long to come.

He was visiting Grandmom, but the occasion wasn't as joyous as the Burundian saying implied. Deo towered over her, his arm around her. He was laughing softly. I thought he was on the verge of tears. I imagined Lonjino was probably there in his mind, as an absence, but for once I knew better than to *gusimbura* him and ask.

Deo had wanted to return to Butanza unannounced, but it seemed as though half the village was waiting for him when we arrived. Every relative still living in the area, and some who seemed to have become relatives since he'd been away, crowded in on him. One after the other, they recited their troubles. An elderly cousin of Lonjino's grasped Deo's hand and said what all the others were indirectly saying: "Give me money. Help me."

Deo escaped up the steep slope of the mountain Runda. "Gosh, I think this is the first time I took this trip in shoes." He pointed to a hillside, a rocky outcropping, the place where Clovis had begun to die, and he lingered at the site of his family's hut, a patch of shrubs in the middle of a pasture. More than a decade of rainy seasons had washed away the ashes of the house. He turned and walked uphill toward a piney woods, but then turned back again and gazed toward the site of the old homestead.

It was getting on toward evening, the shadows of the trees lengthening onto the grassland. Deo was saying that life up here was "harsh," the soil poor, the journeys steep and long just to gather water, and never mind the distances they'd covered taking cows to summer pastures. And then it was as if the words he was speaking carried his thoughts across one of nature's narrow boundaries, like the line between rain and snow. He smiled. "You know, I really love it up here in the evening. It's so quiet and cool and the stars are already out. I remember the first time I saw *étoiles filantes*. What's the English name? Shooting stars. I went running to my father, frightened. 'There's fire coming from the sky!' "

Deo was still smiling as we started back down the mountain, and then the spell was broken.

A couple of boys had been following our little party—out of curiosity, I'd imagined wrongly. Now each in turn sidled up to Deo and told him that their mothers wanted private audiences. Deo turned to me, issuing orders for a quick getaway: "When we get back to Butanza, get right in the car. Tell the others."

He didn't blame the people here. How could they know that back in Iburaya he was just a student with a pocketful of debts? He'd known that this would happen. It was one reason he had stayed away so long. Afterward I asked whether he had told himself he would never come back to Butanza, and whether, now that he had, he regretted his return. He allowed as how the whole experience had been painful, that it was tempting to reject all the obligations of family, and even of affection, and to become a loner in the world, never setting foot in one's old life. But he had tried that strategy, during his first months in New York and often in his mind since then, and had always found it wanting. "It's more painful than 'I'm me, and I come from here,'" he said.

The previous summer, when Deo was working at the PIH hospital in Rwanda, a patient had arrived with a painfully enlarged spleen. The cause was not mysterious; untreated bouts of malaria often lead to splenomegaly. But around the swelling in the patient's abdomen there were several round burn marks, and these puzzled the American doctors. Deo recognized them at once. Someone in the patient's family, probably the father, had heated the end of a metal pipe and applied it to the place that hurt. Deo's own father had done this to him as a boy, applying the red-hot end of a spear around an abscess on Deo's thigh. The pain of the burns, and the hatred he felt toward his father, had obscured the pain of the abscess—temporarily.

"Distracting pain with pain," Deo called this practice. It was common among peasants in Rwanda and Burundi, who had little access to pharmacology but a lot of experience with pain. It was a gruesome and harmful form of palliation, and for Deo it expressed a psychological truth with broad application—that pains exist in layers, with the most excruciating at the top obscuring the pains beneath. So many years of paying attention to the topmost pain of war, he felt, had left many of his people numb to all the rest. In his country now, any death that wasn't violent was accounted "a good death," he said.

I remembered this idea many times while we were traveling in Burundi.

We stayed several days in the mountains of Bururi province. On one afternoon, Deo and his young American friends scaled a cliff beside a waterfall. Deo still relished a hike—against all odds, I would have thought. Above another waterfall and another cliff, he and his party of hikers came upon a settlement of six Tutsi families. Deo had to fend off one of their bulls—"Of course, being a cowboy, I knew how to handle it." He spoke with some of the settlers. They told him they had fled the civil war with their cows and seedlings and ended up there on their mountaintop, in splendid isolation, beyond the reach of any road or even trail. "It's beautiful up there," Deo said, and I wondered if, for a moment, he envied them.

On another day we visited the Séminaire du Buta, a Catholic high school in that mountainous region, one of the best secondary schools in Burundi, and a significant place to Deo's family. It was here, in 1997, that one of his brothers had been killed. (Another brother had narrowly escaped.) This was just the sort of thing one didn't talk about, at least not in Deo's family. He didn't tell me that he had lost a brother at the school, not until after we had visited the place. Even then, he didn't talk about that brother, not what he remembered about him, not what they had done together, nothing. The only things Deo conveyed were affection for him and grief—via silence, as I understood that silence.

An old friend of Deo's family gave us our tour, Abbé Zacharie Bukuru, a tall, broad-shouldered priest. He had been the school's director back in 1997. In the midst of the civil war, brutal on all sides, Zacharie had pulled off something remarkable. He'd managed to make peace within the student body.

He had forbidden the students their radios. Night after night he had cloistered them and let them talk, intervening only now and then to limit the invective between the Hutu and the Tutsi boys. The proof that this had worked arrived in a dreadful way. "Hutu, Tutsi were everywhere here together, praying together. We were an example of unity," Zacharie told me. He added, "They wanted—how do you say in English—*eradicate* this example of living together." By "they" he meant the contingent of rebel Hutu militia which, on the morning of April 30, 1997, came out of the mountains and descended on the school, like the wolf on the fold.

The soldiers busted open the doors to the dormitory, and their commander—weirdly enough, a Rwandan woman, a veteran of that genocide—ordered the students to divide themselves: "Hutu brothers over here, Tutsi cockroaches there." The Hutus would not abandon their schoolmates. The soldiers tried to kill them all. It was said that some of the dying boys quoted Jesus on the cross, crying out to God to forgive their killers because they didn't know what they were doing. There were 150 students at the school. Some were wounded, and many escaped. Deo's brother, the one who survived, the one he could talk about, had climbed down a rope ladder; he got away with a minor injury to his foot and a grave wound to his psyche. In all, forty students were murdered.

Zacharie had been the militia's main target. I didn't ask him how he'd managed to escape. I had the strong impression that he had long been asking himself that question and all its corollaries. He simply began to tell me the story. (Zacharie was at ease in several languages, but not in English, which he spoke out of courtesy to me.)

He was in his bedroom when he heard the first shots. "I said, 'God, what happened?' I said, 'Oh, my children, what can I do?' I wanted to go out, to get to them, to protect them. Then I heard the second gun." He imitated the sound of a heavy machine gun.

He had hidden in the storeroom behind his office. He took Deo and me there. "I was dead! Try to imagine. There was three hundred soldiers here outside. There was perhaps five hundred altogether. They were drunk. Can you imagine? Was terrible. Inferno. They shattered this wall. We have repaired it."

He took us to the memorial, forty crypts painted magenta outside a small chapel. Portraits of the murdered boys were painted on a wall above the altar. "Oh, my poor boys," Zacharie said in a squeaky voice, a choked parody of his deep baritone.

I stared at the faces of the dead students. "You know, Zacharie, just looking at them, I can't tell you which ones were Tutsis, which Hutus."

"Exactly!" said Deo in a loud whisper. Evidently, one was supposed to whisper here. "And neither could the killers!"

"The killers couldn't see the difference, too," whispered Zacharie. "So they ask. Because they can't tell. We are the same people."

Zacharie had presided over the school for two more years, then had retreated to a monastery in France. Homesickness had brought him back. He had arranged for the construction of a small monastery near the school. The building had just been completed. He took us there and gave me a copy of the book he'd written: *Les quarante jeunes martyrs de Buta (Burundi 1997): Frères à la vie, à la mort* ("The Forty Young Martyrs of Buta: Brothers in Life, in Death"). He would spend the rest of his days here, he said. "Praying for the world and for Burundi. I will live here, praying, working, studying. In silence."

FIFTEEN

Burundi,
2006

We had to go to Mutaho. It was the place where Deo's flight had begun, another place he had not revisited. The last he'd seen of Mutaho was on the night of October 22, 1993, when he was running away from it. He had heard a rumor, though, that the former hospital there, the hospital where he'd worked and boarded, had been completely demolished either during or after the war. Supposedly, a new hospital had been erected in the place of the old and bloodied one. If all this was true, no trace would remain of the massacre that he'd escaped all those years ago. But we should make the trip anyway, Deo said.

I had located Mutaho on my map of Burundi. It lay about a third of the length of the country away from our hotel in Bujumbura—that is, we'd be covering about a third of a piece of land roughly the size of Maryland or Belgium. The route looked fairly direct. But our driver said that some of the roads I saw on the map had become dead ends or vanished altogether in the war.

Our driver's name was Innocent. He was another old friend of Deo's family. Like many other Burundians, Tutsi and Hutu, Innocent had lost his wife and children during the civil war. He had met a woman who had also lost her family, and who had been raped by an HIV-positive soldier. Innocent had married her. She had died asking his forgiveness for having given him AIDS. Innocent had told Deo simply, "I miss her so much." Innocent was, I had come to think, completely trustworthy. A careful driver, at least by Burundian standards, judicious, and calm. Innocent said the trip to Mutaho would take about three hours. If we got an early start, we would make it back to the hotel before dark, he said. To me this seemed important. The police were still closing the principal roads from nightfall into the morning.

But we got started an hour later than planned. Then we had to make stops in downtown Bujumbura, to change money and to buy oil and gas. By the time we cleared the outskirts of the city and were riding into the mountains, I felt a little nervous. Would we get lost? Would we make it back before the main roads were closed? Would we run into another impromptu police roadblock, as we had a few days ago? We'd been held up for the better part of an hour while Deo negotiated the bribe.

Deo appeared to be worried, too, but for different reasons.

"Last night I know that I slept, but I had nightmares."

He sat in the front seat. I was in back.

"Well, listen," I said, "if Mutaho starts to really get to you, we just get the hell out of there."

"It's okay."

"I don't care about stopping and seeing some new hospital."

"Let's just see what . . ." His voice died away. He said he'd learned last night that an old childhood friend had been killed. "I didn't know that he was killed." He examined a wad of dog-eared, sweat-stained Burundian francs, murmuring, "They come from dirty pockets and dirty hands. These bills . . ." His voice was soft, a bit raspy, far away: "I didn't know he got killed. But I believe it, of course. I need really to try, to see how many people are still . . . It would be much easier to find out the number of people who are my old friends who are still alive, than to look for the number who have been killed."

A near accident on the road up ahead made me cry out.

Deo sounded half asleep. His voice sounded different today, slow and heavy, as if it were hard to lift. "You know what it is? They are all crazy."

I gazed out at the mountain scenery and talked about bricks. Deo was very interested in bricks—where he could get the best for the least money, for the medical buildings he planned to erect in Kayanza. We passed children dressed in what had been flour sacks, full of holes. It was amazing what bicyclists on these roads carried on their backs and on the frames of their rickety machines—huge bags of charcoal, enormous arrays of jerry cans filled with palm oil, a wooden bed frame. Wherever the road ascended, we'd see half a dozen bicyclists holding on to the backs of trucks. Many riders were half naked, dressed only in dirty shorts and flip-flops. We passed one wearing no shoes at all. Deo gazed out at them. "People who have to live like that, how can they refuse to kill someone?" I knew he only half believed this, and that I shouldn't respond.

We drove an hour or more on the main road that rises from the plain of Bujumbura, the two-lane paved road that runs all the way north through Rwanda. The road clung to mountainsides. Some of the pavement was crumbling at the edges. Parts had been blown up years before, and rough dirt detours, carved deeper into the hillsides, still served. When we turned due east, at a town called Bugarama, the traffic thinned, the woods by the road deepened, the air cleared. We were in high country again, more than a mile high now. "So you see it's different. The smell of the mountains, fresh smell. This area is wonderful," Deo said.

I tried to make some small talk. It came out sounding idiotic. "On your escape, did you ever come to places where you saw spectacular views?"

"No," he said. "I was not paying attention to that."

We rode on in silence for a while. Then he said, "This is an area that I passed through, but I don't remember exactly where." He gazed out his side window. I heard him murmur, "I am so scared."

We didn't talk much the rest of the way. When we crossed the Mubarazi River, Deo made a sound like a stifled cry. This was the river he'd crossed twice the first morning of his escape from Mutaho. I remembered his telling me how he had followed the Mubarazi's valley, strewn with corpses, all of his first full day on the run. He had followed the valley almost to the town of Kibimba. We were entering the outskirts of Kibimba now. Up ahead, beside the road, stood an odd-looking construction: three tiers of square pillars in concentric semicircles, holding up simple friezes. On the front of the foremost frieze, block letters read, "PLUS JAMAIS ÇA!"—"Never again!" Deo told Innocent to pull over beside it.

"This is one of the rare, rare memorial sites," said Deo. It stood across the road from the school he'd seen burning, the school where his cousin Geneviève had been, above the valley where he'd felt as though he were wading through corpses. The school's headmaster had organized the slaughter of the Tutsi students, and had been hanged for it, Deo told me. The memorial's white pillars were streaked with what looked like black mold. Weeds were sprouting among the flat stones in the courtyard out front.

Innocent drove on. At Gitega, Burundi's second city—I hardly noticed the place, and Deo didn't have much to say about it—we turned north onto an orange dirt road.

"My stomach's really feeling bad," Deo said.

I sensed he wasn't talking to me, but I felt I had to respond. "Do you want to go back?" My voice, I'm afraid, sounded hopeful.

"No. No, no, no, no."

"Are you sure?"

"Yes," he said. He added, "I'm going to shut up."

Now he was keeping his word. We rode along mostly in silence. The orange dirt road must have been graded recently. It felt smooth, too smooth, as if we were traveling a little distance above the ground, the SUV sliding around corners like a small plane in the wind. For me, everything began to seem like too much of something—the road too orange, the dust too thick in my nose, the silence too prolonged. I had the feeling that this trip was taking us too far into something and that if I looked back I might see the road closing up behind us. I leaned forward and told Deo, "Maybe we should just go back."

He turned a little toward me, and said, rather sternly, "You may not see the ocean, but right now we are in the middle of the ocean, and we have to keep swimming." It was his way of telling me to shut up. I tried to obey. Now and then he made terse comments: "This is a nightmare area. Many militiamen came from here." "We are passing the road to Bugendena." (I remembered his story of finding the slaughtered family, around dawn, in a village near Bugendena.) "There is the valley of the Mubarazi again." Huge eucalyptus trees lined the sides of the road. We passed a bunch of brick houses, half fallen down, greenery poking up through the remnants of their roofs. "I don't know what I was thinking when I came here," Deo said, as if to himself. He meant back when he was a medical student and had asked to be sent to Mutaho's hospital. He pointed to our left, toward the valley that sloped down from the road, a brushy-looking landscape, the place where his long flight had begun. "I went down here." He added, in a murmur, "Trying to be as quiet as I could."

"To get away from the road?"

"Yes, exactly."

A little farther on, Innocent turned onto a well-tended dirt road, passed through a flimsy gate, and stopped. Up ahead lay the remnants of the hospital. It had not been demolished and replaced after all. Much of what had been here thirteen years ago was gone, but a piece of the original remained, as it happened the very piece in which Deo had lived. And the remnant, a bunch of one-story concrete buildings, had evidently been repaired and repainted, from white to a mustardy yellow. Deo sat silently, staring at the buildings through the windshield. Just then a man crossed our field of vision, paying no attention to us. A farmer perhaps, and he was carrying a brand-new machete, its blade still encased in clear plastic.

"Oh, my God," murmured Deo in English, his voice barely audible. Then he spoke to Innocent in Kirundi. "Look at that."

Deo translated Innocent's response for me: "Maybe this is one of the machetes left over."

"Don't say that, Innocent," Deo answered.

Innocent, it seemed to me, had an abundance of sangfroid, but he knew the history of this place and he had reason to be spooked by the sight of machetes. So he called the man over for a chat, just to ease his own mind, just to make sure, I think, that this was merely a farmer and not a malevolent apparition.

About half a dozen people were sitting on a concrete ledge in front of the hospital. They were staring at us. "So what are we going to do here?" I asked Deo.

He didn't seem to hear me. He had been gazing out the windshield with the lassitude of the bedridden, a little slumped in his seat, a little slack-jawed, and now it was as if he'd been shocked back to action. He sat up. He looked different from any version of Deo I'd known, not so much confident as fierce, under his jaunty black bush hat, in his aviator-style dark glasses. He leaned out the side window and called to the people sitting in front of the hospital. *"Amahoro! Mura kome?"* "Peace! How are you?"

He opened his door. As he closed it behind him, he said, "At this moment, I *don't care*. I want to go inside."

He wasn't speaking to me. I tried to get his attention. "Well, I do care, Deo. So . . ." But he wasn't listening.

A young man came up to us, the person in charge of the facility. The people who worked for him called him "the doctor." ("He's

not," Deo told me. "He's a nurse. He has a tenth-grade education.")
Deo addressed "the doctor" in a friendly, executive way, like a man
giving orders who knows they'll be obeyed. He told "the doctor"
we had come from the United States to look at hospitals, with an
eye to learning more about nutrition programs.

"The doctor" led us inside. I had been struck by the tidiness of
the facility's exterior, its swept grounds, its good repair. The innards
were something else altogether, a warren of narrow interior hallways, empty and echoing, open at their ends to the outdoors. The
walls were streaked with bird shit. From somewhere outside came
the bleating of a goat. There was a screeching of birds, amplified by
the tall narrow concrete walls, and a flock of what looked like spar-
rows flew over our heads. I looked up. Dozens of wasps' nests hung
just overhead, suspended from the high concrete ceilings on immensely long, weblike tethers. I remembered a phrase from the Gos-
pel of Matthew: "Whited sepulchres." ("Whited sepulchres, which
indeed appear beautiful outward, but are within full of dead men's
bones.") I had seen a photograph of a hallway of this hospital taken
after the massacre, with a burned body in the foreground, the whole
picture dark purple in my memory. "What are we doing?" I said to
Deo.

He didn't answer. He was chatting with "the doctor" and trying
the handles of metal doors, opening one door after another, onto
identical-looking rooms, all empty of patients. In several there was
a rusty bed frame but no mattress. In one, there was a cylindrical
piece of equipment, some sort of medical device that clearly hadn't
been used in years—I didn't look at it closely. I felt as if I were holding my breath against the moment when we would get out of there.
Deo was trying another door handle, his false smile for "the doctor" gone for the moment, an alert, angry look passing over his
face. The door wouldn't open. He turned to me, looked me in the
eyes, then looked at the doorknob. I didn't understand right away
that he was showing me his former room, the place where he'd left

his door open and death had passed him by. It was just as well I didn't get his meaning. As it was, I was having a hard time hanging on to a pretense of equanimity.

Deo had tried to describe his nightmares to me. In the telling, they hadn't seemed unusual. Everyone has bad dreams. Even the most sheltered are chased by bogeymen from time to time. Up until now I hadn't fully understood the difference: that even his most lurid dreams weren't weirder or more frightening than what inspired them. He didn't wake up from his nightmares thankful they weren't real. Now, for the first time, I thought I could imagine what it might have been like for him during some of those nights in the comfy Black Hole in SoHo. At the moment, in that corridor of the fake hospital—all that money spent on fixing up an empty shell in a country full of illness—everything felt eerie in the worst sense. It was as if I were looking around inside a dream of Deo's, a dream I was in, and looking around at the cause of the dream simultaneously.

This was a place of unreason, and at the moment I had no faith at all in the power of reason against it. Part of the problem, I think, was that for the moment I didn't trust Deo. The smile he turned on "the doctor" was radiant. I'd never seen him so angry.

Why were there no patients in the hospital? Deo asked.

"The doctor" replied that people had felt reluctant to come here since "the crisis."

La Crise had become the common euphemism for the civil war, the euphemism favored by many Burundians when speaking to strangers, because if you used a more descriptive term you might reveal your ethnicity and which side you'd been on. Oh? Deo said, the light from his smile flaring. What "crisis" was that?

"The doctor" frowned. He must have sensed we weren't the people Deo had said we were. In any case, he had stopped smiling. Deo didn't seem to care. "Do you want to take a picture?" he asked me.

"No," I said. "I left my camera in the car." I muttered, "Let's get out of here." At any moment, I imagined, "the doctor" would go off and bring back who knew what.

Deo didn't seem to hear me. He was telling me what "the doctor" had told him, that the place had been renovated back in 2000.

"I see that it's functioning really well," I replied.

"And the whole thing is empty," Deo went on. We were standing on a concrete porch now, facing an interior courtyard, open to the sun. There was a tree in the middle, and grass. Deo said, "This is where I was. This courtyard was full of bodies. I came out here, and I went this way."

"I think we should go, Deo."

"Yah," he said. But he went on talking, in a low and ruminating voice: "It was much bigger than this. But the site . . . They replaced the windows. Around here, right here, this ground was covered with bodies. I was right here. Around here on these grasses, packed with bodies. They were really just coming down these hallways and knocking down the doors and killing the people inside."

"Let's go back to Bujumbura," I said.

"Mura koze." Deo was thanking "the doctor." Innocent had pulled the car up closer to the building. He had also opened the doors. Clearly, he too was eager to leave. I climbed in. Deo climbed in. Then Deo got out again, with his camera. He strode away and started taking pictures. "The doctor," I saw, had rejoined his crew on the concrete ledge. They stared at Deo.

It seemed as though he took pictures for a very long time, though it was probably only a few minutes before he got back in the car, no longer smiling, but with his jaw still hard.

Innocent had kept the engine running. He said, as he drove out through the chicken-wire gate, "Deo, I don't feel comfortable here."

"Innocent," said Deo, "where in Burundi do you feel comfortable?"

Innocent didn't answer.

As we drove on, Deo looked out at the valley across which he'd begun his long escape, in the dark, almost thirteen years before.

"There were all these drums, and houses around here were burn-ing."

"It was the middle of the night, right?"

"Yah. All day I stayed along the river Mubarazi."

On the way back, Deo wanted to drive through Bugendena, the first town he'd skirted on his escape. Innocent took the turn off the main road, but then I made a fuss. Hadn't Deo heard that Bugendena was patrolled by former militiamen? Hadn't we seen enough for today? I'm afraid I grew vehement.

Deo told Innocent that I was afraid to go on. Innocent told him, "I'm afraid, too." He told Deo, in so many words, "You know, I don't care about myself. Right now I can easily go to Bugendena without you, but I'm just thinking how you survived and now you're going back looking for trouble. Do you know how many people struggled to survive and didn't survive? And now you are coming back here on purpose? It's like you are laughing. This is a stupid idea."

Deo later explained to me, "Innocent was thinking deep about it. And he was warning me. He was just like referring to all these old beliefs, you know?" That is, Innocent accused him of tempting fate or the devil, putting us all at risk by incurring the wrath of the spirit world. I thought I understood. Deo was behaving like one of those arrogant ancient Greek heroes who, victorious in a battle, succumbs to hubris, claims he's mastered fate, doesn't fear Atê's retaliation, and for his stupid boast gets visited by Nemesis. I was inclined to agree with Innocent.

As we drove back on the orange dirt road in silence, I thought that I should start talking about bricks again. Just to change the subject. For the time being, though, I couldn't manage even that. When we hit the paved road, I began to feel relieved, but then Deo insisted that we stop again at the memorial in Kibimba. This time the small shrine made me think of a diminutive Greek temple, on its way to becoming a ruin. Deo took some photographs, as vehicles and bicycles passed by—as, I imagined, the drivers and riders glared at him. When he got back in the SUV, he stared at the message written on the front of the memorial, "PLUS JAMAIS ÇA!" He sniffed, and said as others had before him and others no doubt would again, "I have learned *never* to say, 'Never again.'"

SIXTEEN

Burundi,
2006

Every day in Burundi, Innocent drove us to places that seemed inhabited with Deo's memories, waiting for him to return. The country's lone medical school was an obligatory stop. The Coca-Cola stand was still there, marking the spot where he'd climbed off the army truck when he'd finally made it back from Rwanda. And here across the street was the medical school's main building, where he had studied so assiduously. The building was massive and still looked rather new. "It was so beautiful!" Deo cried, gazing up at it, his eyes fixed on a great vertical crack that some sort of artillery had made in a concrete wall.

In his day, he remembered, more than a hundred faculty had taught here. The school was functioning again but, he said, with only seven full professors. He wanted to go inside. A pair of custodians obliged him. The current students were on vacation. The place was empty. It felt like a ruin. A lock and chain barred the way to one wing, which was in danger of collapse. Tattered curtains hung in the classrooms where Deo had received lectures on basic physiology, pathology, pharmacology. In the laboratory where he'd first seen bacteria swimming in a petri dish, there were no microscopes anymore—all stolen, the custodians said. There were no textbooks or slides for students to study, no slide projector for that matter, and only a small collection of tattered medical journals, which a sign on the library door asked students not to photocopy lest they be damaged.

We walked over to the university hospital, the teaching hospital. I could imagine Deo in a white coat, a student on rounds. As we passed through the rooms, rooms that used to contain only two beds but now had six crowded together, he smiled at patients, offering greetings to each. He stopped at the bed of a young woman. A plaster cast covered one of her legs, from toes to hip. He asked her for her story. She said she'd been tending her bean plants in her roadside garden and had been hit by a passing car, which hadn't stopped. Kindly neighbors had brought her here, but she had spent her life savings, such as they were, for her medical care, such as it had been, and was now in debt.

That woman, Deo said as we walked away, would soon be discharged to a special section of the hospital, equipped with security guards. She would be prevented from leaving until someone paid her bill, and in the meantime would receive no nursing and not even food, unless a friend or relative brought some to her. That was how the medical system dealt with unpaid bills these days.

Detention of indigent patients—imprisonment, really—wasn't exactly the fault of the new Hutu-led government. Given time, perhaps, the new administration would end the practice, which had begun under the previous, mainly Tutsi government. The World Bank and other international financial institutions had insisted, as they had through much of Africa, that Burundi's medical facilities impose "user fees." Some time back, in its zeal to collect those fees, this very hospital, the place where Deo had trained, applied the policy to corpses. The authorities refused to release the bodies of people who died with unpaid bills. Deo had heard the rest of the story, and he told it with a certain grim satisfaction. The morgue was unrefrigerated; when the air in the neighborhood became unbearable, the city's mayor ordered the bodies released. The bankrupt patients were buried, Deo had heard, by prisoners who couldn't refuse the job.

While visiting hospitals on his last trip to Burundi, Deo had met a total of thirty-eight patients in detention at two hospitals, and he'd learned of more than a thousand others in different facilities. Of the detained patients he met, a woman with burns covering half her body stood out for him, as did an elderly woman with a soulful, mournful face. He photographed that elderly woman, then bailed her out, for fifty-seven dollars. He had already made an appointment to talk to the minister of health about his plans for building a clinic. He decided to take the elderly woman along, so she could tell the minister her story.

The security guard outside the minister's office stopped him. "You can't bring her in here," he said.

Deo told the guard that the old woman was the minister's aunt. "The minister will be so happy to see her!"

Deo told me, "If I were living in Burundi, they would have sent me the same day to jail." But the minister, a woman, did listen. The elderly woman had a beautiful face. In Deo's photograph of her, I thought he had captured some of the essence of dignity and sorrow. Maybe the minister saw something like that as well, in the sad, stoic, weathered face across her desk. At any rate, on the following day, 150 detained patients were released from various hospitals. But the policy remained. Before long, 150 new sick detainees would replace them, Deo figured. When he got back to the United States, he thought of trying to raise enough cash to free all the patients, then realized this would only make detentions more lucrative for hospital administrations. For weeks he stole time from his studies at medical school, trying to write a paper on the issue, but to his relief he had recently been upstaged by a detailed exposé from Human Rights Watch.

Many friends and family wondered why Deo kept coming back to Burundi. Many, including his mother, said they wished he wouldn't tempt fate in this way. To me, he said, "But it's my country no matter what. You know?" And as in almost every setting of great poverty, health in his country was dreadful. He had gleaned Burundi's statistics from various sources. These were some he liked to cite at fund-raisers for his yet to be built clinic: an average life expectancy of about thirty-nine years; one in five deaths caused by waterborne diseases or lack of sanitation; severe malnutrition for 54 percent of children under five; for women, a one-in-nine lifetime risk of dying during childbirth; and fewer than three hundred doctors to serve a population of about seven million. And most of those doctors practiced in the capital. Many didn't see patients in public facilities but worked for foreign aid organizations because the salaries were far better.

I think this was Deo's favorite part of the tour he led me on, the part that had to do with public health and medicine. These, I think, were the subjects around which time could reassemble for him, around which past and present and future could begin to seem coherent and purposeful.

It was on our visit to Sangaza that he began to tell me the story of his first attempt to build a clinic, when he was a schoolboy years ago. It seemed as if the story all came back to him there at the site of that attempt—with amusement added, most of the pain of failure withdrawn.

Near the end of his junior year at high school, Deo had said to a bunch of his friends—no doubt one could have heard his father's and grandfather's voices in his—"Instead of wasting time walking around chins up, why can't we build a clinic in Sangaza?" "Chins up" was Deo's term for arrogance; because places in high school were rare, students tended to lift their chins at the thought of manual labor. He won over half a dozen friends, and led a small schoolboy delegation to visit the governor of the province. The governor agreed that if they managed to put up the walls of a clinic, he would supply the metal roofing. Deo talked his father into giving him a little time away from cowherding duties, and the week after school let out, Deo and his friends made bricks. Deo persuaded some of the local women to cook meals for the work crew.

They made a great number of bricks out of wet clay. But they didn't know how to fire them, and they had no money to hire someone who did. A thunderstorm turned all their bricks back to mud. Deo overheard adults talking about "those kids"—kids who didn't know what they were doing, who were just wasting time, just trying to avoid their chores at home. He realized he should try to get the community involved. In the fall of the following year, right before school started, he organized an election in Sangaza. A clinic-building committee was chosen, another largely student work crew assembled. They made more bricks, and this time Deo and the committee managed to get a local craftsman to fire the bricks for a nominal fee. But they had to build a kiln first, and that took many days. By the time the bricks were being fired, the rains had begun. When the rains ended months later, the tall pile of partially fired bricks had collapsed, partway back to mud again.

So Deo and his friends decided to build out of wood. The first week of the next summer vacation, they started cutting trees from the forest next to the graveyard in Sangaza. They cleared a site and carried logs to it, singing traditional work songs. But they hadn't cut nearly enough wood to begin construction before his father's dispensation ended and Deo had to return to cowherding. He had told himself that he would get back to building the clinic someday. And now he was—about sixteen years later, and in Kayanza.

Deo's impulse to public service had been planted by his mother and shaped by Bishop Bududira; in our travels in Burundi, Deo made sure to stop at the small memorial to the bishop, adorned with plastic flowers, in a corner of Bududira's former church. And Partners In Health had given Deo confidence: no one could have worked for that organization without believing in the possibility of building public health systems and hospitals in desperately poor places. When PIH had expanded into Rwanda, Deo had hoped they'd also go to work in Burundi. But now he knew they wouldn't, not right away. The organization was already overextended, with large projects all over the world. He knew that Paul Farmer hoped he wouldn't try to build a clinic on his own, at least not before finishing medical school. But he also knew that if he forced the issue and got a facility started, PIH would help him. Farmer was already giving him advice and had promised to visit the site later in the summer.

At Partners In Health, I think, Deo had discovered a way to quiet the questions he'd been asking at Columbia. That is, he saw there might be an answer for what troubled him most about the world, an answer that lay in his hands, indeed in his memory. You had to do something. And trying again to build a clinic must also be a way, I thought, for him to reach back to his former life and connect it with his new one.

We were sitting one night in an outdoor bar, taking a break from touring. As often happened wherever we were, Deo began talking about his plans for Kayanza. It wasn't my place to worry, I suppose. But I did. He didn't yet have an organization that would finance and construct and staff the clinic he imagined. In fact, he was still trying to decide on a name. He would come up with one, declare emphatically this was it, and then for one reason or another reject it. In the bar, he finally settled on "Village Health Works." I was glad to have the matter settled—for how long I wasn't sure.

The night air was fragrant; I smelled jasmine. The third round of beers had arrived at our table. Deo said, "So my pipe dreams are these. If the Kayanza project is successful, we can expand around, and people will see, 'Oh it works, it's good.' And hopefully the

whole country will begin to understand that you can do this without bringing a hammer, because once you bring a hammer, people
will bring a shield, with another hammer to break your legs. How
can we be healthy and a good society? We can train nurses in
Kayanza and expand all over the country. Let the population know:
'Look, this is what life is.' And those people, they will teach other
people, make people see what is right. And show them the value of
work. And that would erase, not the history, but it would create a
new world, make it peaceful and a wonderful paradise. It's a really
small country. There is no reason why it should be impossible, no
reason at all."

He had been smiling, a faraway look on his face. It faded. "I
know I have these unrealistic beliefs and thoughts, that the world
can be peaceful, can be healthy, people can be humane. But is it fea-
sible?"

"Well, you won't know unless you try," I offered.

"Right. And if you try . . . Sometimes I think, 'Am I crazy?' You
try to save someone and you get killed, by that person. You stay
away, you get troubled, because you are not doing something you
believe in." He laughed. "In the middle of the ocean, and I always
have these thoughts. Goddammit!"

"So here we are off to Kayanza!" cried Deo as we turned off the
paved highway beside Lake Tanganyika. A deeply rutted dirt road
led through a palm grove, a dark and mysterious maze, orderly, fe-
cund. There were seven of us crammed into the SUV. Deo's American medical friends had come with us on this trip, too. This was
what they had traveled to Burundi for, to help him get started on the
clinic. This trip to Kayanza would be the summer's opening ceremony, as it were. I was looking forward to seeing Kayanza, Deo's
adopted hometown, which had clearly replaced Butanza in his af-
fections. More than that, I was looking forward to meeting his parents.

He had told me some of what he knew about their recent past. His father had come all but undone during their several years as refugees, and the nightmarish years of civil war they endured after returning to Burundi, and the loss of practically everything they had worked for all their lives, including most of their cows.

The first time Deo returned to Burundi, on the trip he survived because he didn't take the bus, he found his father drinking heavily and threatening suicide. Deo went back to the United States feeling he had to get his father help. It took a long time, but eventually he made arrangements for his father to see a psychiatrist, in Rwanda's central hospital. Deo flew from New York to Kigali to be on hand. But when he met his mother there, she told him his father would refuse to see him. His father had told her he didn't have anything to give Deo. Therefore, he could not see him.

Deo grabbed a bunch of clothes from his suitcase and put them in a plastic bag, which he handed to his mother. "Just tell him these are clothes you bought for me."

The ploy worked. His father let him into his hospital room and said, his usual commanding tone restored for the moment, "I bought clothes for you. Here." He handed Deo the bag. "Try them on."

That had been another wretched trip. Deo didn't even get to Burundi. His uncle said it was too dangerous, and Deo believed him but also thought, "Too dangerous for me but not for my parents?" And the psychiatrist wasn't much help to his father—less help than Deo's mother, as it turned out. Back in the United States, Deo heard from relatives that one day, enduring another of his father's threats of suicide, his mother had said that if he killed himself, she would follow suit. And it seemed as if his father awakened at least partially to his old self. In any case, he stopped making the threats.

It was his mother, Deo heard, who had managed almost every-thing in the years after she and his father returned from the refugee camps and settled in Kayanza. She milked their few cows and tended the beans and cooked the meals and took care of Deo's two youngest brothers. And she managed their escape, the day when some neighbors warned them that militia were coming. For a time they lived in the forests near Kayanza. They came back to find their house burned. Deo's youngest brothers remembered how anxiously she looked after them, at one point even paying other families in rather distant, safer villages to take them in. She would walk miles carrying food for the boys, food that the foster families often kept for themselves. When the boys decided to come home to Kayanza, she didn't scold them, she simply wept. She and the boys were hiding in a field of maize the next time the militia came and burned their house again.

Deo didn't know much more about those years. He didn't know exactly what his parents had endured in their trek across the mountains to Tanzania, in the refugee camps across the border, in the woods around Kayanza where they often had to hide. He didn't want to know. On that first trip back home, he had learned that his mother had added to her two given names another: the Kirundi word for silence. He didn't ask her the reason. One day some years later, she announced to Deo and one of his younger brothers that she was going to tell her story. Deo couldn't bear to listen. Against all he felt was right and best for her, he turned and walked away, and in a moment his younger brother did likewise, in tears.

But these were acts committed out of too much filial feeling, not too little. Deo had never turned away from his parents in any other sense that mattered. On the contrary, it was because they were in Kayanza that he had adopted the village as his own. The place was certainly remote enough to suit him, I thought, as the suv lurched up and down on the rutted road through the palm grove. Then came a town called Rukomo and another rutted road. There were hot springs nearby, and a good-looking clinic that was underequipped and charged for its services and wasn't much used. A European church group had built that facility, Deo said as we passed, but a Burundian pastor now controlled it. "He's like huge, Bible in his hand, a suit, and five pens in his pocket, and a huge belly." Some time back, Deo said, he had imagined a joint effort to improve the clinic, but the pastor had demurred. Deo remembered arguing: "If tomorrow you don't have a large number of people coming to worship you, don't be surprised. They will be sitting in their houses, in these miserable hospitals, dying. Give them something. At least that way they can show up on Sunday at your church."

The pastor had countered by saying that Deo should tell his American friends to bring him equipment and medicines and then go away.

"I wanted to puke right in front of him," said Deo. "I asked him, 'Are you drunk?'" Deo knew the man didn't drink. Deo had wanted to insult him, and had succeeded.

But he could be diplomatic. The province's new governor, for instance, had become a friend and had pledged to give whatever help she could.

We passed bunches of children. They waved and called, "Amahoro." One called out, "Amahoro! Don't hit my goat!" Deo laughed. "I love kids around here. They greet people." He added, "I feel like, 'Wow, finally, I'm with my people.'"

Deo talked about Kayanza. In the entire village, he said, there was only one Tutsi family besides his own. It seemed that some radicalized children of neighbors had directed rebel soldiers to his family's house during the war, but other neighbors had warned his parents, and after the family house had been burned for the third time, a large group of those country people had banded together and evicted a person who had tried to take his parents' land. This was another reason Deo felt drawn to Kayanza. And so much the better, he said, that 99 percent of its people were Hutu.

At the far edge of Rukomo, the road rose steeply. Trees and brush encroached on it, but it wasn't badly rutted, no doubt because few vehicles used it. Deo remembered hiking up this road—a path, back then—with bags of cassava or sorghum grain on his head. "There were a lot of gorillas here. There used to be many monkeys, running, jumping, crossing." They were all gone now, shot or chased away. But once in a while you could still catch a glimpse of a leopard, like a flash of sunlight in the foliage. Deo said the air up in Kayanza was cooler than down by the lake, and good summer grazing land lay nearby, and the soils were richer and more versatile than in Butanza.

When we crested the last grade, the land opened up onto a broad plateau, and you could see what the Belgians had meant when they'd compared Burundi and Rwanda to Switzerland. You could look down to the east and see Tanganyika's waters, like a cerulean sky. To the west, your eyes climbed tiers of mountains, often shrouded in mist, though not today. Unlike Switzerland, of course, the place lacked just about everything necessary and useful for health: sanitation, medicine, mosquito nets. Most of the people here had no access to clean water. No one had electricity. "Here you are in the land of Joe Conrad," said Deo. "This is the heart of darkness right here."

On the other hand, there was an elementary school, just up ahead. While working at PIH, Deo had managed to save enough of his salary to send about one thousand dollars for that school's reconstruction—money went a long way here. He had also saved enough over the past decade to have his parents' house rebuilt three times. The latest version was brick, with a rusty metal roof and several real windows: a fine house in a village mainly of huts. Deo said he'd made sure it was smaller than previous ones, so it would be less conspicuous. About a year ago, he had told the village elders that he intended to get a clinic built for Kayanza. And the last time he'd come here, with his doctor friends from PIH, hundreds of villagers had turned out to welcome him and his friends. There had even been a band.

There was no music this time, but in a field surrounded by palm trees, another crowd was waiting, hundreds of people at least. They had been waiting there for hours, one of the villagers later told Deo, adding that there had been more than a thousand, but many had left for work. For the moment, though, my attention was fixed not on the crowd, but on Deo. He had jumped out of the SUV, and was surrounded by people he seemed to know well. The couple he was embracing had to be his parents.

I thought I saw a family resemblance. One usually does when one is looking for it. His father was an inch or two shorter than Deo, his mother about the same height as his father and thinner than both. They had dressed for their son. Deo's father was the only man in sight wearing a sport coat—and a fedora, tilted a little backward. His mother wore what seemed like the Burundian standard for women, a blend of modesty and flair, a simple dress for a first layer and, draped over it, a beautiful outer dress with images of birds on branches dyed into the cloth. They were in their early sixties, quite old by Burundian standards, but neither seemed infirm. Both wore glasses, which lent them a slightly studious air.

Deo stood with his arm around his mother's shoulders, introducing her to his American friends and laughing—a long-running laugh, holding a high, soft note. It seemed involuntary. It had a childlike vulnerability. It seemed to say all at once: I'm so happy, so nervous, so excited, and I don't know what to do with all these feelings.

He had told me that on his last visit, he'd held palavers with the village chiefs, making sure his father was included, and had suggested that the villagers start making bricks. Since then, Deo had heard, the town had taken up a collection and bought a load of foundation stones. He'd also heard that his father had largely put aside banana beer and become a leader in the brick-making. He'd heard that neighbors now made an effort to speak to his father, and would invariably say, "Your son is so nice." This was an ancillary benefit he'd hoped for from the project. Ever since he'd learned his parents were alive, he had been trying to purchase a peaceful old age for them. In this respect, it seemed to me, his incipient clinic was already a success.

The size of the crowd, the long wait they'd put up with, made it obvious what the hope of a clinic meant to the people of Kayanza. It also seemed obvious what Deo's leading role in all this meant to his parents. There was a moment, just long enough for a snapshot, when I saw Deo's father and mother turn from looking at their son in order to look toward each other. His mother cocked her head slightly and smiled at Deo's father, and his father beamed back at her.

Then his father was scowling. "Why were you late?" he said gruffly to Deo, and Deo's high soft laugh ran on, as he translated these words of his father's for me. Then Deo exclaimed to me, "He is doing so well! I was so excited to see that. He is doing so great! He was very, you know, for so many years. He's now very alert. He is so happy."

"Come. Come and see the stones," his father said to him.

The foundation stones lay in a great heap, all ready for use—except that they'd been unloaded several hundred yards downhill from the site of the clinic-to-be. When Deo caught sight of the misplaced pile, he halted. "This is so retarded!" He had already examined the bricks that the villagers had made. They stood in a huge rectangular pile near the site, but they had been fired during the rains and though they hadn't turned to mud, they were too soft for structural duty.

But all that was okay, Deo said. The bricks could be used for paving and for the borders of the gardens he planned—vegetable gardens and orchards to supply food to malnourished patients. And the foundation stones could be moved.

The crowd assembled around the misplaced pile of rocks. There were greetings—chants of "Amahoro"—and speeches, which the villagers cheered, and more speeches, and during the course of all this, Deo exclaimed to me, "I am so happ-ee!" He said, "I really get so excited when I see people so excited."

Religious people, I'm told, have their meanest thoughts in church. I found myself thinking that tomorrow morning Kayanza's residents would wake up and still have no doctor or nurses or clean water nearby, just this misplaced pile of rocks. I felt for a perverse moment like reminding Deo of all this. But it was good to see him happy, as always. And after all, he knew far better than I the obstacles he faced.

As we drove away, the figures of the villagers receding in the suv's back window, Deo said to us, his American friends, "Thank you so much." His voice was tiny. It cracked. "Thank you so much for coming to my little village."

SEVENTEEN

Rwanda,
2006

On my map, Deo had traced the path of his escape. The pencil line ran west, then north, from Burundi into Rwanda. We flew to Rwanda from Bujumbura in an old propeller-driven commercial plane. We gazed through the window together. Deo pointed out landmarks below. The paved main road between Bujumbura and Rwanda, rising into the mountains, a road he had crossed in a hurry during his escape. A corner of Kibira, the national forest— he'd traveled through the shadows of its deep green canopy, but you could see great chunks had been burned and cleared since then. We couldn't spot the hospital in Mutaho, but it was somewhere down there, not far away.

Nothing was very far away, unless of course you were on foot and running from people who were trying to kill you. "These are such tiny countries," said Deo over the roar of the engines. "Here we are flying like an old bird. We are in no hurry, but here we are already reaching Rwanda." The entire flight took less than half an hour, and in only about fifteen minutes we had passed over the entire landscape of his journey, a round trip of about 150 kilometers according to my map. The banana grove where the Hutu woman had found him—he couldn't pick it out, of course, but Deo thought it was probably still down there.

"What was it you told her?" I asked over the noise of the plane.

Gazing out, Deo replied, "'I'm too tired. I'm just going to stay here.' And she said, 'No, no. It's not far to the border.'"

He couldn't spot the border river, Akanyaru, which he had crossed two times, but he located Butare, Rwanda's university town, where he had yearned to go, imagining he'd find sanctuary there. Of course there was no trace from the air of the refugee camps, just over the border in Rwanda, where he had languished fearfully for months.

I asked him if he could see Murambi, the place where he had turned around and fled back toward Burundi. But Murambi was off to the east, on the other side of the plane. So for a while longer it remained wholly a place I imagined—a place where Deo had stood in tall grass on a hillside, looking across a valley toward a massacre. "It was night," he had told me. "And it never stopped being night."

Deo had arranged for a driver in Rwanda, who took us the next day to the Murambi Memorial Center. It was in the southwest, about two hours from the capital. Everything in Rwanda, Deo said, was about two hours from the capital. The main part of the memorial was a large two-story building of brick and concrete. A purple banner hung over the entrance. The site was much more elaborate and better cared for than the little memorial we'd stopped at in Burundi on the way to and from Mutaho. But the banner carried essentially the same message, a more explicit version of "Never Again." Deo translated for me: "Never forget the genocide and the people who were slaughtered here."

Looking up at that banner now, with Deo beside me, I thought that in his place I'd find the message ironic. The words weren't meant for people with memories of the kind of thing that had happened here. One's own forgetfulness wasn't the problem for people like Deo.

It was a Sunday morning, still early, and the sounds of a choir came from the town nearby. Deo muttered some imprecations; he was far from irreligious, but he'd acquired a lot of anticlerical feeling, in part because of all the well-attested stories of Rwandan priests aiding and abetting the genocide, and in some cases actually wielding machetes. As we walked toward the memorial building, I thought it was obvious why the *génocidaires* had chosen to lure their victims to this place. It seemed like an ideal ambush site, an all but treeless plateau shaped like the prow of a ship, the land sloping steeply away on three sides. Deo pointed toward the surrounding hills, his hands describing the route he had taken away from here. "I went just down that ravine. Then I went up there just to see, and I heard people dying, and I went down to that bunch of eucalyptus. So, I went down. This way. So all this, I mean, but it's all the same. I just, I feel like I want to throw up."

After a time, I asked again how long he thought it had taken him to get back from here to the Burundian border. He said he thought about four days.

"Oh boy, Deo," I said. "I can hardly imagine. You are one tough son of a gun."

"No, no, no."

"Yes, you are. I mean, so many people would just give up."

"Oh, well, you know, how many times I just thought I *would* give up."

The memorial building was still locked. But after poking around awhile, Deo ran into the man who kept the keys. His name was Emmanuel. Deo had visited this place last summer and had met Emmanuel then. They greeted each other warmly now. Emmanuel was older and thinner than Deo, and he had a deep dent in his forehead, a little round crater, hard not to stare at. Emmanuel, Deo explained, had lived in Burundi for a time but had returned to this part of Rwanda a few years before the genocide. Hoping to escape the slaughter in his village, he had fled with his family here, to the technical school at Murambi. His wife and five children had all died in the massacre. He himself had been shot, but the bullet hadn't entirely penetrated his skull. He'd lain wounded, hidden among a heap of bodies. When the killers had left, he had headed cross-country, like Deo, for Burundi. There his wound was repaired, and after a few years he had come back to Rwanda, and eventually back to this site. He told Deo that he stayed with the dead to repay them, because it was their bodies that had saved him. He also said that his family was buried here, and he was not going to leave them again.

He and Deo talked and laughed like old friends. When they had met here last summer, Emmanuel had recognized Deo's Burundian accent, and had said that Deo looked familiar. Now Emmanuel said that he remembered why: he'd seen Deo on an evening, twelve years and two months back, on the trail that led to this place.

"How do you remember me?" asked Deo.

"Well, you were so skinny. You were like a walking skeleton. Now you're fat. But your face didn't change."

"No, no, no, Emmanuel. You're confusing me with someone else."

"No. We were on that hill over there, and people were coming from many different directions, and I was looking at faces, because I came from here and I was scared. Everyone was afraid of each other. I saw you and I thought, 'I never saw this guy before.'"

"So did you talk to me, or did I talk to you?"

"No. You were not talking. You were sitting down by the path. I could see that you were sick. I told my wife, 'I want to help that boy,' and she was so angry. 'You want to help someone else when you have your own family here?'"

This encounter seemed unlikely, though it was possible. In interviews recorded for the memorial, Emmanuel had said that he'd come here to the technical school, seeking refuge, a couple of days before the grand slaughter had begun. But Deo didn't know for sure when he had arrived in the vicinity. At the time, he hadn't been keeping track of dates. It was, in any case, a story that I thought I would want to believe, if I were Deo. To run into someone who claimed to have crossed his path during that time—this had never happened to him before. It had to make the world feel less lonely.

Before we parted, Deo hugged Emmanuel, then quickly slipped him some Rwandan francs. Emmanuel let Deo and me in to look at the exhibits. Some of the displays offered only a rather simplistic history of the Hutu-Tutsi divide. There were a couple of videos in which survivors—Emmanuel, prominently—described the massacre. There was also an old transistor radio of the kind Deo remembered seeing Rwandan militiamen carrying next to their ears as they walked around refugee camps. The radio had been a primary tool in the genocide, for whipping up murderous fervor and for organizing it. In the museum, you pressed a button and the radio's tinny speaker played the chant that Deo told me he'd heard so often before and during the genocide, like a satanic inversion of a hymn: "God is just. God is never unjust. And we will finish them soon. Keep working, keep working. We will finish them, we will finish them soon. They are about to vanish! They are about to vanish! Don't get tired! You are about to be done!"

We left the museum building by the back, so as not to get Emmanuel in trouble with his boss for letting us in before the official opening time. Crossing a sunlit, tiled floor, we passed a sleeping bag, Emmanuel's bed. "That's how Emmanuel sleeps," Deo told me. "I asked him how can he stay here. He told me, 'This is my home.' And his wife died here and his children, and he's still *here*. And he's still here, you know? I mean, that, as pain goes, that has no word. And he stays here."

Emmanuel's choice did seem strange—to be the keeper of the keys to a place full of bones, some of them his family's. "I can't presume to understand," I said.

"You know, what I *can* tell you is that he's half alive," said Deo. "This is a guy who lost the trunk of his life."

Back behind the memorial building stood rows of narrow, shedlike buildings, each with its own metal door. These, I gathered, had been the dorms and classrooms of the Murambi Technical School. Now each chamber was filled with bones.

We stood in the doorway of one of the rooms, looking in. Bleached-white skeletons lay on wooden tables, a dozen or so per table, all neatly arranged, side by side. Deo took a photograph. He pointed at a mosslike tuft on one of the skulls. "This is hair." He went on, pointing at bones: "You can see like this was a guy. This was like a woman, you can see clothes still. You see a child here."

We went back outside. "So at this site they counted the bodies. Fifty thousand and something people. Most in, I think, one night."

"You said *fifty thousand*?"

Deo led the way to another door. "You can open here and see like skulls. There's some right here. Somehow like only heads. You know. They were chopped."

I went in first. Behind me, I heard Deo murmur that he smelled blood. Then I heard him say, "I think I took enough pictures. I am kind of *sick* of this." Then he was silent. I could hear him make a little cough. By now I knew this meant that he was weeping.

I heard him leave the room. When I looked outside, he was walking slowly, head down, toward the memorial building. Best to leave him alone, I thought.

On the table in front of me lay four rows of skulls, neatly aligned, ten to twelve skulls per row, and behind the skulls, two rows of what I thought were femurs, neatly stacked, hundreds per row. From across the valley to the west came the sound of people still singing hymns. It was utterly silent in the room, except for a sound that for a moment I couldn't identify—a clicking, a ticking, a dripping. It was just the sound of the metal roof heating up in the midday sun and moving against its fastenings. I knew that I knew the sound and its origins, but at the moment I couldn't place it. The room was very clean, and so were the bones. But I could have sworn that I smelled milk. I looked closely at the skulls on the table. Most had cracks in them. Some had big chunks missing. Human beings had taken machetes and rifle butts and those clubs with protruding nails on their business ends that Deo had described to me, and who knows what else—rocks perhaps?—and smashed them into the heads of human beings, and then chopped off these heads, or chopped off the heads and then bashed in the skulls, thousands of times over.

But even while telling myself this, I felt I was a world away from the hospital in Mutaho where Deo's flight had begun. That had seemed like a place of unfinished business. To me, this display of bones, though far more graphic, felt much less uncanny, much less unnerving than that empty remnant of a hospital. Here the evidence of brute, unleashed human energy was all laid out before you, and you could imagine that human reason was putting up a stand against it. This was an intentional place, a museum, a place thoroughly preceded by a story and expectations.

I didn't know how to respond to all these bones. I had come expecting to feel the horror of what Murambi memorialized, but I wasn't sure I felt enough, or if I felt much of anything. A stupid self-consciousness got hold of my thoughts, an invitation to falsity. "I should feel like crying," I thought, and sure enough, I felt tears well up. I went out to look for Deo.

Evidently, the museum had opened. A group of white-skinned people with cameras were coming down the paths toward the school buildings.

EIGHTEEN

Rwanda,
2006

In Burundi, peace was still new, whereas Rwanda had been recovering for more than a decade. What I saw of Rwanda, I saw from the roads we traveled. They were remarkable compared to roads in most other poor countries I'd known, not just paved but smooth and well maintained. And they were patrolled by cops on foot, some of whom were equipped with radar detectors and were actually trying to enforce speed limits—and none solicited a bribe from us. We passed men dressed in pink uniforms, prisoners convicted of crimes in the genocide, working in fields and on public buildings. We passed public attempts at English, which I took as evidence of the flourishing enmity between the French and Rwandan governments: a road sign that instead of "Bon Voyage" read "Good Away," a liquor store named Nigger Boy Saloon, which probably meant that hip-hop had arrived but without translation. There were hilly and mountainous landscapes almost completely covered with crops and banana groves, one-story towns, the occasional monkey by the side of the road, churches everywhere and women walking toward them at all hours of the day.

Superficial impressions of a country at peace. For me, they sat uneasily beside the fact that Rwanda's government had become a pariah in several quarters. A number of scholars and human rights groups accused the Kagame administration of its own unacknowledged atrocities, of discriminating against the mass of Hutus, of rigging elections, of stifling dissent, of disappearing dissenters. Some critics were scornful of the government's yearly commemorations of the genocide and of the continuing village-level trials of small-time *génocidaires*. The government, critics said, was just trying to claim "a genocide credit" that would excuse its autocratic ways, that would allow it to avoid discussion of the crimes Tutsis had committed against Hutus. The critics denounced the government's virtual ban on discussions of ethnicity that diverged from the official line— a ploy, they said, to cover up systematic discrimination against Hutus, which was bound to lead to more violence someday. Official Rwanda was also said to have played an evil role in the rather recent and extraordinarily violent events in the neighboring Congo. The Kagame administration was accused not of having started this ongoing catastrophe, but of escalating it—and also, by a UN panel of inquiry, of having joined various other governments in plundering the Congo's mineral wealth.

Deo had supplied me with the most stinging critique that I'd read, by a Belgian law professor and student of the country named Filip Reyntjens. But Deo also said of Rwanda's president, Paul Kagame, "If he were here, I would give him a hug." To Deo, Kagame and his government were the people who had stopped the genocide, who had managed to bring order back to a shattered, looted country. In Deo's view, the critique contained far too little appreciation for the government's accomplishments—rebuilding institutions virtually from scratch, repatriating about two million refugees, providing security for a traumatized population in the face of persistent armed attacks from genocidal forces in exile. He felt that some critics, especially the French, were just trying to cover up their own failures and crimes, and that human rights groups, as was often the case, had too little sympathy for the problems the government still faced. Deo believed that most of Kagame's efforts were aimed at preventing another slaughter and at promoting prosperity—to Deo's mind, the only way of making the current, fragile peace endure. He did feel it was a mistake for the government to limit discussions of ethnicity, but he understood the impulse. From his summer working for Partners In Health in rural Rwanda, among the indigent sick, Deo had seen the country's poverty firsthand and had heard the murmuring hatreds that might be only temporarily suppressed. When I asked him how long he thought it would take for Hutus and Tutsis to forget, he said, "It will probably take the time the earth has left." But there was no war now. Rwanda now was a paradise compared to the abattoir he'd passed through in 1994, and it left him much more hopeful, he said, than his own homeland, indeed than most of Africa. "Kagame may not be a perfect person," he said. "But at least he gets something constructive done."

It was obvious that Deo also felt grateful for Rwanda's memorial sites. Dozens of mass graves and memorials had been created throughout the country, some large like Murambi and financed by foreign organizations, others modest. "Villages of the dead," Deo called them. Again and again, he directed our driver to memorial sites, sometimes calling for a stop when we came upon one he hadn't planned to see. For instance, the kiosklike roadside memorial in the university town of Butare. The number of dead housed in that little mausoleum made me think it was probably just as well Deo had never made it to Butare back when he was on the run.

Deo had gone to Murambi once already, the summer before, and I thought if I were Deo, I wouldn't want to go again. Actually, I thought if I had memories like his, I would spend the rest of my life as far away as possible from Rwanda and Burundi. But then I entertained the idea that, no, if I had places like Murambi in my past, I might want to revisit them, if only to justify my troubled dreams.

The other memorials we visited weren't on the tour of Deo's life. They weren't places he'd passed through. I know he took me to them partly because he wanted to make me a witness. And I think he had additional reasons. At almost every site we went to, he wept. I don't mean to suggest there was anything insincere or unjustified about his tears—usually, he tried to hide them from me, and when he didn't succeed, he simply said, "Sorry." After a time, I came to think that visiting memorials was in part a willed catharsis. And why wouldn't he have need of that?

Once, when trying to explain how it had felt to be on the run, he put his hand over the top of a teacup, saying, "You are in a closed place, and you don't see anything else, and you don't believe there *is* anything else." When we visited Kayanza, it seemed to me that building a clinic really could be Deo's way out of that cup, his antidote to Mutaho and Murambi, his tool for mending the tear that had divided his life—somehow, I pictured him sewing a patch over the rips in his pants, years back, in his dorm room at Burundi's medical school. But on our drives through Rwanda, I realized again the weight of his memories. The most innocent views from the roads could *gusimbura* him. A bunch of men, probably on lunch break, sitting at the roadside, Deo saying in a small voice, as if to himself, "That's the way the militiamen would sit, waiting for people who were running away." Or a view of farmers walking along with machetes, a ubiquitous sight, Deo murmuring, "Every time I see a machete, I just feel like . . ."

I think he visited memorial sites partly in order to confront the nagging trouble in his mind. To fight back against the invasions of memory.

As for me, I welcomed those stops, at least at first. Inevitably, some people now denied that what had happened in Rwanda was a genocide—arguing either in obvious service of the guilty, or, I think,

in service of the extreme self-pity that admits no suffering as great
as one's own. But no one else, it seemed to me, could doubt the importance of memorial sites like the ones Deo took me to. They were
a means of keeping a history that had to be known. The fact that
mass slaughters hadn't been prevented in places all over the world—
and weren't being prevented now—didn't argue against these attempts to preserve the memories of former massacres and the hope
they represented, that someday "Never Again" might seem like
more than a pious, self-enhancing platitude. And surely these sites
had great value for many survivors, as public recognition of their
suffering, as places to mourn their murdered friends and families.
Surely the sites were psychologically useful for some, as they seemed
to be for Deo.

A lot of Western thought and psychological advice assume that
it is healthy to flush out and dissect one's memories, and maybe this
is true. And yet for all that, I began to have a simultaneous and opposite feeling: that there was such a thing as too much remembering, that too much of it could suffocate a person, and indeed a
culture. Our tour of sites began to seem relentless. Observing Deo's
endlessly renewed sorrow, I found myself thinking that there was
something also to be said for a culture with a word like *gusimbura*.

One day we drove west of Kigali, many miles north of the farthest
point Deo had reached on his escape in and out of Rwanda. We
stopped at a place called Nyange, at a memorial situated at the site
of a former Catholic church, now rubble. On a day in 1994, after
about two thousand Tutsis had taken refuge in the church, its priest
had told the *génocidaires,* "Knock it down. We'll build another."
Everyone inside had died. The guide told us that the ecclesiastical
authorities had in fact tried to rebuild on the site. As we left, Deo
said, in a low, fierce voice, "If I were Kagame, I would rebuild the
church. Out of the bones of the victims."

We drove on. After an hour or so, we began to see glimpses of

Lake Kivu, which marks part of Rwanda's western border. Then a stone church hove into view, on a lovely promontory high above the lake. Deo remembered that this was another memorial site. He ordered an unplanned stop.

A sign stood beside the dirt drive to the church. Deo read from it: "April 17. So eleven thousand, four hundred people in like just one day. Imagine. Eleven thousand people."

I followed Deo to the church's front door.

He peered at a notice posted there, then yelled: "Wah!" He read the message aloud: "'Christian love is what brings us together here.'" The notice also reminded visitors that this was a place of worship, one should behave respectfully. Deo's jaw came forward. In a moment he was snapping pictures, peering in windows, climbing on the roof of the makeshift memorial adjacent to the church. When he got back in the vehicle, his eyes were wet. He said, "We are crazy people."

Deo had planned for us to visit another memorial site that afternoon, another hour or so away. But first we'd have lunch, he decided, in a restaurant down by the lake. The place was nearly empty. We chose a good table, looking west across the waters, in the direction of what used to be named Zaire and is now called the Democratic Republic of the Congo. It is a vast, rich land long beset by tragedies: the long and brutal Belgian occupation, decades of misrule after independence, and recent civil wars of great violence and complexity, wars in which the catastrophes of Rwanda and Burundi had played a terrible part. Something like two dozen proxy armies and militias were still fighting in the Congo. Over the past twelve years, millions had died in the wars and from the starvation and disease that wars bring. I said to Deo that I was confused about current events in that embattled country.

"If you understood the hearts of coltan businessmen, then you'd understand," he said. He was referring to an ore abundant in the Congo, very valuable because it contains an ingredient for making electronic devices like cell phones. Coltan, along with gold and dia-

monds and the influx of armies and militias from Rwanda and Burundi, had provided some of the fuel for the Congo's wars.

"I just mean who's fighting whom," I said. "And—"

Suddenly, Deo was laughing loudly, saying, "Well, the number of
militia groups may be the same number of different types of miner-
als!"

This was amusing, but Deo's laughter seemed oddly misshapen,
out of proportion to the joke. I wanted to find it funnier than I did.

Then beers and food arrived, and for a time Deo spoke about
our plans, about stories he'd heard from his father and grandfather
of traveling to the Congo years ago and finding abundant hospital-
ity. "People opened the door for you even when it was dark."

In a few minutes, Deo was laughing again. He was telling a story
he had told me before, of a colonial who had fought against the end
of Belgian rule in Burundi. Deo was only partway through the story
when his barking laughter began. Supposedly the Belgian had
hanged himself in despair on the day of Burundi's independence.
Since then, Deo said, the man's house had been turned into a restaurant. "The Restaurant of the Hanged Man! You will see it! I'm sure
you will get fish from there! Mr. Maus! He cried! He said, 'I am not
going to leave this country!' I'd say, 'Go back home, man! What's
wrong with you?' It was the first of July 1962! He was so stupid! He
hanged himself! The rope broke! Boom on the rock! He hit his
head!"

Deo quieted. "Ahhh boy," he said.

But then he caught sight of a flock of waterbirds out over the
lake, and it started again. "You wished you could be a bird! Or
even, like, an insect! Because they were not threatened!" Over his
own loud laughter, he went on: "They were not in any danger! In
fact, they were feeding! They were eating to death! From! You
know, bodies! You know?"

While this lasted, I didn't want to look at Deo's face. This was
the Deo I didn't and couldn't know. I didn't know what it was to get

to that place beyond horror. But I realized that for Deo it was a necessary place.

Once more he went silent. He went back to gazing at the lake. I sensed that his need was satisfied for now. He was purged. He'd returned. "You see that little tiny island?" he said in his usual voice. "There's a big one and another one in the middle. It's called Napoleon. Can you imagine? Napoleon hat. Napoleon beret. Those islands belong to Congo, and if you go up north you see Congo in Goma."

He added, "We are not going to see more memorial sites. I guess we have had enough."

"Couldn't be a prettier place for lunch," I offered.

He murmured something about the loveliness of the waters. "A place like this, feeling the waves."

"You like being near the edge," I said.

"Yes." He paused. "I'm actually glad that we didn't go on to another memorial site."

"Me too."

We stared out at the lake. A couple of drab old wooden work boats moved slowly across our field of vision, their engines just within our hearing, heading across Kivu toward the Congo.

EPILOGUE

Burundi,
June 2006–08

For the rest of the summer of 2006, Deo worked on the underpinnings of a clinic in Kayanza. It seemed to him that he awoke every day with a list of ten things to do and was lucky if he accomplished one. When he returned to medical school, he tried by email and midnight phone calls to manage the project. Both endeavors suffered. In November, he withdrew from Dartmouth. He told me once, "If people say, 'Before he died, Deo became a doctor,' that would be all right." In 2009, he would resume that dream, elsewhere. In the interim, he threw himself into clinic-building.

On his trips to and from Burundi, Deo had always dreaded the moment when he had to pass through U.S. Immigration. One time, agents took him to a room and grilled him, trying, he thought, to make him angry, trying, he imagined, to create a pretext for rescinding his green card. And they succeeded in making him angry, but he managed not to let it show. On another occasion, an agent said she'd never heard of a country called Burundi. "Are you sure it isn't Burma?" she asked him. Before he could catch himself, Deo had replied, "Well, it was Burundi yesterday when I left." But she didn't seem to sense that she was being mocked, and let him pass eventually.

It was mostly relief from worries at Immigration that Deo expected to feel when, in 2007, he took the oath to become a U.S. citizen. But he found the ceremony surprisingly moving, and afterward, when he walked out of the huge federal office building in Manhattan, the feeling he'd had for years, the feeling he'd had right up until just a moment ago, came back to him: "You walked around chin up, but in your mind you felt like you were hiding, like you were a criminal." He looked up and down the crowded street. "Hey, I'm like everyone around here now."

In effect, he became at once both an American citizen and a virtual expatriate, spending most of his time on the hilltop plateau of Kayanza, carrying rocks and planting trees and sleeping in a tent.

Deo had been greatly taken with the myth of Sisyphus when he'd encountered it at Columbia. "Pushing the rock" was his term for trying to build a not-for-profit medical facility in a desperately poor country. But the task was more nearly like the labors of Hercules, a succession of varied obstacles. He had to get title to the land, permits to import equipment and medicines, and nonprofit status in Burundi as well as in the United States, and to accomplish any of those tasks, he had to overcome the suspicions, even at first the hostility, of several Burundian officials.

Buildings had to be designed. Materials had to be purchased and trucks rented to transport them, and the trucks were always breaking down. Masons had to be hired. They also had to be supervised. So did one enterprising driver, who would siphon gas from his truck and resell it. And the person hired to supervise the work had to be supervised himself, and eventually fired, because he kept disappearing in the middle of the day to drink banana beer, taking the work crew with him. (One of Deo's brothers, all of eighteen years old, took over the job; he had no experience but could work for free.)

Provision had to be made for sanitation and clean water and, someday, for electricity. Staff had to be chosen and trained. Money had to be raised to pay for all of that and more. And from time to time, Deo had to overcome his own disillusionment. He had imagined many difficulties, but experiencing them was different, sometimes like "a knife in the heart," he said. He shouldn't have been surprised or even upset, but he was both at first, whenever someone he'd considered an ally turned out to be interested only in personal gain.

Alone in his tent, he'd awake in the middle of the night, the world so dark and quiet around him that he'd wonder, "Am I alive?" In the half-awake state of infinite dire possibility, his fears seemed invariably to go to the partially constructed buildings of the clinic. He'd get up and survey the work site with his miner's flashlight, just to make sure the buildings hadn't collapsed, or been stolen.

Deo often complained that progress was slow. To me, it looked rapid. In what seemed like no time at all, he had made allies of many government officials, who on one occasion scotched an attempt by a group of soldiers to appropriate one of the clinic's just finished buildings. Later, after a group of rebels—bandits, really—tried to raid Kayanza, the government provided a constant security detail. It was reported that the president himself had good words for the project. Friends at Partners In Health offered counsel and help with every conceivable problem and also training for nurses and community health workers. Members of Deo's family did various jobs. A host of Deo's American friends came over to work, while others raised money back in the United States. As for the villagers, Deo often said they were what kept him going—their misery on the one hand, and their wild enthusiasm on the other.

He had established a committee of villagers and given them a real say in the affairs of the clinic. Women and children were the majority in the community, so he figured that women, and through them children, should hold the majority in the committee. But the men dominated the meetings anyway. So, over vehement protests from the men, he abolished that committee and created a women's committee and a men's committee, and since then the women had taken over. It wasn't as if many men didn't pitch in, but it was the women's committee that mainly organized volunteer work crews, advised Deo on the village's needs and desires, and, perhaps most important, managed relations between the clinic and the village. When one of the soldiers guarding the clinic remarked, "We don't have much to do," Deo figured this was mainly thanks to the women. They had worked hard from the start, he told me. "But now they get to talk, too, and direct the clinic." The women made up a song that the volunteer work crews would sing as they weeded the lawn and tended the gardens that were spreading all around the new buildings. The song went like this: "This project was brought here by Jesus Christ. We are thrilled. This project is beautiful. This place is beautiful. Kayanza is beautiful."

Speaking at a fund-raiser in New York, Deo told this story:

"This past summer, we needed some help to make a road that goes to our site passable. A friend of mine told me, 'Well, Deo, there's a great Belgian construction company that builds roads in Burundi and Rwanda and the Congo,' and I was so excited. So I went to talk to the representative of the company. He sent someone to look at the road and estimated a cost of at least fifty thousand U.S. dollars. Not to pave the road, but just to widen it and make it passable. I went back frustrated, wondering how to tell the Kayanza community this bad news. As I was explaining this to them, one woman with a baby crying on her back said to me, 'You will not pay a penny for this road. We become so much sick because we are poor, but we are not poor because we are lazy. We will work on this road with our own hands.' The next day a hundred sixty-six people showed up with pickaxes, hoes, machetes, and other tools. One of the volunteers was a woman who came to work with a sick child.

When a friend of mine and I looked at the baby, we saw that the baby was sweating. I then asked the mother why she came to work with a child that sick. And she said to me, 'Well, I've already lost three children, and I know this one is next, whether I stay at home or come to work here. So it's better for me to join others and make my contribution, which hopefully will help to save someone else's child, who will be sick but alive when you have a clinic in Kayanza.'

"The entire road, six kilometers long, was rebuilt by these people with machetes and hoes. The same day the road was finished, the representative of the Belgian road construction company called me to negotiate the price. You can imagine how I felt to get that call from him. I said to him, 'Thank you so much for your call, but it's already done.' He was obviously shocked and said to me, 'What do you mean? Who did it? We are the only road construction company in the entire region!' And I said, 'Not anymore.'"

At the same fund-raiser Deo compared Kayanza to "a small sunflower seed, no bigger than the tip of my finger." He went on, "But the sunflower seed, as everyone will tell you, has the potential to grow into an enormous flower that is bigger and taller than any of us here." He imagined the spread of this enterprise, of a close alliance with the Ministry of Health, of an expansion to the large, underfunded district hospitals where someday indigent patients would no longer be detained. For the time being, though, the medical staff at Kayanza was obliged to sleep on the floor of the storage building.

But by November 7, 2007, when the clinic opened for patients, there were three buildings ready for use and a moderately well-stocked pharmacy. The pastor from Rukomo had objected to the clinic's tapping the water pipe that ran from the mountains and through Kayanza, but the government had overruled him. Water now flowed into a brand-new, fifty-thousand-liter tank with its own internal filtration, enough to provide safe water for most of Kayanza and some of Rukomo. An African-American doctor named Dziwe Ntaba, an old friend of Deo's, left his job in New Jersey and came to work full-time and for no pay at the clinic. For the foreseeable future the whole operation would depend on private donations—but by the winter of 2008 no longer entirely on flashlights. Paul Farmer asked a nonprofit organization called the Solar Electric Light Fund to take on Kayanza, and SELF found a donor named Lekha Singh, who gave the money to buy a generator and fuel for the time being, and also the money for a solar-powered, ten-kilowatt electrical system, to be installed by the summer of 2009. A company named Sonosite donated most of the cost of a compact, versatile imaging machine. Paul English, the founder of Kayak.com, provided computers and a satellite system so that Kayanza could manage its medical records and communicate with the rest of the world. And Paul Farmer persuaded national and international health authorities to make the clinic eligible for inexpensive supplies and drugs, including free medicines for AIDS and tuberculosis.

By the summer of 2008, Village Health Works had begun administering AIDS medications to fifty-seven patients. The clinic had an ambulance, beds for ten patients, and thirty-three community health workers. It had a growing vaccination program, a deworming program, and a program to curb malnutrition. It had six Burundian nurses and a Burundian doctor, as well as Deo's American medical friends, and it had a new building for all of them to sleep in, in beds. The clinic was receiving an average of forty-seven patients a day, and sometimes as many as ninety—about twenty thousand individual patients in its first year. They came on foot and in the baskets that serve traditionally as stretchers—one man, near death, was brought encased in a bag, ingeniously strapped to a platform, itself ingeniously attached to the back of a bicycle.

Everyone who made it to Kayanza was seen for free, by a doctor or nurse. All were asked to pay for their medicines, if they could. Not always, but often, it was the best-dressed people, even people who drove up in their own vehicles, who claimed they couldn't pay. The staff usually sent those people off with only a prescription, to fill elsewhere. The staff had lists of the poorest people in the area, and it wasn't hard for Deo to spot the others who were truly destitute, as he circulated among the crowds that gathered outside the clinic every morning. It seemed as if the poorest were often the ones who would insist on paying for medicine, the ones to whom he and the staff would say, "No, no, go and buy some beans instead."

Some patients traveled long distances on foot, usually in groups, some even from Tanzania, and some crossed the lake from the Congo and hiked up to Kayanza. Deo always asked these people, "How did you hear about us?" The usual answer was a phrase that meant literally, "When you're miserable, you lose your head." That is, a person in misery forgets to be silent and talks to everyone. Because those patients had long return journeys, it was decided that they would be seen first in the mornings. The women's committee joined in creating this policy, and when some of the villagers objected, it was the women's committee who explained and calmed them down.

Some people visited not for medical help, but only to look at the clinic. When Deo asked one of these travelers why he had come, the man replied, "To see America."

This made Deo happy, since he was a full-fledged American now. But other testimonials seemed more important. For instance, from a driver who, Deo believed, was a former Hutu militiaman. After making a few trips to the construction site, the man came up to Deo and said he was puzzled. Ninety-nine percent of Kayanza was Hutu, but Deo was a Tutsi, wasn't he? Told this was true, the driver walked off literally scratching his head. The next time he arrived, he volunteered to help out with the planting at the site. One elderly patient told Deo that he'd been fighting and killing Tutsis ever since 1965. The man had scars all over his body to prove it. He told Deo, "I wish I had spent my life trying to do something like this." He was already getting free care and medicine. So Deo figured his words were at least partly sincere. He said to Deo, "If I could prolong my life, I would do nothing but work with you guys."

A lot of people in Kayanza, it seemed, were astonished by Deo. One villager said, "Many others went abroad, but most of them have not returned to show us how we can improve our situation. We have never seen before an educated man like him hiking around in the mountains, up and down, to talk with people in their households. When we are working, he does not cross his arms. He works with us, so that the work can be done quickly. We hope that other people will see how he behaves, and then imitate him."

One day a woman approached Deo with her head bowed and said, "You don't know me, but I want to say that I am so sorry for what happened." Deo suspected that she was confessing to some offense against his family during the war. Her words worried him. If people thought he planned revenge, they might try to kill him first. But it seemed to Deo that Kayanza was becoming a "neutral ground," a place where Tutsis from the mountains and Hutus from the lakeside could mingle without fear. A place of reconciliation for everyone, including him. And he hoped he wasn't dreaming. "What happened happened," Deo said to the woman. "Let's work on the clinic. Let's put this tragedy behind us, because remembering is not going to benefit anyone."

ACKNOWLEDGMENTS

My thanks to all of the people whose names appear in this book, and my thanks for various kinds of help to: Joyce Apfel, Robert Bagg, Jolanta Benal, Georges Borchardt, Alice Bukhman, Gene Bukhman, Evan Camfield, Ed Cardoza, Benjamin Dreyer, Paul English, John Farber, Elliot Fratkin, Bob Freling, Philip Gourevitch, Tony Grafton, John Graiff, Jonathan Harr, Chris Jerome, Frances Kidder, Nathaniel Kidder, Diantha Kidder, James Leighton, Alastair Maitland, Craig Nova, Rachel Rackow, Mike Rosenthal, Natasha Ryback, Haun Saussy, Mary Kay Smith-Fawzi, Basil Stamos, Sara Stulac, and Peter Uvin. I am also immensely grateful to a number of Burundians, but I think it best not to mention them by name.

Special thanks, once again, to Stuart Dybek and to Kate Medina. I also want to thank Richard Todd for all that he has done on my behalf, with a patience that has lasted thirty-five long years.

SOME HISTORICAL NOTES

The "ethnic" compositions of Rwanda and Burundi, past and present, aren't precisely known. The estimates most often cited are based on a census conducted by the Belgians near the end of colonization. Subsequent estimates have been colored by the ideologies and interests of various governments and are therefore unreliable.

According to a widely respected historian of the precolonial era, Jan Vansina, the meanings of "Hutu" and "Tutsi" changed over the centuries but generally described "relative categories," not geographical origins or clans or tribes. Certainly, most objective differences between Hutus and Tutsis had disappeared over the centuries before Europeans colonized the kingdoms of Rwanda and Burundi. Hutus and Tutsis spoke the same language and practiced the same religions. They shared the same taste for banana beer and the same proverbs and for the most part the same territories. They intermarried, too—more commonly after colonialism, at least in Rwanda. This ensured that by the time of Deo's youth it was hard to tell Hutus and Tutsis apart simply by looks, stereotypes notwithstanding.

Before colonialism, though, other distinctions had been established. These were social, economic, and political. People who mainly herded cattle were called Tutsis, and "Hutu" had come to designate people who mainly farmed the land. There were many exceptions, and it wasn't as if "Hutu" and "Tutsi" described genetic predispositions for plants and cows, but very broadly speaking, the aristocracy was drawn from the population of cow-owning Tutsis, and their inferiors or dependents were predominantly Hutu farmers.

By the late nineteenth century, before colonization, the categories Hutu and Tutsi had become "absolute" in Rwanda, Vansina writes. By the time the Europeans arrived, Rwandans were not only "conscious of a great divide between Tutsi and Hutu," but the "antagonism between these two social categories had already broken into the open."

In Rwanda, the king and aristocracy were Tutsi, and it seems the social hierarchy was more rigid than in Burundi. There, power lay less with the king than with the small princely class, descendants of kings, known as the ganwa. The ganwa and the king stood apart from the ethnic categories, and they ceased to be either Hutu or Tutsi. The various rivalrous groupings of ganwa needed all the support they could get, from Hutus as well as from Tutsis. Hutus occupied important positions, especially in the system of justice. So the oppression of Hutus in Burundi was both less onerous than in Rwanda and not as neatly identified as a Tutsi oppression. And the very complexity of Burundi's social hierarchy also seems to have muted ethnic hostility. Tutsis were divided into at least two different classes, the Tutsi-Hima and the Tutsi-Banyaraguru, and both Hutus and Tutsis belonged to lineages of varying status. "Lineage affiliations," writes the scholar René Lemarchand, "could rectify and even reverse the formal rank-ordering established through the caste system."

But the European colonists administered Rwanda and Burundi as one, and the effects of colonization, though not identical in each country, were profound in both.

In one of his books, Lemarchand quotes a German duke, who described the landscape of the colony Ruanda-Urundi in 1910 this way: "A hilly country, thickly populated, full of beautiful scenery, and possessing a climate incomparably fresh and healthy; a land of great fertility, with watercourses which might be termed perennial streams; a land which offers the brightest of prospects to the white settlers." But comeliness was an incidental matter. The two little agrarian kingdoms were scraps in Europe's carving up of Africa, potential sources of labor and further opportunities for the Christianizing enterprise.

Vansina writes that both kingdoms had known cattle raids and small wars. Colonialism appears to have introduced new levels of violence and tools for violence. A chronicle assembled by a Western scholar named Roger Botte contains many entries like this one, from the time of German rule:

> 1908. Burundi. From 31 March to 18 May, Grawert leads a new expedition against the princes of the northeast. This expedition provokes the *Rumanymasunsu* famine, which takes over the preceding famines and sweeps across the region. It reaches horrendous proportions because of the terrible losses incurred by the war—"the natives were slaughtered *en masse* with gun or machine-gun shots"—and the pillage of enormous herds—"4,613 head of cattle and 3,659 head of small livestock."

According to Vansina and others, it is wrong to imagine, as some have, that the Europeans created either the distinction or the "mutual hostility" between Tutsis and Hutus. He writes, of the situation in Rwanda, "The Europeans merely adopted a practice they found on the spot and the terminology they used to express it derived from the speech of the local elites." But the Europeans added poison to that terminology. To the Rwandan elites, writes the scholar Mahmood Mamdani, the distinction between Tutsi lords and subject Hutus had been conceived as an indigenous difference, a difference that existed among a single people, among relatives, as it were. The Europeans made the distinction into something it had never been, into a racial difference.

European colonists brought a myth with its own long history, a myth tailored to account for what looked to them like an anomaly: civilization in darkest Africa, kings and aristocracies and peasants, an advanced social order a little like Europe's. Tutsis, many colonists seem to have believed, descended from the biblical Ham, the banished son of Noah. Tutsis had degenerated through long contact with the inferior race of native blacks, the Hutus. But Tutsis were still Caucasian under their black skins. Most likely they had come from Ethiopia, but the important point was that they had come from elsewhere on their civilizing mission. A Belgian who was for many years in charge of administering Burundi, Pierre Ryckmans, described the situation as he saw it in 1931. (He used the terms "Batutsi" and "Bahutu," derived from the Kirundi plural.) "The Batutsi were destined to rule; their mere demeanor lends them considerable prestige over the inferior races that surround them. . . . There is nothing surprising about the fact that the less shrewd, simpler, more spontaneous, and more confiding Bahutu braves let themselves be enslaved." These ideas in themselves had consequences. But the administrative changes that embodied the ideas, the changes that the colonists imposed, mattered more.

The Germans and their successors, the Belgians, never occupied the colony in large numbers. Until the late 1930s, they were fewer than one thousand. They ruled, as is often said, indirectly. Essentially, they placed power in the hands of aristocratic Tutsis in Rwanda and of the ganwa and Tutsi aristocrats in Burundi. They left the shells of the old kingdoms in place, but made the system of government more remote from the population. And ethnicity became a central fact of life. The Belgians classified the natives ethnically—through a census, completed in the 1930s. From then on, every Rwandan and Burundian had a single fixed identity, inscribed on a card. More than ever before, one's chances depended on whether the card read Hutu or Tutsi.

Not all Tutsis benefited. "Ordinary Batutsi who lived on the hills (who constituted at least 90 percent of all Batutsi) were invisible," writes the historian Jean-Pierre Chrétien—invisible, that is, to the colonists. The great majority of Tutsis remained cow-keepers, many of whom did some farming, and, as before, they shared with Hutus the same religions (some 70 percent professed Christianity by the end of colonization), the same language, and the same hills. Many also shared harsh treatment from the Tutsi chiefs. But if you were a Hutu, your prospects were very grim. What little the colonist provided in the way of higher education, the real ticket to power and privilege, was reserved for a handful of Tutsis—and, in Burundi, for ganwa as well as some Tutsis. Most of the Hutus with important public positions lost their jobs and were replaced by Tutsis. Hutu farmers were forced to plant certain crops for the benefit of the colonist. The precolonial practice of enforced communal labor was greatly extended. All Tutsis were excused, but Hutus were obliged to work for nothing, as virtual slaves, sometimes for three days out of every six, on projects designed by the Belgians or the Tutsi chiefs. The Belgians gave the ganwa and Tutsi chiefs considerable autonomy—to extract this forced labor, to collect taxes from the peasants (more than occasionally with whips and canes)—and many chiefs grossly abused their power. One result of all this appears to have been periodic famines. Another was great resentment among Hutus, at least in Rwanda.

Historical inevitability is a fiction. But it is hard to read about the colonial past of Rwanda and Burundi and not imagine that it sealed the future.

According to the *Historical Dictionary of Burundi*, the Belgian settler Albert Maus is said to have been "pathologically anti-Tutsi."

Supposedly, he killed himself on learning of the victory of Prince Rwagasore's political party in 1961.

Rwagasore was married to a Hutu and made his party multi-ethnic. He was very unpopular with the Belgian administrators because he demanded immediate independence for Burundi. According to the *Historical Dictionary*, there is some evidence that the Belgian Resident in Burundi encouraged Rwagasore's political rivals to murder him: "Rwagasore must be killed!" the Resident supposedly said, adding, "Once the deed is accomplished, the lake is not too far away."

———

There has been considerable debate as to the nature of the violence that immediately followed the assassination of Burundi's President Ndadaye in 1993, particularly the massacres of Tutsis that occurred in many locales. Some have insisted that these were "spontaneous." Others have said that there was considerable planning involved: that Hutu extremists seized the occasion to try to carry out preexisting plans for the extermination of Tutsis.

In July 1994, a group of human rights specialists from various countries issued a report on the aftermath of the assassination (Human Rights Watch and others, *Commission internationale d'enquête sur les violations des droits de l'homme au Burundi depuis le 21 octobre 1993*, Rapport Final, July 1994). It is an incomplete account of the massacres, but its tone seems evenhanded. It blames "important officers of the Burundian army, including the chief of staff," for the assassination, which the officers, all of them Tutsi, surely knew would set off violence throughout the country. It also blames Hutu "provincial and local authorities" as well as the Hutu government ministers who fled Burundi and used Rwandan radio to "broadcast appeals for resistance." The report states: "The ministers who made appeals for resistance could have used the same means of communication to call for an end to the massacres." The report's summary goes on:

In those places where a large number of Tutsi were killed, an important minority of local government officials participated in the summary executions or incited others to carry them out. In these communes, the killings began with detaining the Tutsi as hostages, often in public buildings. Tutsi government employees also used their positions and the resources of their posts to facilitate the killing of Hutu. These findings call into question the thesis that the violence was spontaneous, at least as a general explanation for the killings.

The Tutsi army, as it happened, reacted rather slowly. But around the time Deo crossed the border into Rwanda, back in 1993, fleeing Burundi, the army was following its old pattern:

The army and police used excessive and unnecessary force, including heavy machine guns of 14.5 mm and 20 mm cannons, armored vehicles, and helicopters, against a civilian population that was usually trying only to flee or to protect itself. The army and the police attacked communities where the Tutsi had been detained or killed. But they intervened also in communities where there had been no killings, thereby introducing the very violence that they were supposed to be quelling. In some cases they killed the civilian population themselves, and in some cases they provoked reprisals against the Tutsi.

Rwanda's genocide began about six months after Ndadaye's assassination, in April 1994, with the murder of Rwanda's president. Burundi's president, Ndadaye's appointed successor, also died in the crash. Arguments as to who shot down the plane still continue, along with arguments as to how many were killed in the ensuing four months of slaughter. Most of the victims were Tutsis. But many Hutus were also killed, for opposing absolute Hutu power before the genocide, for being suspected of moderate views, for refusing to participate in the killing. Maybe some were killed for trying to save Tutsis. Some Hutus killed other Hutus for their land and possessions. Some Hutus died simply because they were mistaken for Tutsis.

It appears that a faction of Rwanda's Hutu political elites began planning the extermination of Tutsis and Hutu enemies around 1992, two years after the expatriate and mainly Tutsi army, the Rwandan Patriotic Front, invaded from Uganda. Some historians say that the RPF played an essential role in the genocide, by introducing violence into the situation. But from all I read, it seems as if Rwanda was by then already saturated with violence and the threat of violence. In any event, Rwanda's genocide was, without any doubt, a state-sponsored slaughter. The faction that controlled the government saw its power and privileges threatened—by discontent and anger among the Hutu population, by an economic decline that fed popular unrest, and by international pressure that Rwanda become a multiparty democracy, pressure that increased after the invasion by the RPF. In August 1993, Rwanda's president and the RPF signed a peace agreement, which would have ended the existing dictatorship. To the ruling faction, the agreement was anathema. In his book about the genocide, Philip Gourevitch writes that the preparations for mass slaughter got fully mobilized only after the peace agreement was signed—"only when Hutu Power was confronted by the threat of peace."

The RPF invasion exacerbated the country's economic problems. Mahmood Mamdani and others write that the fact of the invasion— its violence, the masses of internal refugees it created—was probably a temporary boon to the government, lending it legitimacy and popular support. The invasion also provided the extremists an ideal basis for a well-orchestrated campaign of virulent anti-Tutsi propaganda. The assassination of Ndadaye in Burundi in 1993—and the arrival in Rwanda of hundreds of thousands of Burundian Hutu refugees—gave anti-Tutsi propagandists additional material for ar-

ticles in *Kangura* and broadcasts on Rwanda's hate radio. More-
over, it is said that a number of Burundian Hutu refugees joined in
killing Rwandan Tutsis.

A lot of the writing on Rwanda's genocide can be seen as a search
for causes of the violence, with some authors emphasizing one
cause, others adducing concatenations of causes, primary and secondary: colonialism's legacies (especially the propagation of the
myth that Tutsis were a superior race of alien invaders); past and
present violence that hardened ethnic prejudice and helped to beget
further violence; political opportunism that took advantage of a
largely uneducated population, imbued, some have said, with the
habit of obedience; overpopulation, environmental degradation,
and economic distress that led to competition for dwindling resources; the harmful and appalling role played by France and the
criminally negligent response of the United Nations, the United
States, and other Western powers, both to warnings of genocide and
to the mass slaughter itself.

Of the scholars I read, Peter Uvin takes the greatest pains to ad-
duce the possible causes and to discriminate among them, dismiss-
ing several that are widely mentioned. (The notion, for instance,
that Rwandan peasants participated in mass violence because of
their culture of obedience: "This is the same population that spends
an inordinate amount of time and energy disobeying the messages
that come from above," writes Uvin.)

Uvin writes extensively about the role of international development aid—work in which he himself once participated, in both
Rwanda and Burundi. As in Burundi, Rwanda's economy and government were entirely interwoven with foreign aid and dependent
on it. The administration of that aid, Uvin writes, was a vehicle "for
exclusion and for the reproduction of privileges for a small elite."
What Uvin calls "the development enterprise," far from improving
the lives of the majority, increased inequality and fostered "preju-

dice, humiliation, and infantilization" among the peasant majority. To summarize Uvin's argument: international aid, all unwittingly, fostered "structural violence," an essential element in the acute violence that overwhelmed Rwanda in 1994. Structural violence was, undeniably, the substrate on which long-standing institutionalized prejudice operated. "If one recognizes the condition of structural violence, one can understand that profound racist prejudice and outbursts of murderous violence are part of a continuum of ever-present violence in which violence is the answer to violence, and in which victims temporarily become perpetrators and then victims again."

SOURCES

African Rights. *The Cycle of Conflict: Which Way Out in the Kivus?* Kigali, December 2000.

Agathonrwasa.blogspot.com. "Titanic Express Massacre, December 28th 2000." http://agathonrwasa.blogspot.com/2005/05/titanic-express-massacre-december-28th.html.

Botte, Roger. "1889–1930: Chronology of a Slow Assassination," parts I and II. *The International Journal of African Historical Studies* 18, no. 1 (1985), pp. 53–91, and 18, no. 2 (1985), pp. 289–314.

Bukuru, Zacharie. *Les quarante jeunes martyrs de Buta (Burundi 1997): Frères à la vie, à la mort.* Paris: Editions Karthala, 2004.

Chrétien, Jean-Pierre. "Burundi: The Obsession with Genocide." *Current History* 95, no. 601 (May 1996).

———. *The Great Lakes of Africa: Two Thousand Years of History.* Trans. Scott Straus. New York: Zone Books, 2003.

Dallaire, Romeo. *Shake Hands with the Devil: The Failure of Humanity in Rwanda.* New York: Carroll & Graf, 2003.

Des Forges, Alison. "Burundi: Failed Coup or Creeping Coup?" *Current History* 93, no. 583 (May 1994).

———. "The Meaning of 'Hutu,' 'Tutsi,' and 'Twa.' " In *Leave None to Tell the Story,* pp. 31–35. New York: Human Rights Watch, 1999.

Deutsche Presse-Agentur. "Belgian Airline Suspends Burundi Flights After Plane Hit by Gunfire." December 5, 2000.

Eggers, Ellen K. *Historical Dictionary of Burundi.* 3rd ed. Lanham, Md.: Scarecrow Press, 2006.

Farmer, Paul. *Infections and Inequalities.* Berkeley: University of California Press, 1999.

———. "An Anthropology of Structural Violence." *Current Anthropology* 45, no. 3 (June 2004).

Franck, Karen A. *Nancy Wolf: Hidden Cities, Hidden Longings.* London: Academy Editions, 1996.

Greenhouse, Steven. "Gristede's Deliverymen to Share in $3.2 Million Wage Settlement." *The New York Times,* December 18, 2003.

Gourevitch, Philip. *We Wish to Inform You That Tomorrow We Will Be Killed with Our Families.* New York: Farrar, Straus and Giroux, 1998.

Human Rights Watch. *A High Price to Pay: Detention of Poor Patients in Burundian Hospitals.* Human Rights Watch report, vol. 18, no. 8(A) (September 2006).

Human Rights Watch/Africa Watch, Ligue des Droits de la Personne dans la Région Des Grandes Lacs, Centre National pour la Cooperation au Développement, Fédération Internationale des Droits de l'Homme, Organisation Mondiale Contre la Torture, Nationaal Centrum Voor Ontwikkelingssamenwerking, and NOVIB. *Commission internationale d'enquête sur les violations des droits de l'homme au Burundi depuis le 21 octobre 1993.* Rapport Final, July 1994.

International Monetary Fund. IMF Country Report No. 05/329, September 2005.

Kinzer, Stephen. *A Thousand Hills: Rwanda's Rebirth and the Man Who Dreamed It.* Hoboken, N.J.: John Wiley & Sons, 2008.

Klippenberg, Juliane, Jean Baptiste Sahokwasama, and Joseph

Amon. "Detention of Insolvent Patients in Burundian Hospitals." *Health Policy and Planning* (2008), pp. 1–10.

Lemarchand, René. *Rwanda and Burundi.* New York: Praeger, 1970.

———. *Burundi: Ethnic Conflict and Genocide.* New York: Woodrow Wilson Center Press, 1996.

———. *Ethnicity as Myth: The View from Central Africa.* Occasional Paper, Centre of African Studies, University of Copenhagen, May 1999.

Malkki, Lisa H. *Purity and Exile: Violence, Memory, and National Cosmology Among Hutu Refugees in Tanzania.* Chicago: University of Chicago Press, 1995.

Mamdani, Mahmood. *When Victims Become Killers: Colonialism, Nativism, and the Genocide in Rwanda.* Princeton, N.J.: Princeton University Press, 2001.

Melvern, L. R. *A People Betrayed: The Role of the West in Rwanda's Genocide.* London: Zed Books, 2000.

———. *Conspiracy to Murder: The Rwandan Genocide.* London: Verso, 2004.

Newbury, Catharine. *The Cohesion of Oppression: Clientship and Ethnicity in Rwanda, 1860–1960.* New York: Columbia University Press, 1988.

Newbury, David. "Precolonial Burundi and Rwanda: Local Loyalties, Regional Royalties." *The International Journal of African Historical Studies* 34, no. 2 (2001).

Nkurunziza, Janvier D., and Floribert Ngaruko. *Explaining Growth in Burundi: 1960–2000.* The Centre for the Study of African Economies Working Paper Series, no. 162 (July 20, 2002).

Pan African News Agency. "Britain Sues Recalcitrant Burundi Faction Leader." November 29, 2002.

Philbert, Nkanira, et al. *Dusome: Igitabu c'umwaka wa gatatu.* Nyakanga: B.E.R. Bujumbura, 1993.

Pottier, Johan. *Re-Imagining Rwanda: Conflict, Survival and Disinformation in the Late Twentieth Century.* Cambridge, England: Cambridge University Press, 2002.

Prunier, Gerard. "Burundi: A Manageable Crisis?" London: WRITENET (UK), October 1994.

———. "The Great Lakes Crisis." *Current History* 96, no. 610 (May 1997).

———. *The Rwanda Crisis: History of a Genocide.* London: C. Hurst & Co., 2005.

Reyntjens, Filip. "Rwanda, Ten Years On: From Genocide to Dictatorship." *African Affairs* 103 (2004), pp. 177–210.

Rodegem, F. M. *Sagesse Kirundi: Proverbes, dictons, locutions usités au Burundi.* Annales du Musée Royal du Congo Belge, vol. 34, no. 8. Tervuren, Belgium, 1961.

Swain, Jon. "British Family of Aid Worker Identify Killer." *The Sunday Times,* January 11, 2004. http://www.timesonline.co.uk/tol/news/world/article992717.ece.

Uvin, Peter. *Aiding Violence: The Development Enterprise in Rwanda.* West Hartford, Conn.: Kumarian Press, 1998.

———. "Ethnicity and Power in Burundi and Rwanda: Different Paths to Mass Violence." *Comparative Politics* 35, no. 2 (April 1999).

———. "On Counting and Categorizing the Poor: Census and Power in Burundi and Rwanda." In *Categorizing Citizens: The Use of Race, Ethnicity and Language in National Censuses,* ed. David Kertzer and Dominique Arel. Cambridge, England: Cambridge University Press, 2001.

———. *Life After Violence: A People's Story of Burundi.* London: Zed Books, 2008.

———. "Structural Causes, Development Cooperation and Conflict Prevention in Burundi and Rwanda." Paper commissioned by and presented at Wilton Park Conference 889—Conflict Prevention and Development in Africa: A Policy Workshop, November 2008. http://www.wiltonpark.org.uk/documents/conferences/WP889/participants/participants.aspx.

Vansina, Jan. *La légende du passé: Traditions orales du Burundi.*

Musée Royal de l'Afrique Centrale, Archives d'Anthropologie, no. 16. Tervuren, Belgium, 1972.

————. *Antecedents to Modern Rwanda: The Nyiginya Kingdom.* Madison: University of Wisconsin Press, 2004.

Waugh, Colin M. *Paul Kagame and Rwanda: Power, Genocide and the Rwandan Patriotic Front.* Jefferson, N.C.: MacFarland & Co., 1995.

Weissman, Stephen R. *Preventing Genocide in Burundi: Lessons from International Diplomacy.* Peaceworks No. 22. Washington, D.C.: United States Institute of Peace, July 1998.

Wilson, Robert. "Little Truth and No Reconciliation." *The Guardian,* December 23, 2006. http://www.guardian.co.uk/commentisfree/2006/dec/22/littletruthandnoreconcilia.

Wolf, C. P. "They Are Filling In the River! Ecology Action in Athens, Ohio." *The Post* (Athens, Ohio), supplement to issue 95 (1971).

Workman, Daniel. "World's Poorest Countries: Lowest GNP Nations Highlight African Poverty," October 22, 2006. http://international trade.suite101.com/article.cfm/worlds_poorest_countries.

ABOUT THE TYPE

This book was set in Sabon, a typeface designed by the well-known German typographer Jan Tschichold (1902–74). Sabon's design is based upon the original letter forms of Claude Garamond and was created specifically to be used for three sources: foundry type for hand composition, Linotype, and Monotype. Tschichold named his typeface for the famous Frankfurt typefounder Jacques Sabon, who died in 1580.